Mac
at Work

David Sparks

WILEY

Wiley Publishing, Inc.

To Daisy, Samantha, and Sarah.

The three best reasons to turn off my Mac.

Mac
at Work

Mac at Work

Published by
Wiley Publishing, Inc.
111 River Street
Hoboken, N.J. 07030
www.wiley.com

Copyright © 2011 by Wiley Publishing, Inc.

Published by Wiley Publishing, Inc., Indianapolis, Indiana
Published simultaneously in Canada

ISBN: 978-0-470-87700-5

Manufactured in the United States of America

10 9 8 7 6 5 4 3 2 1

For general information on our other products and services or to obtain technical support, please contact our Customer Care Department within the U.S. at (800) 762-2974, outside the U.S. at (317) 572-3993 or fax (317) 572-4002.

Wiley also publishes its books in a variety of electronic formats. Some content that appears in print may not be available in electronic books.

Library of Congress Control Number: 2010939959

Trademarks: Wiley, the Wiley logo, and related trade dress are trademarks or registered trademarks of John Wiley & Sons, Inc. and/or its affiliates in the United States and other countries, and may not be used without written permission. All trademarks are the property of their respective owners. Wiley Publishing, Inc. is not associated with any product or vendor mentioned in this book.

Colophon: This book was produced using the ITC Giovanni typeface for the body text, Gotham for the titles, Rotis Semi Serif for the captions and sidebar text, and Rotis Sans Serif for the table text.

Acknowledgments

This book is the result of a two-year campaign to document the fact you *can* work on your Mac. I had a lot of help along the way.

A person does not get the gumption to write a book without some amazing teachers. I've had several, including my mother, Jean Sparks, who stayed up many late nights teaching her dense son to read, and Dr. Ronald Peterson, a college professor who became a lifelong mentor and friend.

I would like to thank Wiley Press, particularly Aaron Black, for taking a chance on an unpublished author and championing *Mac at Work* from the beginning. Many thanks also go to my capable editorial team, Galen Gruman and Carol Person, for their advice and support throughout this journey. This book is better as a result of their talents (and patience). I had additional proofreading help from Jeanelle Cameron. Thanks also go to E. John Thawley III for my photograph.

Additional thanks for permission to use their photography in this book to Apple (Figures 1-1 through 1-6, and portions of Figures 2-5, 2-6, and 20-1) and Livescribe (Figure 10-9).

Finally, I want to thank my family (especially Daisy, Samantha, and Sarah), friends, the MacPowerUsers.com community (particularly Katie Floyd), and the MacSparky.com readers for hanging in there with me while I spent my nights and weekends writing 90,000 words.

Credits

Acquisitions Editor
Aaron Black

Editorial Director
Robyn Siesky

Business Manager
Amy Knies

Senior Marketing Manager
Sandy Smith

**Vice President and
Executive Group Publisher**
Richard Swadley

**Vice President and
Executive Publisher**
Barry Pruett

Editor
Carol Person, The Zango Group

Technical Editor
Galen Gruman, The Zango Group

Design and Layout
Galen Gruman, The Zango Group

Cover Designer
Michael E. Trent

**Copy Editing, Proofreading,
and Indexing**
The Zango Group

About the Author

David Sparks is a trial attorney in Orange County, California, where he's been eating other lawyers' lunch for years using Macintosh computers. David is also the editor of www.MacSparky.com (where he writes about Apple technology and productivity) and a co-host of the popular "Mac Power Users" podcast (www.macpowerusers.com).

David speaks and writes often about Apple technology. David is a frequent speaker at the annual Macworld Conference and Expo and a regular faculty member for the American Bar Association's TechShow, the premier legal technology conference, where he speaks on the Mac, iPhone, iPad, and productivity.

contents

Chapter 7: Macs and Mobile Devices   93

Chapter 8: Talking to Your Mac   103

Part III: Basic Business   113

Chapter 9: Task Management   115

Chapter 10: Notes and Outlines   131

Part IV: Advanced Business 207

Chapter 15: Spreadsheets 209

Chapter 16: Databases 223

Chapter 17: Project Management 235

Chapter 18: Billing and Invoicing 247

Chapter 19: The Paperless Mac 257

Part V: Advanced Topics 267

Chapter 20: Networking 269

Chapter 21: Synchronization 281

Chapter 22: Windows on Your Mac 293

Chapter 23: Security 309

Why *Mac at Work?*

Because everyone needs an advantage.

A few years ago, I spoke at the American Bar Association's technology conference about how I use my Mac to run circles around other lawyers. This conference happens once a year and is ground zero for cutting-edge legal technology. When I started talking to these Mac lawyers, however, their ugly secret was revealed: although they were using Macs, the only software they had was Word, Excel, and PowerPoint. They were missing out on all the fantastic Mac software. It was like buying a Ferrari, but only driving it in the parking lot.

The Apple Macintosh is a fantastic computer. Not just for its traditional constituents (graphics designers, musicians, and students) but for everyone. Macs are some of the best designed computers available today. The operating system, also created by Apple, integrates seamlessly with the hardware. Everything just works. Moreover, there is a rich ecosystem of software developers for the Mac that have adopted Apple's standard of excellence. Mac software isn't just functional, it is magnificent.

The word is getting out. Macs are showing up in boardrooms, courtrooms, offices, and even enterprise networks. The Mac is a serious business tool. So can you take advantage of this superior hardware and software to up your game at work? Absolutely. I've been using my Mac at work for years.

This book is intended as a resource, not an encyclopedia. You are not going to learn about every Mac application available for each topic covered. Instead you will discover a selected group of applications that work. This is important. I have gone down the dark and ugly road of bad software. With this book, you get the benefit of my travels.

You can read this book cover to cover or treat it as a reference. Do you suddenly find yourself looking for paperless solutions and not know where to start? Read Chapter 19. Need to figure out e-mail? Jump to Chapter 5. You get the idea.

Whether you've been using a Mac since 1984 or are simply considering switching to a Mac, this book is for you. You'll learn to work more efficiently with superior results than your unfortunate competitors saddled with Windows PCs. This book shows you the way.

If you are ready to pull your Ferrari out of the parking lot, keep reading.

Conventions

Throughout this book, I describe how to use the mouse and keyboard shortcuts for many of the applications covered. In doing so, I use the following terms to explain mouse and keyboard actions.

Mouse Conventions

I'll be asking you to use your mouse to run your Mac and all the applications that help you get work done. When I do, I use the following terms:

▶ **Click:** Most Mac mice have only one button, but some have two or more. If you have a multibutton mouse, quickly press and release the leftmost mouse button once when I say to click the mouse. (If your mouse has only one button, just press and release the button you have.) If you are using a MacBook laptop, click the trackpad.

▶ **Double-click:** When I say to double-click, quickly press and release the leftmost mouse button twice (if your mouse has only one button, just press and release twice the button you have). On some multibutton mice, one of the buttons can function as a double-click (you click it once, the mouse clicks twice); if your mouse has this feature, use it — it saves strain on your hand. You can also double-click a MacBook trackpad.

▶ **Right-click:** Right-clicking means clicking the right-hand mouse button. On a Mac's one-button mouse, hold the Control key when clicking the mouse button to achieve the right-click effect. On multibutton Mac mice, Mac OS X automatically assigns the righthand button to Control+click. On a MacBook's trackpad, hold the Control key when clicking the trackpad. Newer MacBooks can also be configured to right-click by tapping the lower right corner of the trackpad or tapping with two fingers.

▶ **Drag:** Dragging is used for moving and sizing items in a document. To drag an item, position the mouse pointer on it. Press and hold down the mouse button, and then slide the mouse across a flat surface to drag the item. Release the mouse button to drop the dragged item in its new location. You can also drag using the trackpad in the same fashion.

Menu commands

The commands that you select by using the program menus appear in this book in normal typeface. When you choose some menu commands, a related pop-up menu appears (these are sometimes called *pull-down menus*). If I describe a situation in which you need to select one menu and then choose a command from a secondary menu or list box, I use an arrow symbol. For example, "Choose Edit ▶ Paste" means that you should choose the Paste menu option from the Edit menu.

Keyboard conventions

Sometimes, it is easier to invoke a keyboard shortcut than to take your hands off the keyboard and drill through menus with the mouse. The following keys are typically used in keyboard shortcuts.

▶ **The Command key**, which is indicated on keyboards and program menus (and thus in this book) by the symbol ⌘. On older Macs, the Command key has an Apple logo (⌘) on it, while some newer Macs' keyboards use only the label "Command."

▶ **The Shift key** is displayed in menus by the symbol ⇧.

▶ **The Option key** is displayed in menus by the symbol ⌥.

▶ **The Control key** is displayed in menus with the symbol ^.

▶ **The Tab key** is used both to move within fields in panels and dialog boxes and to insert the tab character in text. iTunes and many other Mac programs indicate it in menus with the symbol ⇥.

▶ **The Return key** is used to apply a dialog box's settings and close the dialog box (equivalent to clicking OK or Done), as well as to insert a hard paragraph return in text. In many Mac programs, it is indicated in menus by the symbol ↵. Note that there is another key labeled Enter on some keyboards, in the numeric keypad. This keypad Enter (indicated in menus by the symbol ⌤) usually works like the regular Return.

▶ **The Delete key** deletes text, one character at a time, to the left of the text-insertion point (like the Backspace key on PCs). On the Mac, programs like iTunes use the symbol ⌫ in menus to indicate Delete. To delete forward (to the right of the text-insertion point, like the PC's Del key does), you can use the Delete ⌦ key on some Mac keyboards.

If you're supposed to press several keys at the same time, I indicate that by placing plus signs (+) between them. Thus, Control+⌘+A means press and hold the Control key and the Command key, then press the A key. After you've pressed the A key, let go of all three keys.

I use the plus sign (+) to join keys to mouse movements. For example, Option+drag means to hold the Option key while dragging the mouse.

I also provide Web addresses and, sometimes, programming code or text you must enter into some dialog box or other program interface. I do that by formatting such text in a typewriter-like font `like this`.

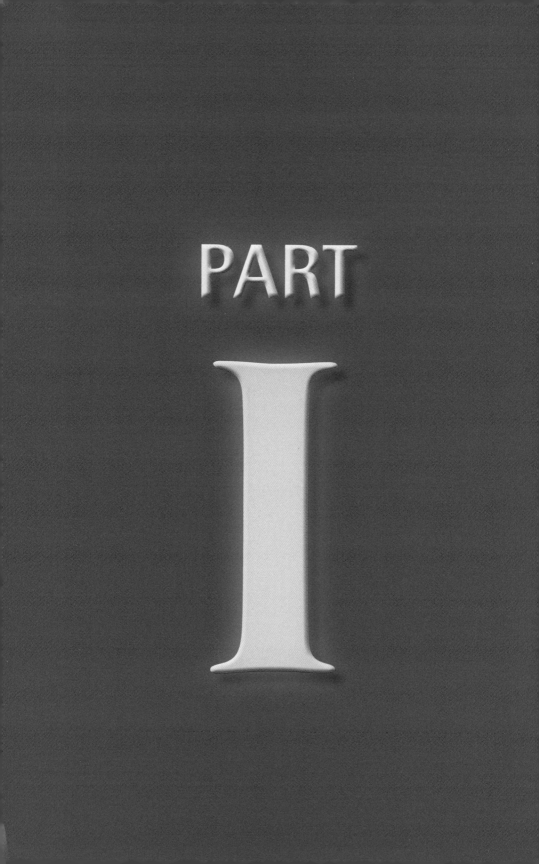

PART

I

Mac Fundamentals

A Tour of the Mac

S o you've decided to use a Mac at work. Great decision. Once you get your hands on the fantastic Mac-only applications in this book, you are going to dazzle your bosses, co-workers, and clients. Now you just need to decide which Mac is right for you.

The Mac Family

There was a time when Apple had so many different Mac models that you needed a slide ruler to pick the right one for you. Fortunately, that is no longer the case. The current Apple product line is streamlined, with each Mac designed to serve a different role. Apple sells both laptop and desktop Macs.

The desktops

If you work at a desk and don't need the portability of a laptop, you get the most bang for your buck with the Mac desktop line. There are three categories of desktop Macs: the Mac Pro, the iMac, and the Mac Mini.

The Mac Pro

The Mac Pro, shown in Figure 1-1, is Apple's top-of-the-line desktop machine. It features an industrial aluminum design and looks like it came off the set of a science fiction movie. Apple let its hardware engineers go nuts with the Mac Pro. Every new Mac Pro model gets the latest and fastest processors. The Mac Pro has options for the most processing cores and memory of any Mac available.

If you've ever worked on the inside of a computer, you will be surprised the first time you open a Mac Pro. The inside looks like it was laid out by a very small, very skilled city planner. Gone is the usual spaghetti jumble of wires and plugs. The Mac Pro is the most upgradable desktop Mac.

But with high-end performance comes a high-end price: The Mac Pro starts at $2,499. Once you begin upgrading, that price goes up. You can customize your Mac Pro to include faster components — and end up spending more than $10,000 on a Mac Pro. You will also need to buy a monitor.

As wonderful and shiny as the Mac Pro is, it is also delicious overkill for most of this book's readers. The Mac Pro is ideal for heavy video editing, 3D graphics, intense gaming, and other heavy, processor-draining tasks. If you want to make

FIGURE 1-1

The Mac Pro

FIGURE 1-2

The iMac

the next *Avatar*, the Mac Pro is for you. For most mere mortals, however, an iMac better suits your desktop needs.

The iMac

The iMac was the computer that saved Apple (see the sidebar "A Macintosh History Lesson"). The current iMac, shown in Figure 1-2, features an aluminum-and-glass design and is an "all-in-one" computer. It includes the computer, an LED monitor, and an optical drive all in one nifty design that is not much bigger than a standard flat-screen monitor. The high-end iMacs pack a lot of punch and can do complex computing tasks. Even the lower-end iMacs can handle less-complex video and photo editing.

Apple has three models of iMacs, ranging from $1,199 to $1,999. The first has a 21.5-inch display and the other two have a 27-inch display. Apple lets you configure the iMac when you buy it at the Apple Store; options include faster processors, better graphics, and more memory. Except for adding memory, the iMac is difficult to upgrade, so make sure to get it with the options you'll want for the entire lifetime of the machine. Whatever options you get, note that the entire line of iMacs is fully able to run all the software mentioned in this book.

The Mac Mini

The Mac Mini, shown in Figure 1-3, is Apple's least expensive Mac, starting at $699. You have to add your own display, keyboard, and mouse. The device itself more closely resembles a space-age cigar box than a computer. Although the Mac Mini is not as powerful as the iMac or Mac Pro, it can handle typical computing tasks, such as word processing, spreadsheets, e-mail, and the Internet with no troubles. Mac Mini upgrade options are limited to memory and hard drive. (The newest Mac Mini opens from the bottom — much easier!) Apple recommends any upgrades or repairs to a Mac Mini be done by an Apple-authorized technician.

FIGURE 1-3

The Mac Mini

A MACINTOSH HISTORY LESSON

Once upon a time, people said that if you wanted a computer, you needed a multimillion dollar budget and a team of engineers. Then two guys named Steve (Steve Jobs and Steve Wozniak) started selling the first personal computer, the Apple 1. It came in a plywood case.

Next, Apple released the Apple II and started a revolution. Computers of that era ran on the command line using obscure textual codes, which was empowering for nerds and baffling to everyone else. In 1986, Apple started another revolution with the Macintosh, the first consumer computer with a graphical user interface. In other words, it gave us the mouse.

Although the Macintosh changed the world, Apple soon fell on hard times and the two Steves left the company. By the early 1990s everyone was predicting Apple's demise.

In 1997 Steve Jobs came back to Apple and kicked off a reboot of the company, including the release of the iMac. The company is now more successful than ever with Macs, iPhones, iPods, and iPads. The Mac's market share is on an upward march. Indeed, the Mac is now entrenched at work.

The laptops

Laptop usage increases every year. Computers have evolved to a point that laptops have enough power to satisfy the computing needs of most people. Apple has three categories of laptops: the MacBook, MacBook Pro, and MacBook Air.

The MacBook

The MacBook is Apple's entry-level laptop. Shown in Figure 1-4, the MacBook starts at $999 and features a 13-inch screen. The MacBook is the only plastic computer in Apple's laptop line. Although it is technically the low-end Mac, that isn't a fair description. The MacBook is enough computer for most Mac workers. Indeed, much of this book was written on a MacBook.

FIGURE 1-4

The MacBook

FIGURE 1-5

The MacBook Pro

The MacBook Pro

The MacBook Pro line starts at $1,199 and includes three aluminum-and-glass notebooks in 13-, 15-, and 17-inch varieties. The MacBook Pro, shown in Figure 1-5, is carved out of a single piece of aluminum and is thus extremely rigid. The MacBook Pro also includes better video performance for video editing, 3D gaming, graphics, and advanced photo editing. As with the MacBook, the memory and disk storage are both user-upgradable in the MacBook Pro.

The MacBook Air

The MacBook Air series, shown in Figure 1-6, starts at $999 and is the ultimate traveling Mac: One model weighs just 2.3 pounds and the other 2.9 pounds. With its slim design and light weight, a MacBook Air takes very little space in your bag. But to get this small size, the MacBook Air has performance compromises and so is not as powerful as the MacBook or MacBook Pro.

The MacBook Air's thinness also creates physical compromises: Not all USB cables can plug into their USB ports due to the cramped space around them, and

FIGURE 1-6

The MacBook Air series

the MacBook Air requires a separate adapter for an Ethernet cable (a big issue for older models that had just one USB port). For basic computing tasks — e-mail, Internet, word processing, spreadsheets, and presentations — the MacBook Air can do the job. If you are planning to do video editing, however, move along. Nothing in the MacBook Air can be upgraded, so be sure to order enough RAM and storage.

Which Mac is right for you?

Picking the right Mac depends on your particular needs. Do you want the mobility of a laptop or the luxury of a 27-inch iMac screen? Do you revel in owning the fastest, screamingest computer money can buy, or do you want the least-expensive machine to satisfy your needs. The best way to decide is to get your hands on a few Macs and figure out what model fits you the best.

Although this book is about the Macintosh, I'd be remiss not to mention that Apple has a few other products that complement your Mac. The iPhone, iPad, and iPod Touch all synchronize with your Mac and, to a limited extent, become an extension of your computer. You can learn more about your Mac and mobile devices in Chapter 7.

Installing, Removing, and Updating Applications

This book covers a lot of Mac OS X applications. So let's review installing, removing, and updating applications on the Mac.

Installing applications

Mac applications install from disk image (`.dmg`) files. Sometimes, Mac OS X developers compress the installation files into a Zip compression package. The Zip file needs to be decompressed to get the disk image file. To do that, just double-click the Zip file, and Mac OS X will extract the disk image file.

Once you have the disk image file, you are ready to install the application. There are two ways to install software from a disk image: an installation bundle and a Mac OS X installer.

Installers are the easiest. You double-click the installer icon and the installer walks you through each step of the process. When completed, the application and its supporting files are all where they need to be. Installers are normally used by more complicated applications, such as Adobe Creative Suite.

Most Mac OS X applications don't have a full installer but instead use *application bundles*. The bundle opens a Finder window or folder that contains the application file. Quite often, as shown in Figure 1-7, the application

FIGURE 1-7

The mounted disk image for an application (in this case, OmniOutliner)

automatically opens a Finder window. Regardless, you then copy the application to its desired location, which is almost always the Applications folder.

Once the application is where it belongs, you can eject the disk image using the Eject icon next to the disk name in the Finder's Sidebar. You can also eject an image by clicking the disk image and pressing ⌘+E or dragging the disk image to the Trash.

Ejecting the image after installation is important: Novice users usually don't realize they need to put the new application in their Applications folder, and so they instead run the application from the mounted disk image. Doing so is dangerous: You can't always count on the disk image being there, and it may cause problems with the application's data files.

If you want your application to remain in the Dock, that quick-access bar at the bottom of the screen, you can drag it there from the Application folder or Control+click or right-click the icon in the Dock while the application is running and choose Options ▸ Keep in Dock, as shown in Figure 1-8.

Removing Mac OS X applications

Mac OS X does not have a dedicated application uninstaller. This often surprises Windows switchers, but the reason for its omission is simple: It is not

FIGURE 1-8

Keeping an application icon in the Dock

necessary. To remove most Mac OS X applications, you just drag them to the Trash. (Some applications — typically those installed via an installer — come with an uninstaller app; use that if it exists.)

Some developers have released applications that clean up after deleted applications by tracking down and deleting their support files. AppZapper ($13;

A TOUR OF THE MAC OS X USER INTERFACE

Below at left is the Finder and below at right is an application, with the most common user interface elements identified; the only common element not shown is the dialog box,

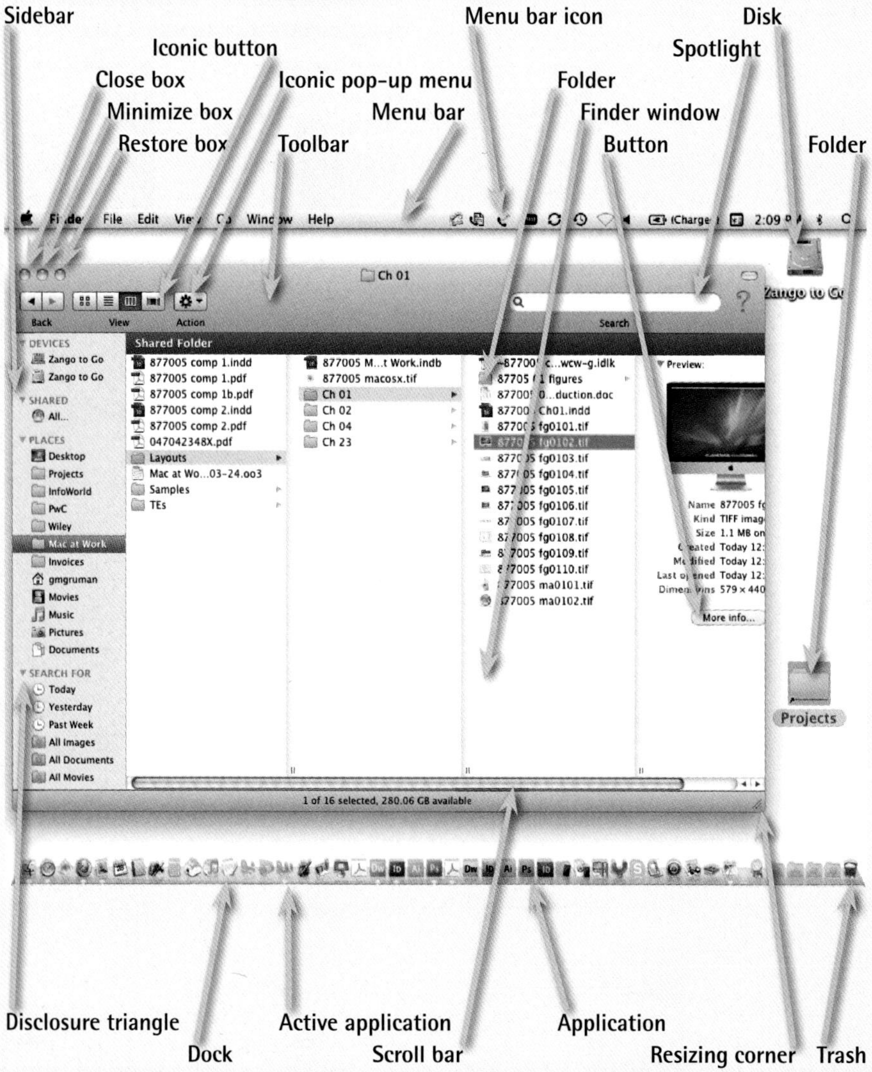

Sidebar

Iconic button

Close box

Iconic pop-up menu

Minimize box

Menu bar

Restore box

Toolbar

Menu bar icon

Disk

Spotlight

Folder

Finder window

Button

Folder

Disclosure triangle

Active application

Application

Dock

Scroll bar

Resizing corner   Trash

`www.appzapper.com`) is a good tool. Hazel (`www.noodlesoft.com/hazel`), covered in Chapter 3, also cleans up after deleted applications.

Getting Mac OS X updates

Updates relating to Apple software are provided automatically in the Software Update utility (choose ⬛ ▸ Software Update). Even if you don't run the updater,

which is like a panel except that when it is open, no other controls are accessible within the application.

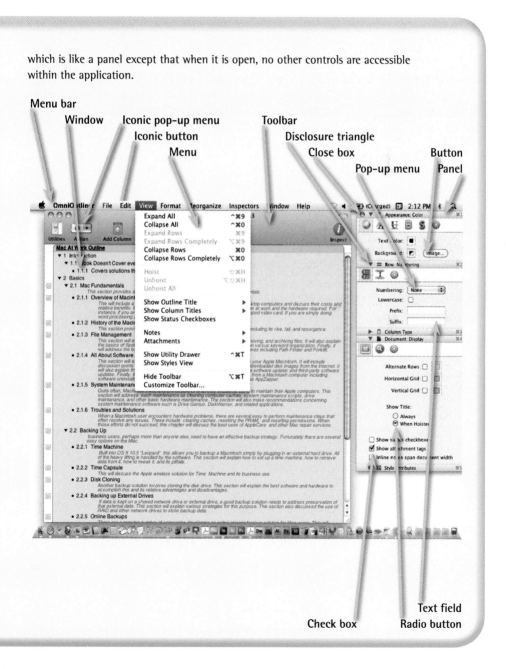

Menu bar
Window   Iconic pop-up menu   Toolbar
Iconic button   Disclosure triangle
Menu   Close box   Button
Pop-up menu   Panel

Text field
Check box   Radio button

Mac OS X periodically checks for you and reports when there are updates. You should always apply security updates as soon as they become available. With other updates, wait a few days until after Apple releases them before installing. Why? Because these upgrades are tested only with a limited number of users and so sometimes include glitches. You are better off letting someone else find out first.

Most software applications periodically check to see if there are updates for those applications. When updates exist, they prompt you to download and install them.

File Management

Moving files around Mac OS X follows the same user interface paradigms found in the first Macintosh. Indeed, if you could teleport a 1984 Mac user to the present, he would have no trouble copying files. In Mac OS X, files are objects that can be moved or copied between folders and disks, as well as to and from the Desktop. Mac OS X automatically creates folders in your user folder for the most common file types, such as Documents, Music, Pictures, and Movies. If the Finder is too constraining for you, PathFinder ($40; www.cocoatech.com) is a powerful replacement.

One change to Mac OS X that a 1984 time traveler would appreciate is the addition of Spotlight. Spotlight is a systemwide search that indexes your files and data. Whether you are looking up an Address Book entry, an e-mail you received last week, or a draft sales proposal, you can usually find it by typing the name in the Spotlight search bar and pressing Return or clicking the Spotlight iconic button (the magnifying glass icon) at the top-right corner of your screen. The point of Spotlight is to help you avoid having to drill through Finder windows — and it usually works.

Spotlight also is an excellent application launcher. If you type the first few letters of an application, Spotlight finds it; you can then launch it by pressing Return. To perform this magic, Mac OS X automatically indexes every file you save. Address Book, for example, adds each contact's name to the Spotlight index. Some applications, such as Default Folder X (covered in Chapter 3), let you add additional terms to the Spotlight index. You can manually add terms to a file's Spotlight index in the file's Info window (displayed by selecting the file and pressing ⌘+I).

Maintenance and Troubleshooting

One of the biggest challenges for Windows users switching to Mac OS X is accepting the fact there simply isn't much maintenance on a Mac. There are, however, some basic maintenance and troubleshooting tools worthy of a mention.

Basic maintenance

Mac OS X has three built-in scripts that run on a daily, weekly, and monthly basis. These scripts clean out system files and preferences so Mac OS X runs optimally. Most users aren't even aware they exist.

The operating system is supposed to run these scripts in the background, usually in periods of low activity, quite often in the middle of the night, if your Mac is on then. If you have a laptop or a Mac that is frequently turned off, there is a possibility your Mac will not run these scripts as often as it should.

You can check these files on your own Mac by looking at the script logs to determine the last time they were modified. You do this by choosing Go ▶ Go to Folder in the Finder and typing in /var/log/. Once in this folder, you can select the daily.out, weekly.out, and monthly.out files and open an Info window (select the file and press ⌘+I). When looking at the file information, the date last modified tells you the last time the script ran.

If your are not running on the usual daily, weekly, and monthly routines, it is not the end of the world. Your Mac won't implode and cats won't start living with dogs. Just leave your Mac on overnight. You can also manually run these scripts a variety of ways. My favorite method is using the application Maintenance (www. titanium.free.fr). Maintenance is a free application, although a donation is requested by the developer. (There are many such useful "donationware" applications for Mac OS X.)

Maintenance, shown in Figure 1-9, allows you to perform several functions on your Mac, including manually running the Mac OS X daily, weekly, and monthly scripts. Maintenance can perform other useful Mac maintenance tasks:

▶ **Repair permissions:** Mac OS X assigns access privileges, known as *permissions*, to applications, folders, and files. The operating system manages these permissions automatically, but occasionally the permissions

---

FIGURE 1-9

The Maintenance application window

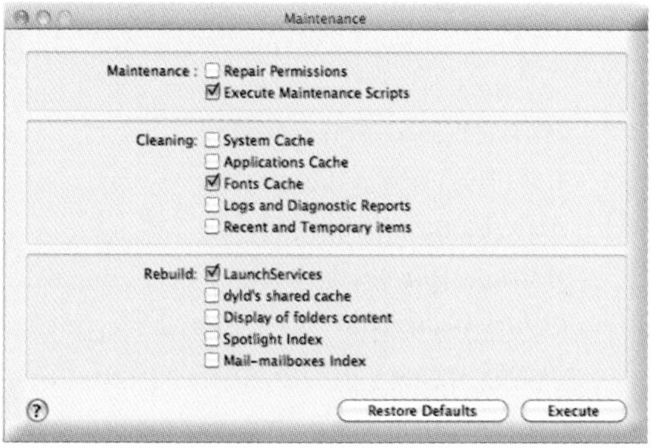

get corrupted. (Corruption was more of a problem with earlier versions of Mac OS X than it is today.) Errors in the permissions can manifest themselves in several ways, from slowing down your Mac to prohibiting certain applications from starting. In addition to repairing permissions in Maintenance, you can also repair permissions using Apple's Disk Utility. Repairing permissions is not a normal maintenance issue but can be used to troubleshoot odd behavior. It is also a good idea to repair permissions before doing any major software or operating system upgrade.

▶ **Cache cleaning:** Caches are files containing commonly used system resources. For example, the browser caches files from your most frequently visited Web sites. When you return to a site, your browser does not have to re-download every file associated with that site; it loads them from the cache and then downloads only changed or new elements for that site. Mac OS X creates caches for system files, applications, and font files. It is a common myth that cleaning cache files is necessary maintenance in Mac OS X. This is not true. Cleaning out the cache files usually slows down your Mac. When you delete them, Mac OS X must then go through the time-consuming act of rebuilding them. (Your Mac created those cache files for a reason.) Although not necessary for maintenance, cleaning caches is appropriate when experiencing problems. Cleaning the font cache, for example, often solves text-related problems.

▶ **Launch Services directory:** Launch Services is the directory that tracks the available applications for the Open With contextual menu option when you Control+click or right-click on a file. If you find you are getting multiple instances of applications in this menu option, use this command to rebuild the directory and remove the duplicate entries.

▶ **Spotlight index:** The Spotlight index is Mac OS X's index of your files and directories. Rebuilding the index should only be necessary when you detect corruption with your Spotlight searches.

 To get at deeper level system repair, try Onyx (donation requested; www.titanium.free.fr), by the developers of Maintenance. But beware when using Onyx: It can modify essential system files, so if used improperly, Onyx could destroy data and harm your Mac. Make sure you know what you are doing before you start pushing buttons — and always back up first (see Chapter 2).

Disk defragmentation

Hard disks don't usually keep files together. When you write a file to the disk, it takes blank space wherever it may find it; thus, large files may be split up into multiple pieces. It is like reading a book where you are required to turn forward 20 pages, then back 30 pages, to continue. When files get heavily fragmented, the disk has to work harder to read them by jumping to multiple locations, which slows performance.

Windows switchers to Mac OS X often look for defragmentation tools. Mac OS X, however, performs its own defragmentation, so user interference is generally not necessary. I don't defrag my Mac hard disks. In fact, the few times I've bothered to defrag a Mac OS X hard disk, I've never experienced any noticeable improvement in performance.

The exception is if you work with a lot of large files or routinely keep your disk nearly full. In that case, iDefrag ($30; `www.coriolis-systems.com/idefrag`) is a good tool. Before defragmenting your disk, however, make certain to back up everything.

Getting help

One advantage to buying Apple hardware is the company's excellent customer support. So many Mac workers have had such bad experience with computer repair with other computers that they sometimes overlook this advantage.

If you are having trouble with your Mac, take it into your local Apple Store or call Apple and send it in. Note, however, that Apple does not generally offer priority service. Moreover, Apple does not offer same-day service for repairs at the office like some PC manufacturers do. So you could experience longer downtimes when you need upgrades and repairs.

Backing Up

Even more valuable than your shiny Mac hardware is the data you create on it. At any time, your Mac may contain that vital customer list or the last three months' sales figures. Although a computer can always be replaced, critical data cannot. In this chapter, you will learn about the most common backup tools and recommended backup plans.

Why Back Up?

Your computer data is important, and your hard disk is going to fail. Hopefully that failure will be sometime after you are done with your computer but oftentimes it is not. The trouble is, you don't know when that failure is going to take place. Most disks are sold with one-, three-, or five-year warranties, but those are just estimates. The only thing certain is that your disk will fail sometime between the next few years and the next few seconds. You can survive this inevitable disk failure with a reliable backup plan.

Apple's Backup Tools

The reason so few computer users historically have had a backup plan is because, until recently, backing up was hard. The software was cryptic and unfriendly. Worse yet, there was no simple way to test your backup to know if it even worked. People didn't trust their backup, so they didn't bother. Apple provides several products to address these difficulties, including a simple and reliable backup system that comes free with Mac OS X: Time Machine.

Time Machine

Starting with Mac OS X 10.5 Leopard, Apple built a painless and reliable backup plan into every Mac. The first time you plug an external hard disk into your Mac, Time Machine asks if you want to make it your backup disk. With one click, Time Machine formats the external disk and begins backing up the full contents of your Mac; Figure 2-1 shows the Time Machine settings dialog box.

FIGURE 2-1

Time Machine's settings

After initiating a Time Machine backup, you don't need to adjust another setting. The first backup takes several hours because it is copying everything on your Mac to the backup disk. After the initial backup, Time Machine backs up just new and changed files every hour, which usually takes just a few minutes. If your disk fails, you use Time Machine to restore your replacement disk.

FIGURE 2-2

Time Machine's recovery interface.

In addition to worry-free backups, Time Machine also keeps versions of your files. This allows you to restore older files that were later modified. So, using Time Machine, you can recover an older version of your sales proposal that you hacked to pieces six hours ago in a caffeine-induced haze of overzealous editing.

To recover your files from Time Machine, navigate to the folder containing your now emasculated proposal and activate Time Machine. This opens the Time Machine recovery interface, shown in Figure 2-2. You can then scroll back in time using the time bar at the far right (here, by six hours), select your file, and click Restore. Time Machine replaces your current version with the older one and you can pick up where you left off. You can use the same technique to recover files you deleted, even if you emptied the Trash in the meantime.

The biggest advantage of Time Machine is that it takes zero user configuration. You plug it in and it just works. If, however, you want to customize your Time Machine, you can. The Time Machine system preference has an option that allows you to exclude (or add) data to the backup list. Also, if the hourly backup is overkill, you can run the free TimeMachineScheduler (free; www.klieme.com) utility, which allows you to adjust the backup frequency to between one and 12 hours.

Restoring files with Time Machine

Restoring from a Time Machine backup is simple. After installing a new startup disk on your Mac (such as to replace a failed one or to simply use a larger disk in place of the original one), you have to reinstall Mac OS X. The installer will ask if you have a Time Machine backup; if you do, it is just a matter of plugging in the Time Machine disk and letting the installer do the work. Do note that depending on the size of your disk, the entire process takes a few hours — but you don't have to reinstall anything manually this way.

External disks and Time Machine

Time Machine backs up externally connected disks, not just your Mac's internal disk. For example, if your work files are on an external disk and then you add a second external backup disk, Time Machine will back up both the internal and the external disks. Just make sure your Time Machine disk is large enough to accommodate both the internal and the external disks. For example, if you have a 250GB internal disk and 250GB external disk, you should have a backup disk of at least 1TB — double the capacity of the disks you're backing up.

However, Time Machine only works for disks physically connected to your Mac. If you have data on a network disk not physically connected to your Mac, Time Machine will not back it up.

Time Capsule

Time Machine is a fantastic backup system; it solves the simplicity and reliability problems that have prevented users from backing up in the past. However, laptop owners often forget to stop and plug in their external Time Machine disk. If you don't plug the disk into your laptop, the backup doesn't happen and so your data is at risk.

Apple has a wireless solution: Time Capsule (`www.apple.com/timecapsule`), a wireless router with a built-in hard disk. Once the Time Capsule is on your network, Time Machine recognizes it and offers to wirelessly back up to it. Because the backup is done over a wireless connection, you don't have to remember to plug the backup disk into your laptop. Apple sells 1TB and 2TB versions of the Time Capsule for $299 and $499, respectively. Because multiple Macs can back up to a single Time Capsule, it is an excellent low-cost backup solution for a small office running several Macs.

However, do note that wireless backup speeds are significantly slower than a directly connected USB or FireWire hard disk. If you are using a Time Capsule,

WHICH HARD DISK FOR TIME MACHINE?

When choosing an external disk for your Time Machine backup, there are two considerations to note: capacity and connection type.

Because Time Machine keeps multiple versions of your data, the backup disk needs to hold more information than the disk in your Mac. A good rule of thumb is to get a disk at least two times the capacity of your Mac's internal disk.

The two primary external hard disk connection types are USB and FireWire.

USB: Universal Serial Bus (USB) is the most common hard disk connector and can be found on every currently shipping Mac. Some USB disks are bus-powered, which lets them run without being plugged into the wall. USB disks are generally cheaper but usually a bit slower than FireWire disks.

FireWire: FireWire disks come in two flavors: 400 and 800 Mbps (megabits per second), and each has a different style of port. Currently shipping Mac Pros, iMacs, and MacBook Pros support FireWire 800 ports only, but older Macs have FireWire 400 ports. (There are adapters that let you connect FireWire 400 disks to FireWire 800 ports and vice versa.) For several technical reasons, FireWire disks are generally faster, but they are also more expensive than USB disks of the same capacity. A faster disk is useful for speedier backups, but not essential.

Both USB and FireWire are adequate for Time Machine backups. If you can afford FireWire disks, you'll find that they not only back up faster but also don't slow your Mac down during backup as the use of USB disks can.

make sure your backups are completed before closing the lid on your MacBook and running out the door; otherwise, you may lose important data. You can tell that the backup is finished when the Time Machine icon in your menu bar stops spinning.

Cloning Your Mac

Another backup solution involves making a copy of your internal hard disk, often called *cloning*. A cloned disk is an exact copy of your internal disk, so if your internal disk fails, you can boot from your cloned disk (just press and hold the Option key during startup to get a choice of startup disks connected to your Mac, and then click the desired disk; in this case, the clone) and have immediate access to your backed-up data and files. If your internal hard disk crashes, you can be up and running from the cloned disk in five minutes or so. Another benefit of a clone is that you can easily browse the contents of the backup without having to load separate software. A cloned disk can be plugged into any Mac and easily browsed through the Finder.

Because it is an exact copy of your internal disk, a clone does not contain prior versions of your data, as a Time Machine backup does. So a cloned disk is best suited as a safety copy of your Mac startup disk, such as before upgrading the OS or installing security or encryption software that can sometimes make a disk unusable. A cloned disk lets you continue working in your old configuration while you figure out what went wrong on your upgraded or secured original disk — or decide to replace that corrupted original disk's contents with the clone disk's backup. Of course, you can use a Time Machine backup for the same purpose.

One of the best cloning tools for the Mac is SuperDuper ($28; `www.shirt-pocket.com`). SuperDuper simplifies the process of cloning your Mac. It can be configured so you just plug in your external disk and the application does the rest. SuperDuper also includes a built-in scheduler, shown in Figure 2-3, which allows you to automatically clone your hard disk every day at a convenient time.

FIGURE 2-3

The SuperDuper scheduler

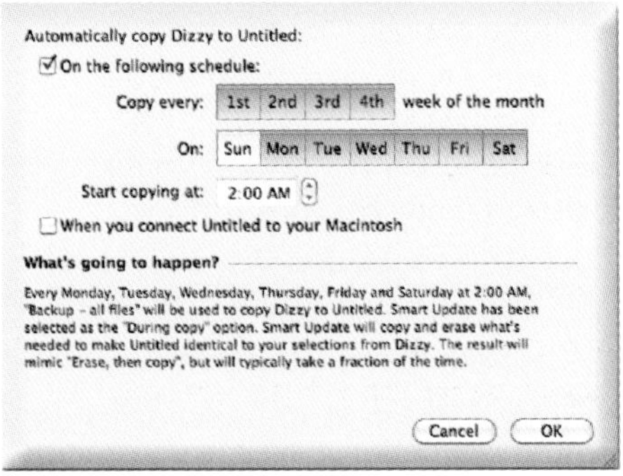

Automatically copy Dizzy to Untitled:

☑ On the following schedule:

Copy every: 1st 2nd 3rd 4th week of the month

On: Sun Mon Tue Wed Thu Fri Sat

Start copying at: 2:00 AM

☐ When you connect Untitled to your Macintosh

What's going to happen?

Every Monday, Tuesday, Wednesday, Thursday, Friday and Saturday at 2:00 AM, "Backup - all files" will be used to copy Dizzy to Untitled. Smart Update has been selected as the "During copy" option. Smart Update will copy and erase what's needed to make Untitled identical to your selections from Dizzy. The result will mimic "Erase, then copy", but will typically take a fraction of the time.

Cancel   OK

DISK STATUS AND RECOVERY

Although your hard disk can fail without any warning, there is a protocol to check the status of your disk called S.M.A.R.T., which stands for Self-Monitoring, Analysis, and Reporting Technology. This can sometimes give you the advance warning you need to prevent disaster.

You can check the S.M.A.R.T. status of your disk in Mac OS X's built in Disk Utility. S.M.A.R.T. is used to find predictable disk failures that result from mechanical wear and degradation of the disk. If S.M.A.R.T. reports a problem with your disk, back it up immediately and then replace it soon. S.M.A.R.T., however, is not perfect and will not predict all disk failures. Disks are always subject to unpredictable failures.

If you experience a disk failure and have no backup, get your Mac to an authorized technician. There are several "Hail Mary" techniques, including putting the disk in the freezer, they can try. If an authorized repairperson can't help, you can submit the disk to a disk recovery company, such as Disk Savers (`www.disksaversdatarecovery.com`). Disk recovery services cannot always deliver, and when they do they can cost hundreds and even thousands of dollars to recover the disk's data. You are much better served putting your own backup system in place so when a disk goes bad, you can discard it and move to a backed-up copy.

One strategy many Mac workers use is to run an hourly Time Machine backup of their Mac throughout the day and script SuperDuper to make a clone on a separate backup disk once a day in the middle of the night.

Although cloned disks are a terrific backup solution, you must be careful when you are experiencing computer problems. When you clone a disk, you make an exact duplicate of the existing data. If your Mac's internal hard disk is corrupted, those corruptions are copied onto the clone disk. Although it is usually a good idea to immediately back up if you begin having trouble with your Mac, backing up with a clone disk may replace a prior uncorrupted version of your data with a new corrupted version. For this reason, if you are using a cloned backup strategy and your Mac is out of sorts, make your emergency clone backup to a separate disk and keep your prior, uncorrupted version intact.

File-Specific Backup

If you just want to back up specific folders or groups of data, use ChronoSync, from Econ Technologies ($40; `www.econtechnologies.com`).

ChronoSync lets you designate particular folders and files for backup. It looks at any source available in the Finder, including files and disks on your network, and copies the files to any location you designate. It can both back up and synchronize

FIGURE 2-4

The ChronoSync interface

data, and it includes scripting and scheduling components. For example, if you want to just back up your budgeting and spreadsheet files to a network disk every six hours, ChronoSync can do so automatically. As shown in Figure 2-4, with a little tinkering, you can set up an automated network backup system.

The only limitation of ChronoSync is that it only sees the files and disks mounted on your Mac or on your local network. Using ExpanDisk ($20; www. expandisk.com/mac), you can mount Internet-based storage, such as Amazon. com's cloud-based S3 storage, to your Mac as if it were a local disk.

Network Data Backup

A networked Mac office also requires reliable backup. Most network storage products include their own backup systems. Some of the most common devices are RAID 1 backup drives, available from many vendors, and Drobo from Data Robotics.

A RAID (Redundant Array of Inexpensive Disks) Level 1 drive is an external hard drive that includes at least two hard disks. The disks are formatted to make two copies of all data. RAID disks can be connected to the network server. When choosing a RAID 1 drive, make sure it includes hard disks with network-class warranties (usually five years) and an idiot-proof system, like a red light, for notifying you when the disk fails.

Not all RAID is created equal. Make sure your backup RAID disk is configured as RAID 1. A RAID 0 configuration, for example, is very fast but provides no backup whatsoever.

Another popular tool for Mac workers is the Data Robotics Drobo drive. Drobo (www.drobo.com) is an external disk enclosure that holds between four and eight hard disks. Like a RAID 1 drive, the Drobo makes an extra copy of all the data you throw at it. One of Drobo's primary benefits is that, unlike a RAID 1 disk, Drobo does not require matched disks; you can fill a four-bay Drobo with disks of different capacities. When you start running out of space, the light next to the smallest disk turns yellow; you then pull out that disk and replace it with a bigger one and Drobo does the rest.

Online Backup

There are several online services useful for backing up key files. Two of the most popular for Mac workers are Apple's MobileMe (www.apple.com/mobileme) and Dropbox (www.dropbox.com). Although the primary selling point of these services is the ability to share files among multiple computers (these services are featured in Chapter 21), they also offer an efficient method for offsite backup of your critical files.

Both services offer the ability to create a virtual, cloud-based storage disk on your Mac. Dropbox always keeps a local copy on your internal disk and the cloud-based copy. MobileMe also allows you to keep a local copy of the data. Before leaving town or after hitting a key milestone, drag a copy of your file to this virtual disk. The service does the rest, copying it to the Internet and tucking it away safely in your account. If you later lose your local copy, you simply log on to your MobileMe or Dropbox account and download the saved copy.

Dropbox offers a free 2GB account, but for $100 a year, you can increase the online storage to 50GB (or 100GB for $200 per year). If you are running a small office, Dropbox could be used as a cloud-based server storage site. Dropbox also keeps versions of your files much like Time Machine so you may restore older versions of your files. MobileMe costs $99 per year for 20GB of storage, though that amount includes any e-mail you send and receive via a MobileMe e-mail address.

Offsite Backup Services

There are also several companies offering Mac users more systematic online backup services. Two of the most popular are Mozy (www.mozy.com) and Backblaze (www.backblaze.com). With these services, you pay a monthly $5 fee and designate certain portions of your hard disk for backup. The service software installed on your internal disk sends your data through your Internet connection to the backup company's data servers. If your office burns down or there is a burglary, your data is preserved safely offsite.

Offsite backup technology is emerging and there are some issues to consider before jumping in.

Privacy and security

Make sure the service has a privacy policy that keeps your data secure and private. The better services will allow you to encrypt the data with your own password before uploading it.

Backup speed

The amount of time it takes to make a significant upload to an online backup service is not measured in minutes or hours, but days and weeks. Be prepared. Some services, such as Backblaze and Mozy, install an application on your Mac that trickles the data up to the online storage in the background. Backblaze even allow you to change the amount of system and bandwidth resources devoted to the upload so you can throttle it up during slow periods.

Download speeds are also slow when recovering files from an online backup. Some services compensate for this speed by offering to send your data on an optical media or a portable hard disk for an additional fee. Of course, if you get your data back by mail or download, you will not have immediate access to it.

Backup Strategies Compared

Each strategy is summarized in Table 2-1. As you can see there are good and bad points for each backup system. There is no single best solution. Indeed if you pick just one solution, you are making a mistake.

Backup redundancy

Keeping your data backed up to just one place is dangerous. Backup disks and media, by their very nature, are not used often and you don't want to wait until after your hard disk fails to discover your backup is corrupt. Likewise, in the event of a disaster or theft, quite often the backup disks are also lost. For critical data, one backup simply is not enough. The best backup systems are redundant with copies of the data at different locations.

External hard disks are a cheap and a fast alternative for offsite backup — just be sure to store the disks offsite! Using backup applications, such as SuperDuper or ChronoSync, you can automate the process of making an external backup of your Macs or server attached RAID disks on a regular basis. The most recent version of SuperDuper can automatically start the application,

TABLE 2-1

		Summary of Backup Strategies			
Backup Strategy	System Backup	File Versions	Internet Storage	Wireless	Multiple Macs
Time Machine	✔	✔	—	—	—
Time Machine with Time Capsule	✔	✔	—	✔	✔
Cloned Backup	✔	—	—	—	—
Online Backup	—	some	✔	some	—
Network Storage	—	—	—	some	✔

mount the backup disk, make the backup, and then dismount the disk without ever requiring you to touch the keyboard. If you don't want to buy another hard disk, you can also make offsite backups with optical media, such as recordable CDs and DVDs.

Sample backup plans

Having surveyed the most common backup solutions and understanding the importance of redundancy, here are some sample backup plans.

TEST YOUR BACKUPS

No matter how you go about making backups, it is important to routinely test them to verify the data was copied and is available to be restored. How you test your backups depends on their format.

Time Machine: Testing your Time Machine backup just requires opening the Time Machine application and browsing the files to make sure everything works. If your Mac is out of commission, you can restore from or browse the Time Machine backup from a new installation of Mac OS X. You can also access your Time Machine backup from a different Mac. To do so, connect your Time Machine disk to the other Mac and while holding down the Option key, click the Time Machine menu bar icon and choose Browse Other Time Machine Disks. Your Time Machine backup should then appear.

Cloned hard disks: You can test your cloned disk by plugging it into your Mac and exploring it using the Finder. If your cloned disks spend a lot of time on the shelf, it is important to routinely make sure they still work. Hard disks at rest often remain at rest — permanently.

Optical media: There are a lot of opinions about exactly how long a DVD or CD will retain the data written to it before "bit rot" corrupts the data. Rather than push the envelope with your important data, you should copy the data to new discs every few years.

The home office's backup plan

This backup plan is for a Mac worker who runs a consulting business from her home. She has an iMac at her desk and a MacBook for the road. The data on both Macs is usually the same, but she wants to have multiple backups. Her backup gear includes a 1TB external FireWire disk, a 320GB USB-powered portable external disk, and a 500GB external hard disk. Her backup plan covers both Macs.

First, she attaches the 1TB FireWire disk to the iMac. She splits it into 320GB and 680GB partitions. The first partition is assigned to a SuperDuper mirror backup that runs every day at 2:00 a.m. The second partition holds the Time Machine backup. (Ideally, of course, she would have the Time Machine and SuperDuper backups on separate physical disks.)

She uses the 320GB portable USB disk to back up her MacBook with Time Machine. She keeps this disk in a drawer and attaches it to her MacBook every few nights. This way, if she loses her MacBook, she doesn't lose the backup.

Because she is the cautious type, she also runs a ChronoSync script on the external 500GB disk every few weeks. This disk does not get a clone or Time Machine backup. Instead, it holds essential work files, archives, and work in

FIGURE 2-5

A home office backup strategy diagram

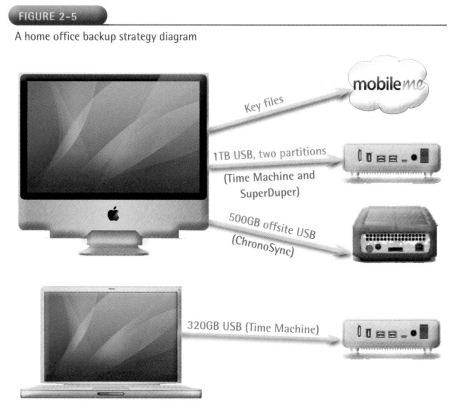

Key files

1TB USB, two partitions
(Time Machine and SuperDuper)

500GB offsite USB
(ChronoSync)

320GB USB (Time Machine)

FIGURE 2-6

An office's backup diagram

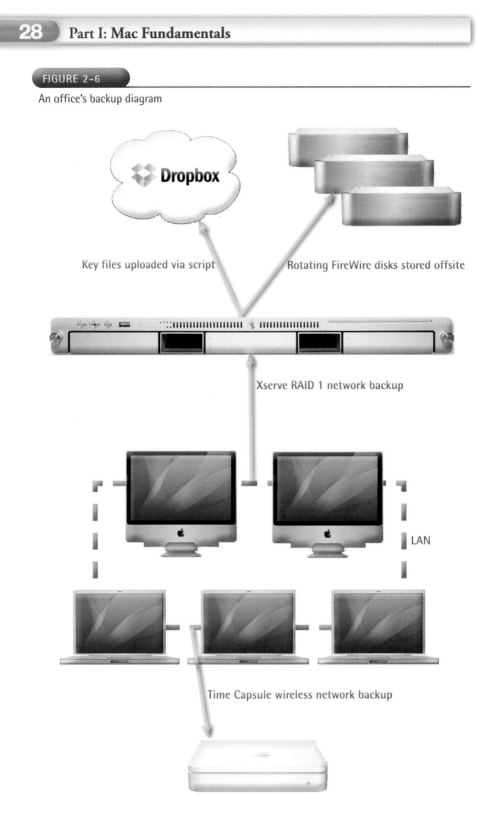

Key files uploaded via script

Rotating FireWire disks stored offsite

Xserve RAID 1 network backup

LAN

Time Capsule wireless network backup

progress. She also backs up her personal music, pictures, and video. Once this backup is made, she leaves it with her brother, who keeps it in his closet. This is her offsite backup.

For the really important files, she also uses her MobileMe account to copy files to her iDisk. In the event all her computers simultaneously combust, she can still access those files from the Apple servers.

Using this plan, illustrated in Figure 2-5, her key files are located on her iMac, her MacBook, two different Time Machine backups, a SuperDuper backup, on the MobileMe servers, and in her brother's closet. With very little effort, this Mac worker has a complete backup system.

The Mac office's backup plan

In this example, there is a small office running a Mac network. There are five Macs — a variety of iMacs and MacBook Pros. All the Macs are networked through an Apple Xserve server (which Apple stopped selling in early 2011 in favor of the Mac Pro and the Mac Mini running Snow Leopard Server). The users have little involvement with the backup plan. All files stored on the network server are located on a RAID 1 storage drive. Everything attached to the network is backed up. Furthermore, every other night, the server copies the RAID 1 data to a series of external hard disks that are rotated and kept offsite.

The office also runs a script that synchronizes key financial and client files to a paid Dropbox account, providing immediate cloud-based access to key files from anywhere. Finally, even though employees are supposed to keep all their data on the Xserve RAID disk, there is a 2TB Time Capsule in the office that wirelessly backs up the Macs' internal hard disks for any data that does not get to the server. This backup plan is illustrated in Figure 2-6.

For a backup plan to be successful, it needs to be both easy and redundant. This is why Apple's inclusion of Time Machine was one of the single best improvements to Mac OS X. Using the tools described in this chapter, you should have no trouble developing your own solutions and backing up.

Useful Utilities

pple is conservative about adding features to Mac OS X. But, when Apple finally does add a feature to the operating system, it is designed to be easy to understand and use. Time Machine (covered in Chapter 2) is a good example: To back up your Mac, you plug in an external drive and click one button. Sometimes, however, you need tools that go a bit deeper. As a result, there are several third-party utilities that are too geeky for conservative Apple but just the thing to help power users work faster and more efficiently. Although these utilities don't fit in any specific chapter of this book, they are all useful to Mac workers. So they get their own chapter — this one!

TextExpander

Typing is a drag, especially when you find yourself typing the same bits of text over and over again. TextExpander ($35; www.smilesoftware.com/textexpander) handles such repeated typing for you. Shown in Figure 3-1, TextExpander lets you create extended text entries (called *snippets*) that are automatically created when you type a predefined key combination.

For example, when you type the letters HmAdd, TextExpander could replace the letters with your home address. HmAdd is one of my snippets, along with WorkAdd, Cell#, and Office#. The idea is simple: Any bit of text you type repeatedly gets a keyword and, in the future, typing that keyword instructs TextExpander to do the typing for you. Creating new snippets is easy in TextExpander, as shown in Figure 3-2.

The Content field holds the text that you want TextExpander to type for you. You can make the snippet plain or formatted text. You can also make the snippet AppleScript code or a shell script. I always get a certain amount of pleasure typing long bits of text into the Content field knowing I will never have to type that text again.

The Label field lets you identify the snippet and the Abbreviation is the keyword that TextExpander will look for, like HmAdd, to autofill the snippet. You can optionally organize your snippets into groups. I recommend you do so because you will quickly amass a lot of them, and organization helps.

FIGURE 3-1

FIGURE 3-1

TextExpander

FIGURE 3-2

Creating a snippet in TextExpander

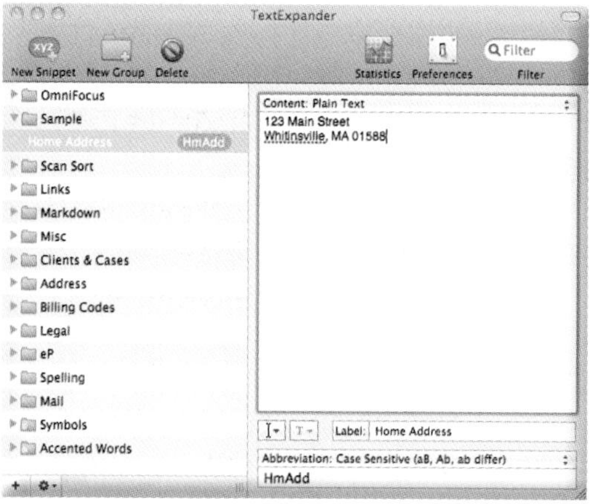

You can create snippets for any kind of text. An advertising executive might have snippets for a market research report. I have snippets that create contract text and legal documents. Use your imagination: A snippet can be a four-letter word with foreign characters or a 20-page specimen sales report.

TextExpander lets you specify the position of the cursor in your completed snippet. This is useful if you want to place the cursor in the middle of an expanded snippet. There is also form support, which allows you to embed blank fields in a snippet and fill them in later.

TextExpander really proves its usefulness when you're working with e-mail. If you repeatedly type the same e-mail messages, it is easy to automate the process with snippets. Customer service and support e-mails, for example, lend themselves to TextExpander automation. I know of one company that answers 90 percent of its customer e-mail from a list of TextExpander snippets.

TextExpander can also replace your e-mail client's signature support. The problem with most e-mail clients is that they blindly add the same signature to every e-mail from a given account. Some e-mails, however, don't need your full e-mail signature, so you have to later delete or modify the signature. Instead, disable your e-mail client's signature support and use TextExpander. I have three professional signatures that can each be triggered as a snippet at the end of e-mails. You can also create signatures appropriate for business associates, vendors, customers, family, and friends and then selectively apply the snipped to any e-mail.

You can organize snippets in folders keeping groups of snippets (such as e-mail, billing, and report text). TextExpander offers several predefined snippet groups that you can add to your snippet library. Just choose File ❿ Add Predefined Group and then choose the group you want to add.

Predefined groups include spelling-correction snippets that automatically fix common misspellings. For example, `freind` will be replaced with `friend`. There is also an accented-words snippet group that will turn `cafe'` into café and a symbol snippet group that will change text into common symbols, such as `iinfinity` into ∞. (The double `ii` in `iinfinity` lets you type the word infinity without triggering the snippet.)

If you are a Web programmer, there are CSS and HTML snippet groups that will create automatic CSS and HTML markup styling for Web pages. Typing `h1`, for example, expands to `h1 { }`, with the cursor positioned between the brackets.

TextExpander also has the ability to automatically enter dates and times in a format that you choose. Setting up an automatic date or time entry, shown in Figure 3-3, is not difficult. I have a snippet that creates a date and time string that I can add to any document when recording an entry. This snippet, shown in Figure 3-3, is activated by typing `.dts` and produces an entry that looks like this: `2010-12-18 11:01:50`.

Your snippet library can be synced with all your Macs using the MobileMe or Dropbox syncing services (both are covered in Chapter 21). There are also TextExpander iPhone and iPad applications that let you use your snippet library on your mobile devices. You can share your snippet library between a Windows PC and your Mac using Dropbox and a Windows application, Breevy ($30; `www.16software.com/breevy`).

TextExpander even keeps track of how much time you've saved by using snippets instead of typing. As I write this sentence, TextExpander has typed 3,415

FIGURE 3-3

Creating a date and time string in TextExpander

snippets totaling 201,253 characters and saved me eight hours of typing in the last nine months.

Default Folder X

The built-in Mac OS X Open and Save As dialog boxes can, at best, be described as spartan. Every time you open one, you find yourself wasting productive time drilling for a folder to save or open your document. Default Folder X ($35, www.stclairsoft.com), shown in Figure 3-4, is a utility that replaces the default Open and Save As dialog boxes, giving them a much-needed function overhaul.

The Default Folder X Open and Save dialog boxes includes a series of buttons on the right side. The top iconic button is the default folder icon, which allows you to specify a directory for saving items by application. Gone are the days of always starting in the Documents folder. Using Default Folder X, you can specify that, for example, iWork Pages opens and saves to one folder while iWork Numbers saves and opens to a different folder.

The second iconic button opens a directory to your hard disk and Home folder. This is similar to clicking the My Computer icon on a Windows PC.

The third iconic button provides a list of favorites. You can mark any folder as a favorite using this iconic button and later navigate to it with one click. I mark

FIGURE 3-4

The Default Folder X Save dialog box

active case folders as favorites along with several other folders I frequently click to in the Open and Save dialog boxes.

The final iconic button presents a list of recent locations. When you have your head down on a big project with multiple files and applications squirreled away in different places on your Mac, clicking this button will let you immediately access those most recently used folders.

FIGURE 3-5

Previewing a file with Default Folder X

In addition to using the iconic buttons to find specific folders, you can also point Default Folder X to a specific location by clicking on the location in a separate Finder window.

The bottom of the Default Folder X Save dialog box includes a Spotlight comment field that lets you attach Spotlight tags (covered in Chapter 1) to your files as you save them. The bottom of the Default Folder X Open dialog box gives you a preview of the highlighted file (shown in Figure 3-5), and displays permissions, comments, information, and tags.

Default Folders X also installs menu bar and Dock icons that give you access to the Default Folder X shortcuts outside the Save As and Open dialog boxes. One measure of Default Folder X's usefulness is the not-so-silent groan I make every time I work on a Mac without it and have to open or save a file.

Hazel

Hazel ($22; `www.noodlesoft.com/hazel`), shown in Figure 3-6, is an appropriately named system preference that does the housekeeping on your Mac. Instead of watching rooms, Hazel watches folders and cleans up all the files in those folders pursuant to your instruction. For example, you could have Hazel take all the image files in your Downloads folder and move them to your Pictures folder, as shown in Figure 3-6.

In Figure 3-6, Hazel is examining the contents of the Downloads folder and this rule description is, appropriately named, Move Images. Hazel then constantly examines the contents of the Downloads folder for image files. The second condition requires that the file be more than a day old. This way, Hazel won't file the image away before you have a chance to access it yourself. Assuming Hazel finds a file that is both an image and more than a day old, it moves the file out of your Downloads folder and into you Pictures folder. If there is already a copy of that image in the Pictures folder, Hazel throws it away.

FIGURE 3-6

A sample Hazel script

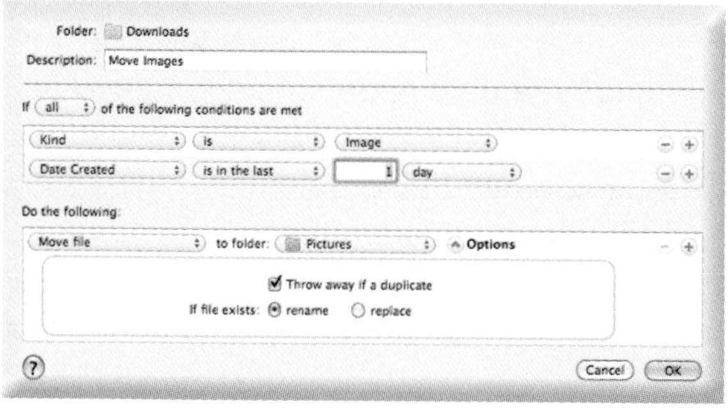

| Folder: | Downloads |
| Description: | Move Images |

If (all) of the following conditions are met

| Kind | is | Image | − + |
| Date Created | is in the last | day | − + |

Do the following:

| Move file | to folder: Pictures | ⌄ Options | − + |

☑ Throw away if a duplicate

If file exists: ⦿ rename ◯ replace

(?) (Cancel) (OK)

FIGURE 3-7

A Hazel script that files documents by name

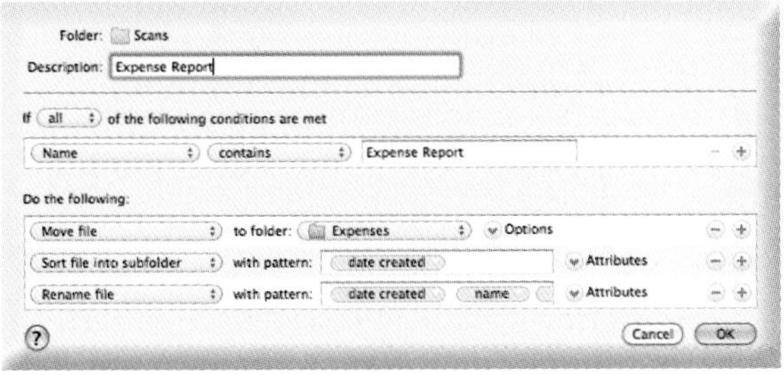

Hazel doesn't just look at a file's type. It can also look at a file's extension, name, date, label color, and a variety of other criteria. Using Hazel, you can develop some sophisticated strategies for automatic file organization. For example, you can create a rule where Hazel looks at the file names in a given folder and sorts the files accordingly, as Figure 3-7 shows.

This rule picks any file that includes the words "Expense Report" in its name and moves the file to the Expense folder. The destination folder can be anywhere your Mac can see, including your network server. Next, the rule sorts the file into a subfolder based on the year. If there is no subfolder for the year of the file, Hazel automatically creates one. Finally, Hazel renames the file, inserting the date before the name. (When setting up the date string, don't forget to add a space or hyphen between the date and name.)

Hazel can be set to run the rules automatically or on your command. The application runs in the background and uses few processing cycles. I've run Hazel automatically for years and never noticed it bogging down my Mac.

Nearly any file management you repeatedly do can be automated with Hazel. I have rules that empty my Trash every few days, sort my Downloads folder, and sort all my scanned files to subfolders. These examples only scratch the surface; Hazel can also set color labels and add Spotlight comments. It even integrates with the iLife library, allowing you to send files into iPhoto and iTunes.

If you are trying to break yourself of the habit of accumulating files on your desktop, Hazel can lend a hand. You can instruct Hazel to automatically file documents according to type (putting .doc files in a word processing folder, for example) or sweep all the desktop files into a separate sort folder for later processing. If you are brave, you could tell Hazel to throw any file that remains on your desktop for more than seven days straight into the Trash.

If you don't already have a program to delete applications, like AppZapper (covered in Chapter 1), Hazel has a feature called AppSweep that sniffs out application support files when you delete an application and gives you the option to trash them.

Hazel excels at handling the tedious computer management tasks that get in the way of doing work, or having fun, with your Mac.

LaunchBar

LaunchBar ($35; `www.obdev.at/products/launchbar`) gives you ninja-like abilities to operate your Mac quickly without ever touching the mouse.

The most common use is application launching. To load applications, activate LaunchBar (the default shortcut is ⌘+spacebar) and type in the first few characters of your favorite application. If your chosen application is at the top of the list, press the Return key. Otherwise, you can use the ↓ key to move down and select the application and launch it with the Return key, as shown in Figure 3-8. The next time you type the same search string, LaunchBar remembers your preference and places the application you chose at the top of the list. Also, LaunchBar doesn't just match text alphabetically; it looks logically at your applications in comparison to your shortcut. For example, when I type of, LaunchBar displays OmniFocus.

The ability to quickly launch applications is nice, but that capability is already built into Mac OS X with Spotlight (covered in Chapter 1). In addition to indexing applications, LaunchBar also indexes files, Web sites, contacts, calendar entries, and your iTunes library. LaunchBar then makes it easy for you to find and access all that information using a few keyboard shortcuts.

For example, in addition to just opening applications, you can open applications with specific recently used files. If you activate LaunchBar and type pag to get Pages and then press the spacebar, LaunchBar shows you a list of the most recently opened Pages files. You then press ↓ to move to the file you want and press Return. LaunchBar then opens the selected file in Pages. This is much faster than opening Pages and then going to the Open dialog box and clicking through folders to find your file. Note that for this to work, the application must use the Mac OS X Recent Items framework. Nearly all applications do, but, unfortunately, Microsoft Office does not.

LaunchBar indexes all your bookmarked and recent-history Web sites. So if you need to quickly navigate to a Web site, activate LaunchBar and start typing the Web site's name. Once the site appears in the LaunchBar search window, press Return and LaunchBar opens your default browser and loads the selected page.

You can also do Web searches from LaunchBar: Just activate LaunchBar and type in your desired search engine. Typing goo is enough to pull up the Google search engine. Then press the spacebar and LaunchBar gives you a line to type in your search query, as shown in Figure 3-9. Once you've typed in your search, press Return and LaunchBar opens your browser, goes to Google, and performs your search, displaying the results. LaunchBar supports many common searchable databases with this technology, including Wikipedia, Amazon.com, iTunes, Google Images, and eBay.

LaunchBar is also useful for accessing information from the Mac OS X Address Book. LaunchBar indexes all your contacts, so if you activate LaunchBar and begin typing the name of a contact in the LaunchBar search menu, you can open that person's card in Address Book or press the spacebar to get his or her contact information. From there you can press Return on the e-mail address to automatically open a new e-mail addressed to that person in your default mail client. If you press Return when on the person's phone number, the person's

FIGURE 3-8

Launching applications with LaunchBar

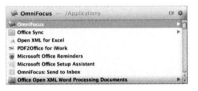

FIGURE 3-9

A LaunchBar Google search

FIGURE 3-10

Displaying a contact with LaunchBar

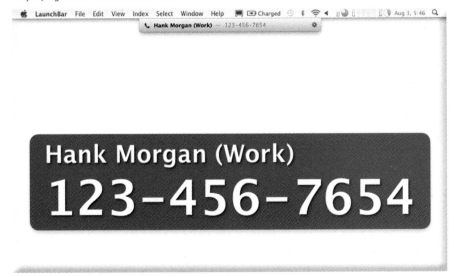

name and phone number are displayed in large text on your Mac's screen so you can dial your phone from across the room, as shown in Figure 3-10.

You can add calendar items and to-dos to iCal using LaunchBar. To do so, you must use LaunchBar's calendar syntax. For example, to set a lunch appointment with Jean on May 8 on your personal calendar, activate LaunchBar, select your personal calendar by typing `personal`, press the spacebar, and type `Lunch with Jean @ Jan 12 12-1pm`. Once you get the hang of it, entering events is faster with LaunchBar than opening iCal and creating events. To-dos are easier: Again you select the calendar for the to-do item and then just type the to-do. For example `Write Smith report !!` adds a to-do item with medium priority.

If you don't want to drill through the Finder for a file, you can search your Mac's file system using LaunchBar. If you need to open your Pictures folder for example, activate LaunchBar and type `pictures`. LaunchBar displays your Pictures folder from your Home folder. You can then press Return to open the Pictures folder in the Finder or press → to start navigating the Pictures folder in the LaunchBar window. If you activate LaunchBar and press the ~ (tilde) key, LaunchBar jumps to your Home folder. Mac OS X's Quick Look feature also works from LaunchBar, so if you have a file selected in the LaunchBar window, pressing the spacebar previews the file. With a little practice you can navigate to any file on your Mac using just your keyboard much faster than using the Finder and a mouse or trackpad.

In addition to navigating to files, LaunchBar lets you manipulate them. If you have an image file on your desktop, for example, you can select it (by clicking it with the mouse or using LaunchBar) and then act on it with LaunchBar by pressing and holding ⌘+spacebar for a few seconds activating LaunchBar's Instant Send mode. You can tell an item is tagged for Instant Send by the orange arrow icon in the LaunchBar window. You can then navigate to a different location on your Mac using LaunchBar (such as the Pictures folder) and press Return. LaunchBar then gives an option to copy or move the file from the desktop to the chosen destination. Instead of moving the file, you could instead type in a contact name and automatically attach the file to an outgoing e-mail. Once you get the hang of it, you will be surprised how fast you can manipulate files.

Another LaunchBar feature is the ability to save the Clipboard history. Every time you copy a new item into your Clipboard, the prior contents are flushed from memory. When you find yourself switching your clipboard between several items, it becomes maddening. LaunchBar can remember up to 40 items on your Clipboard and what applications they came from. You can access all these clippings by activating LaunchBar and typing `ClipboardHistory` (I use the shortcut ch). LaunchBar then gives you a list of the most recent clippings, as

FIGURE 3-11

LaunchBar's Clipboard history

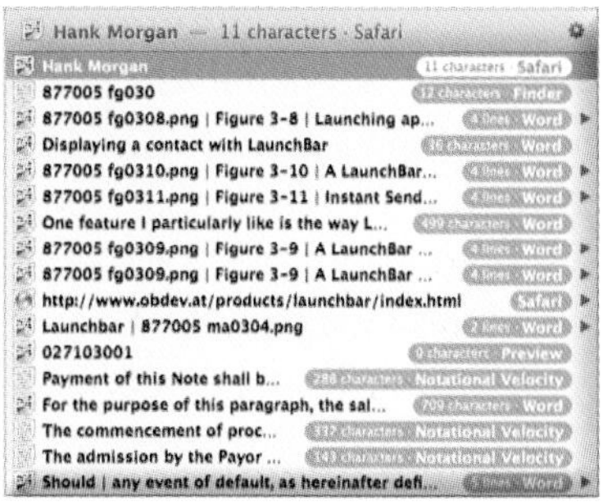

shown in Figure 3-11. You can scroll down the list with the arrow keys or type a few letters from a particular entry to make LaunchBar focus on it. Once you've found the entry you want to use, press Return and LaunchBar pastes it in your current application. LaunchBar also lets you set a preference that all text is copied and pasted as plain text; this helps when moving text between word processors and the Web.

LaunchBar has many additional tricks up its sleeve. You can resize an image by selecting a file, activating LaunchBar, and typing `resize`. You can create an archive by selecting multiple files, activating LaunchBar, and typing `zip`.

There are several competing application launchers for Mac OS X, but none of them works with LaunchBar's panache. Once you get the hang of LaunchBar, you can make your Mac dance using your keyboard. I have baffled many long-time Mac users with my lightning-fast Web searches and file manipulations using LaunchBar.

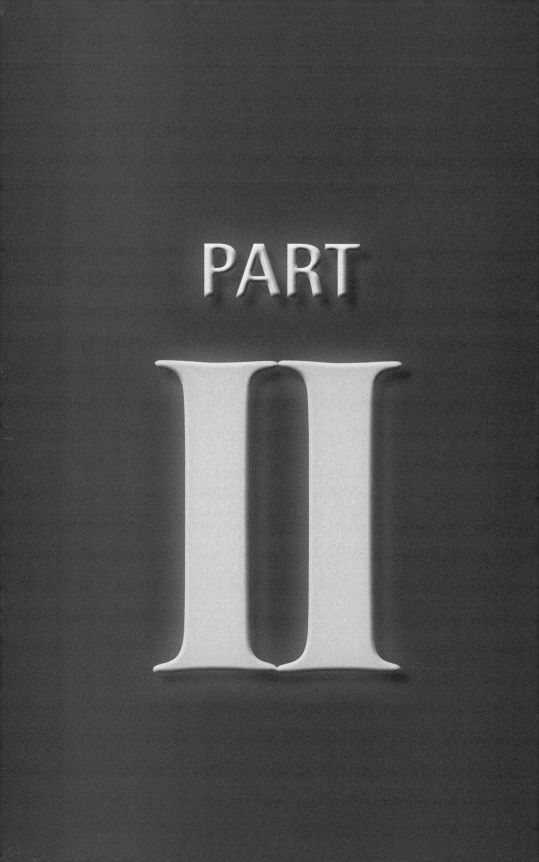

PART

II

Communications and Connections

The Internet and Your Mac

ne of the reasons for the resurgence of the Mac OS X platform is the Internet. As we do more of our computing through Web browsers and Internet portals, our operating system becomes less important. When you read the *New York Times* on the Internet, it doesn't care whether you are using Windows, Linux, or Mac OS X to do so. This gives Mac workers the freedom to use Mac OS X. This chapter explains the best ways to access the Internet from your Mac.

The Web Browser Options

Although Internet Explorer rules Windows, there are several browsing applications on the Mac OS X. Three of the most popular Mac browsers are Apple Safari, Mozilla Firefox, and Google Chrome.

Apple Safari

Safari (free; www.apple.com/safari), shown in Figure 4-1, ships on every new Mac. Safari, designed by Apple, includes the best Mac OS X Internet browser integration. For example, Safari works out of the box with the built-in Mac OS X downloads stack. It also works natively with Apple's Mail application, allowing you to e-mail a link or contents of a page. You can even save photos from Safari directly to iPhoto. Safari is also very automation-friendly and accepts instructions from Automator and AppleScript, both of which are explained in Chapter 24. Safari also integrates the Mac OS X Dashboard with the Web clippings feature that turns a Web page into a Mac OS X Dashboard widget accessible for quick reference. If you use Safari and also use a Windows PC, there is a Windows version that follows most of the same interface guidelines as Safari on the Mac.

Font rendering runs deep in the Mac OS X DNA. This is apparent in Safari, which renders fonts beautifully with its own anti-aliasing. Safari is also intelligent about the way it prints Web sites, auto-shrinking when appropriate.

Safari is based on WebKit, an open source Internet rendering engine. WebKit is the foundation of Safari on the Mac, iPhone, and iPad. It is also the engine used for Google's Chrome, covered later. With WebKit, Apple, which was legendary for its proprietary systems when the Mac was first released, now finds

FIGURE 4-1

The Safari main window

itself at the leading edge of open Internet standards. Safari supports numerous experimental properties such as text and object effects that enhance the browsing

FIGURE 4-2

Safari's Top Sites view

FIGURE 4-3

The History Cover Flow view in Safari

experience. Unfortunately, not all Web sites are compliant with these emerging properties. Some sites, particularly high-security and financial sites, may not render in a WebKit-based browser. Mozilla's Firefox, explained later, does normally render these sites.

Safari supports extensions (also called *plug-ins* and *add-ins*). Apple has a Web site with a collection of some of the most popular Safari extensions (choose Safari ▶ Safari Extensions Gallery or visit `http://extensions.apple.com`). Using extensions, you can add features to the browser.

Extensions are a new addition to Safari 5, so developers are just starting to sink their teeth into the capability. Still, extensions already exist that add security, bookmarking, productivity, shopping, and translation tools. My favorites include the following::

▶ **AutoPagerize.** Some Web sites use a practice of paginating their articles, requiring you to click through multiple pages (and multiple ads) to complete the article. AutoPagerize automatically assembles multipage articles into one page.

▶ **A Cleaner YouTube.** Have you noticed how messy YouTube is? When you go to watch a video, you are bombarded with additional information. A Cleaner YouTube removes the junk and lets you watch just the video.

▶ **Google Reader Styles.** This extension cleans up the otherwise uninspiring Google Reader (covered later in this chapter) Web view.

▶ **InstaPaperBeyond.** This extension adds keyboard shortcuts to the Instapaper service (covered later in this chapter), making navigation much easier.

Other popular Safari extensions include 1Password (covered in Chapter 23) and ClickToFlash (covered later in this chapter).

In Safari, you can start browsing where you left off by choosing to reopen all the windows from your last session in the History menu. Another useful feature in Safari for Mac workers is the built-in PDF-rendering engine. This allows you to view PDF documents in Safari without going to an outside application or add-in. You can open the PDF in Preview, covered in Chapter 12, or save it to your Mac for later use.

Safari's Top Sites feature, shown in Figure 4-2, allows users to get an attractive page with small images of their favorite Web sites. Top Sites can be configured to your favorite sites and is easily navigable with one click. The Cover Flow view, shown in Figure 4-3, allows you to flip through sites in your browsing history. Because Safari keeps an index of all the content in the page history, you can even search for individual words contained on the pages.

Mozilla Firefox

Mozilla's Firefox (free; www.mozilla.org), shown in Figure 4-4, is an open source browser and was the first real alternative to Internet Explorer on Windows

FIGURE 4-4

The Firefox main window

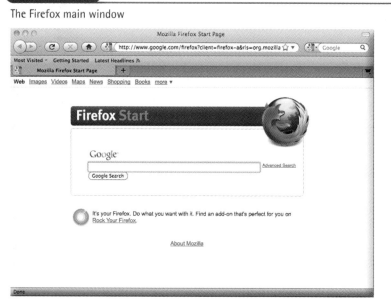

FIGURE 4-5

The Wired-Marker Firefox plug-in

since the original browser, Netscape Navigator. Because it has such penetration on the Windows platform, Firefox works with just about every Web site. If you come across a site that doesn't load in Safari or Chrome, try it in Firefox.

Firefox is also the most extensible browser available for Mac OS X. If you like to customize your browser, Firefox is for you. There are multiple add-ins for every conceivable use. At the time of this writing, there were more than 6,000 add-ins available for Firefox. Additionally, there are thousands of themes to change the look of the application. If you want your browser to feature unicorns and cupcakes, you can do it with Firefox.

The following add-ins are particularly helpful for Mac workers (you can find most Firefox add-ins at `http://addons.mozilla.org`):

▶ **Merriam-Webster** (`www.merriam-webster.com`) puts a dictionary in your browser.

▶ **DeeperWeb** allows you to navigate through Google search results using tag clouds.

▶ **FastestFox** speeds up Firefox with several tweaks and improvements.

▶ **Wired-Marker** installs a highlighter in your browser. You can mark up a page in different colors and the page is automatically saved in a scrapbook, as shown in Figure 4-5.

▶ **Converter** lets you convert units, time zones, and currency on any Web site.

▶ **Adblock Plus** stops a lot of advertising before it gets to your browser.

FIGURE 4-6

The Chrome main window

FIGURE 4-7

Chrome's New Tab window

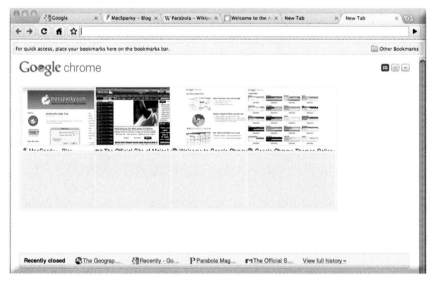

▶ **Greasemonkey** allows you to drastically change the functionality with downloaded JavaScript programs.

Because Firefox add-ins work on all platforms, it is a popular browser for people who use both Windows and Mac OS X; they can have the same browser experience on both machines.

Google Chrome

Google recently launched its own browser, Chrome, shown in Figure 4-6. Chrome for the Mac (free; www.google.com/chrome) simplifies the traditional browser interface. The search bar and address bar are combined into one box, called the Omnibox. You can type a Web address or a search query in the same place, and Chrome is smart enough to do the right thing. The Chrome address bar also displays the security level of the current site and allows you to bookmark pages.

The Chrome browser's New Tab button works much like Top Sites in Apple's Safari, opening a preview page of several sites available to you, as shown in Figure 4-7. Also like Safari, Chrome uses WebKit as its rendering engine.

Google Chrome runs each browser tab in its own block of memory. This technique, called *sandboxing*, makes for a stable browsing environment. If you have seven tabbed pages open and one page crashes, Chrome flushes the memory for that single tab and keeps the remaining six tabs open. This sandboxing also makes your browser more secure: If a hacker gets into your sandboxed Web page, he usually can't get any further than the tab assigned to that particular page. This partitioning of the browser is a significant advance in browser technology. Indeed the WebKit team has announced that it will adopt this feature, so it will also be in Safari, and Firefox is sure to follow suit.

Although Chrome doesn't offer the slick user experience you get with Safari's Cover Flow view, Chrome does a good job indexing and searching visited sites. You shouldn't be surprised; Google is the undisputed king of search.

Where Safari offers the best integration with Mac OS X, Chrome has the best integration with the cloud-based Google applications such as Gmail, Google

BOOKMARK SYNCING

Because there are several attractive browser options on the Mac, you may find yourself using multiple browsers and if you do, you will want to share your bookmarks among them.

When syncing bookmarks between multiple browsers, one popular tool is Xmarks (free; www.xmarks.com). This Internet-based service installs on your computer and keeps your bookmarks in sync. It is multiplatform, so if you use a Windows PC at your desk and the Mac on the road, you will have no trouble sharing your bookmarks.

If you're not comfortable synchronizing your bookmarks through the Web, a local tool is Agile Web Solutions' All Bookmarks (free; www.agilewebsolutions.com/allbookmarks). This application puts all your bookmarks in your menu bar for use in any Web browser installed on your Mac.

If you just use Safari but have multiple Macs, an iPad, or an iPhone, you can sync your bookmarks with Apple's MobileMe service ($100 per year; www.apple.com/mobileme). MobileMe is a subscription service that has several additional benefits as referenced throughout this book.

Docs, Google Reader, and the ever-expanding Google cloud-based software library. If you rely on the Google applications, Chrome is probably the right browser for you.

Chrome is also extensible. Although it does not have the exhaustive add-in library available to Firefox, there is an active community of Chrome developers. There are add-ins for Twitter and many Web social networking services, as well as feature improvements, ad blockers, and enhancements. One of the best is SearchPreview, which allows you to see thumbnail images of the Web sites generated in response to your Google search.

Despite its newness, Chrome is making an impression with innovative security and stability features, making it a favorite for many Mac workers.

Choosing a browser

I have not said which browser is fastest because there is no clear winner. There is a constant arms race among the various browsers over which is the fastest. Every time a new version of any particular browser comes out, it is claimed to be the fastest, until the next browser's update shows up. All three Mac browsers are fast. More important, with modern computer processors, there isn't much of a difference between the slowest and fastest browser.

The real choice is about features and stability. Firefox is the most extensible and most likely to open any Web page you throw at it. Safari masters the Mac OS X experience and integrates throughout the operating system. Chrome features some great new technologies and the Google Web experience. They are all free, and the best way to choose is to try them out and see what works best for you. There is no wrong decision. And you can use more than one if you like.

Taming Flash

Adobe Flash is a programming environment that allows Web developers to make animated graphics for the Internet, as well as other interactive items. When you log onto a Web site and there are popping lights, jumping boxes, and moles to whack, most likely there is a Flash animation involved. Flash is the programming environment of choice for many advertisements and complex animated Web pages.

Unfortunately, Flash doesn't always run efficiently on the Mac. Moreover, not all Flash programmers are created equal. Once you start opening multiple tabs and have several Flash instances running on your Mac at the same time, your browser — and your Mac in general — may slow to a crawl. Because Flash animations are processor-intensive, running them for extended periods makes your Mac run hotter, requires the fans to run more often, and reduces the

FIGURE 4-8

Setting rules in ClickToFlash

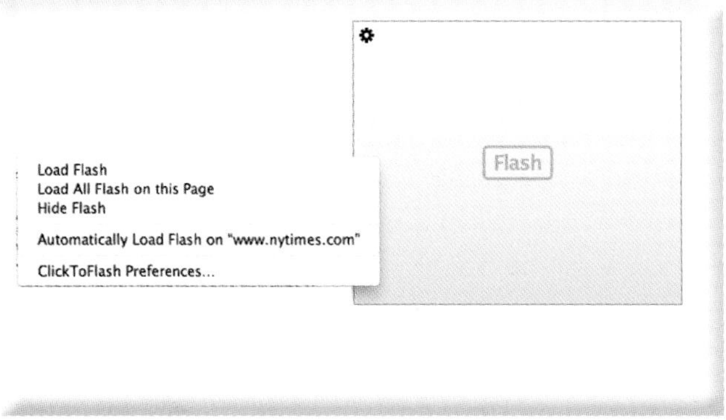

available battery life on your MacBook. Flash also can present a security risk as some hackers exploit Flash as a point of entry into your computer.

One of the best methods to ensure efficient browser performance is to stop Flash in its tracks. For Apple Safari, use the shareware add-in, ClickToFlash (www.clicktoflash.com). Once installed, ClickToFlash blocks all incoming Flash animations. When your page loads, you just see an empty box with the word "Flash" written in the middle, as shown in Figure 4-8. If ClickToFlash blocks a Flash animation that you do want to see, just click the blank space and the animation loads. If you Control+click or right-click on a blocked Flash animation, you can instruct ClickToFlash to always allow (or to always ban) Flash animations on certain Web sites, as shown in Figure 4-8. An additional benefit is that ClickToFlash also strips the Flash out of YouTube, allowing you to watch dogs surf without overloading your Mac.

Because ClickToFlash stops Flash animations until you specifically authorize viewing them, your browser is much less likely to get bogged down. Stopping Flash results in a more stable and secure browsing environment for you and much less work for your Mac, which will run cooler and longer. If you are using Firefox or Chrome, use the Flashblock extension for the same purpose. It is not as feature-rich as ClickToFlash but it does block Flash.

Once you install a Flash blocker, you will be amazed at how much more stable your Web browsing is and surprised by how infrequently you need to click the box and let Flash loose on your Mac.

If you really want to declare war on Flash, you can also install BashFlash (www.bashflash.com). This shareware application installs to your menu bar and gives you feedback as to how much work Flash is giving your Mac. It works with both Chrome and Safari. If the menu bar icon turns red, Flash is using a lot of system resources. With two clicks on the menu bar icon, you can kill all active Flash animations.

By using a Flash blocker with BashFlash, you can limit your exposure to Flash animations in your browser and make sure the Flash code you do let through to your Mac doesn't get in your way.

RSS

Do you have a lot of bookmarks and find it tedious clicking them to see what is new? You are not alone. If you had even 15 Web sites that were relevant to your industry and worth checking on a daily basis, you could spend hours just clicking to see what is new. Fortunately, there is a solution for this called RSS, which stands for Really Simple Syndication.

An RSS document, usually called a *feed*, is a bit of Web code that includes a list of articles and their text from a blog or Web site (sometimes summarized) along with the author and publisher data, as shown in Figure 4-9.

You give an RSS reader a list of your favorite Web sites and it pulls the feeds from those sites, giving you a list of new articles from all your favorite Web sites in one location. This allows you to keep up with all your important Web sites with just a glance, and it saves you the trouble of the bookmark tango.

On the Mac, there are several RSS readers. My favorite is Google Reader (free; www.google.com/reader), shown in Figure 4-10. You can set up Google

FIGURE 4-9

A sample RSS feed

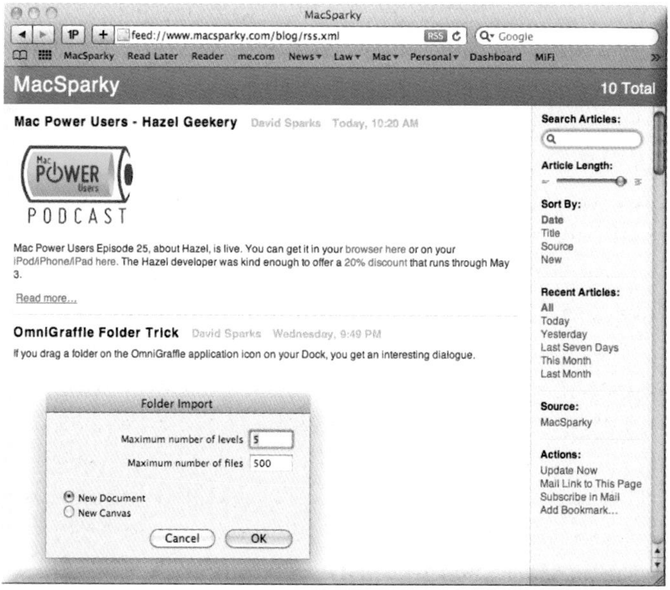

FIGURE 4-10

Google Reader

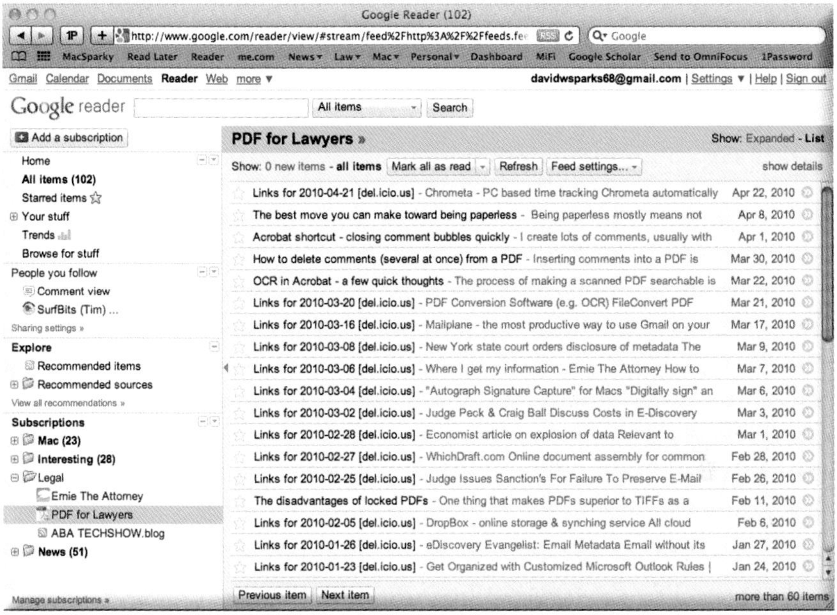

Reader as part of your free Google account and check your feeds from any Web browser. Google Reader also has several social networking features, allowing you to share and mark feeds for other people.

One of the primary advantages of using the Google Reader service is the ability to synchronize with multiple devices. There are Google Reader clients for the iPhone, iPad, and Windows, so you can stay current with your feeds from any device.

Some users prefer a dedicated Mac OS X application to read their newsfeeds. There are several native Mac OS X applications that synchronize with Google Reader. My favorite is NetNewsWire (free; www.newsgator.com/individuals/netnewswire), shown in Figure 4-11.

Another option is Fever ($30; www.feedafever.com). Fever is set up on a Web server. You tell Fever which feeds are the most important and it automatically filters the news for you. Fever uses an interesting temperature metaphor to bring what it believes are the most important news items to your attention: Articles of interest may be set at 101 degrees, whereas something that Fever thinks you must read immediately might be set at 106 degrees.

Once you discover the magic of RSS, you will begin to notice the RSS logo at all your favorite Web sites. It is so easy to click that RSS button and add the feed that before long you will find yourself with 200 RSS subscriptions, and when you open RSS feed reader over your morning tea you will discover there are 1,732 unread articles from the last eight hours. It is really easy to go overboard with

FIGURE 4-11

NetNewsWire's main window

NetNewsWire (97 unread)		
Subscribe New Folder Refresh All	Mark All As Read Next Unread Post to Weblog	Search
Latest News	**PDF for Lawyers – 40 news items**	**Date**
Flagged Items	Links for 2010-04-21 [del.icio.us]	22 Apr 2010
Clippings	The best move you can make toward being paperless	08 Apr 2010
Interesting	Acrobat shortcut – closing comment bubbles quickly	01 Apr 2010
Legal	How to delete comments (several at once) from a PDF	30 Mar 2010
ABA TECHSHOW.blog	OCR in Acrobat – a few quick thoughts	22 Mar 2010
Ernie The Attorney	Links for 2010-03-20 [del.icio.us]	21 Mar 2010
PDF for Lawyers	Links for 2010-03-16 [del.icio.us]	17 Mar 2010
Mac	Links for 2010-03-08 [del.icio.us]	09 Mar 2010
News	Links for 2010-03-06 [del.icio.us]	07 Mar 2010
	Links for 2010-03-04 [del.icio.us]	05 Mar 2010
	Links for 2010-03-02 [del.icio.us]	03 Mar 2010
	Links for 2010-02-28 [del.icio.us]	01 Mar 2010
	Links for 2010-02-27 [del.icio.us]	28 Feb 2010
	Links for 2010-02-25 [del.icio.us]	26 Feb 2010
	The disadvantages of locked PDFs	11 Feb 2010

Brilliant wireframes, diagrams, and designs made easy. OmniGraffle for Mac and iPad. Ads via The Deck

97 unread Default (3.2)

RSS feeds. When you have too many feeds, you either spend your whole day catching up (and get nothing else done) or you don't bother reading any of them and lose the benefit of RSS. So put yourself on a data diet: Pick the feeds that are particularly relevant to your industry and stick with those.

Instapaper

Once you become Internet-savvy with your customized browser and efficient RSS workflow, you will discover there are a lot of interesting articles you want to read. The trouble is finding a time and a place to read those articles. Instapaper (free; www.instapaper.com) is a great tool.

As part of the Instapaper account setup, you copy a special bookmark named Read Later to your browser's bookmarks bar. This special bookmark, called a *bookmarklet,* has a bit of JavaScript code in it. After you copy the bookmarklet into your bookmarks, anytime you find an interesting Web article that you don't have time for, you just click the Read Later button to have that JavaScript push a copy into your Instapaper account. Instapaper then does its best to remove the Internet noise and show you just the article text and any inline pictures. You can later log in to your Instapaper account and read the articles at your leisure. If you own an iPhone or iPad, there is also an Instapaper application that allows you to synchronize your Instapaper articles to those mobile devices.

Instapaper is very useful to Mac workers: No matter what your profession, using the Web to intelligently find, filter, and absorb information is within your grasp on the Mac.

Web 2.0 and the Future

Although the Internet started life as a pipe of information, it has become so much more. There is an emerging group of Internet-based software applications that work out of your browser and are licensed with a monthly fee. This *software-as-a-service*, or SaaS, model seeks to replace the traditional approach of buying software licenses for your office computers and servers. Instead, companies and users subscribe to software from an online vendor. This book addresses several of the popular Internet-based (or *cloud*) applications in their appropriate chapters, such as Google Docs in Chapter 11.

There are certain benefits to software as a service. It is, by its very nature, multiplatform. These applications run on Windows, Mac OS X, Linux, and mobile operating systems — as long as they follow accepted Web standards, of course. These services also are low-maintenance. The software is upgraded and maintained by the software vendor on its servers. No longer do you have to bring in IT staff in the middle of the night because your key application decided to stop behaving. Also, if your staff is mobile, it gives them easy access wherever they are, as cloud-based data is accessible from anywhere there's an Internet connection. In some cases, it can replace costly data servers in your office.

Despite these benefits, software as a service is not a solution for every company. Data security may require that you keep everything on your local servers. Also, this is an emerging field, and often the cloud-based software lack features found in traditional local applications. Regardless, as browsers become more powerful, the move toward cloud-based software is going to accelerate.

The Internet is a blessing and a curse for Mac workers. It offers a wide variety of tools and services to allow us to get work done more easily, but it also constantly threatens to drown us in information. Using the tools from this chapter, you should be able to tame the Internet on your Mac.

Using E-mail

E-mail is, for many Mac workers, their primary mode of communication. Although e-mail is now firmly entrenched in the workplace, few Mac workers have given much thought about how to manage their e-mail efficiently. This chapter will make you an e-mail power user, explaining how e-mail works, showing you some of the best e-mail clients on the Mac, and offering tips to make e-mail work for you.

E-mail Protocols

One of the benefits of using a Mac is you don't have to spend much time thinking about the underlying technologies of how it works. That is what you pay Apple for. E-mail, however, is different. After someone clicks Send and before a message arrives in your inbox, it is parked somewhere on the Internet. The purpose of your local e-mail application (often called the *mail client*) is to talk to the mail server holding your message and successfully get it delivered to your computer. The technology used by the Internet to deliver that message to you is called an *e-mail protocol*, and there are several popular ones: POP, IMAP, Gmail IMAP, and Exchange. Picking the right protocol is essential to efficiently managing your e-mail.

POP and IMAP are the most common protocols used in small businesses as well as by Internet-based e-mail services used by individuals and businesses alike. Microsoft's proprietary Exchange is typically used by larger companies, and I cover it and other corporate e-mail technology later in this chapter.

POP e-mail

The POP (Post Office Protocol) e-mail protocol dates back to 1984. The goal of the POP protocol is to get the e-mail off the Internet e-mail server and onto your computer. When using a POP server, your computer sends a message asking for new messages, and the POP server sends the messages to the local client. Usually, a POP server sends the entire message to your computer without keeping a copy on the mail server. This made a lot of sense when everyone used just one computer. All the messages came to one place, and you always had local access to all your mail.

But once you start adding laptops, smartphones, and iPads, a problem arises: Messages are scattered across several devices. For example, when your iMac connects to a POP mail server and retrieves your e-mail, the POP server dutifully drops that e-mail in your inbox and deletes it from the server. When, three hours later, you check e-mail on your MacBook, the POP server reports there is no e-mail: It has already discarded the e-mail downloaded to your iMac. A few hours later, you check your e-mail again, this time on your iPhone; there's a new message from a co-worker that was sent after you checked your e-mail on the MacBook. The server sends that message to the iPhone and deletes it, so now neither the MacBook nor iMac will get it when you next check for e-mail on them. Before long, you have your e-mail split among several devices, and not one device has everything.

It didn't take long for people to realize this was a problem. One solution is to tell the POP server to keep copies of all e-mail (usually, for a specified period, such as a week or month). This way, each e-mail gets delivered to all devices. But this workaround can prove troublesome: The POP mail server has no idea what you do with the e-mail after it is downloaded to your device. So, if you read and move the message into a folder on your iMac, when you get e-mail later on your iPhone, the POP server doesn't know that and shows the message as unread in your inbox. That can be confusing — requiring you to remember which messages you've read and dealt with previously.

By default, a POP server deletes any message on the server that you delete on your mail client, which helps ensure that you see specific spam messages just once. But many people configure the POP server to keep deleted messages for a day or a week as a safety precaution in case they deleted a message by accident and want to get it from the server's Trash folder. In that case, all your devices get the deleted spam messages as well — at least until the server finally deletes them.

The bottom line is that there isn't enough communication between the mail client and POP server to manage mail across multiple devices.

IMAP e-mail

IMAP (Internet Mail Access Protocol) solves the POP problem. The idea behind IMAP is to not remove the message from the server after sending it to the e-mail client, but instead to leave it on the server so it's available for any and all devices that check e-mail on that account. Because the server retains the e-mail, each of your devices can download a copy and remain synchronized with each device and the server.

IMAP also synchronizes folders (POP does not). So, if you create an e-mail folder called Action on your iMac using an IMAP mail account, the IMAP server synchronizes that folder and its contents to your MacBook and iPhone. Say that you read a message on your iMac and move it to the Action folder; the server sees this and moves the message to the Action folder on the server. The next time your MacBook and iPhone access the e-mail server, their Action folders are updated to include that message.

In addition to keeping your work e-mail organized, IMAP synchronization helps you out with spam: Once you delete a spam e-mail on, say, your iPhone, it goes in the trash on the IMAP server and you will not see it when checking e-mail on your other devices.

Mail Clients

There are several popular mail clients available for your Mac to manage your e-mail accounts. The most commonly used clients in the workplace are Apple Mail, Gmail, and Microsoft Outlook/Entourage.

Apple Mail

Mac OS X ships with its own e-mail client, Apple Mail, which is shown in Figure 5-1. Apple Mail is a full-featured mail client that works with POP, IMAP, and Exchange mail servers. Although Apple's marketing focuses on Mail's consumer features, it is fully capable of being used for work.

FIGURE 5-1

Apple Mail

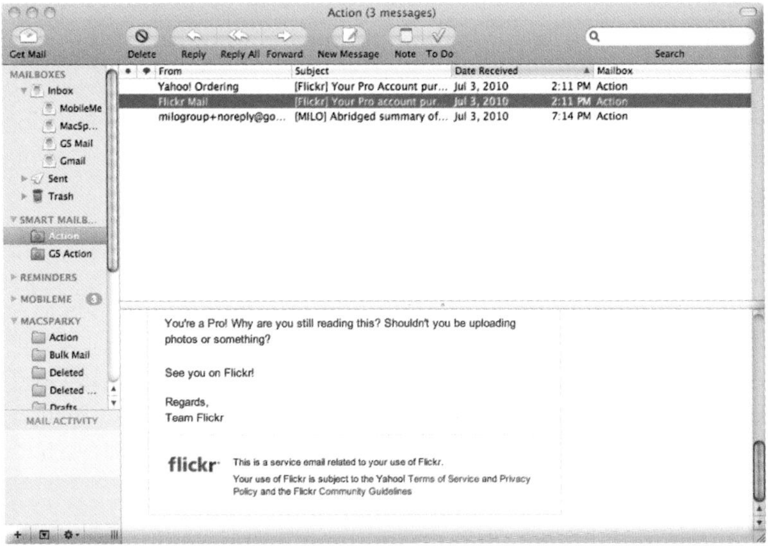

FIGURE 5-2

The Apple Mail Account settings

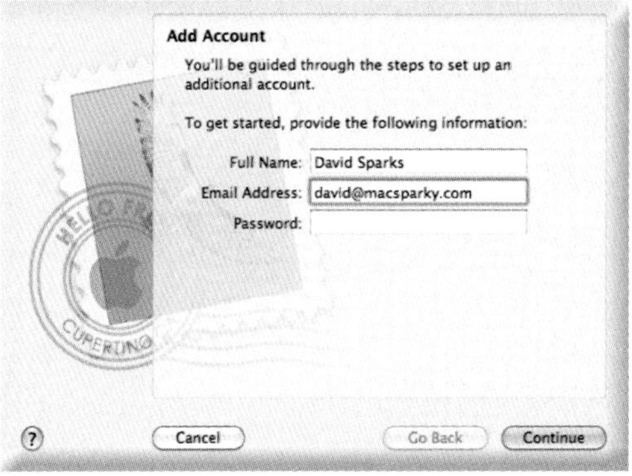

You set up accounts in Apple Mail in the Accounts pane of the Preferences dialog box, shown in Figure 5-2. For MobileMe, Gmail, Yahoo, and AOL accounts, setup is automatic: Type in your account name and password, and Mail does the rest. For other POP and IMAP mail services, you need to provide your mail server details, which should be available from your mail service provider. Apple Mail also works with Microsoft Exchange, as covered later.

If you use multiple accounts, Mail tracks each account separately and lets you set different server rules, such as how long to keep deleted messages, for each account.

Composing a new e-mail in Mail is intuitive: As you start typing a recipient's name, Mail follows your keystrokes and tries to fill in the name from your Address Book database and Mail's own list of recent correspondents. Mail also looks for groups from your Address Book. If you create a group of 12 people called Smith Account in Address Book, typing Smith Account in a Mail recipient field adds all 12 members. Alternatively, you could open Address Book and drag people (or groups of people) into your message's recipient fields.

If you want to add an attachment to your message, drag the file in from the Finder or your Desktop. If you want to add a link, click and drag the address from the Safari or Firefox address bar straight into the body of the message. Mail lets you embed a Web link in your e-mail. To do so, select the text where you want to include the link and press ⌘+K. Mail opens a dialog box in which you can insert a Web link. The linked text then displays in blue in the recipient's mail box, and clicking on the words opens the Web link. This is especially useful when sending long links.

To add photos, click the Photo Browser button in the Mail toolbar (or choose Window ▶ Photo Browser) and a photo browser listing your iPhoto and Aperture libraries appears. Mail lets you set an image size in the lower-right corner of the

FIGURE 5-3

Using data detectors in Mail

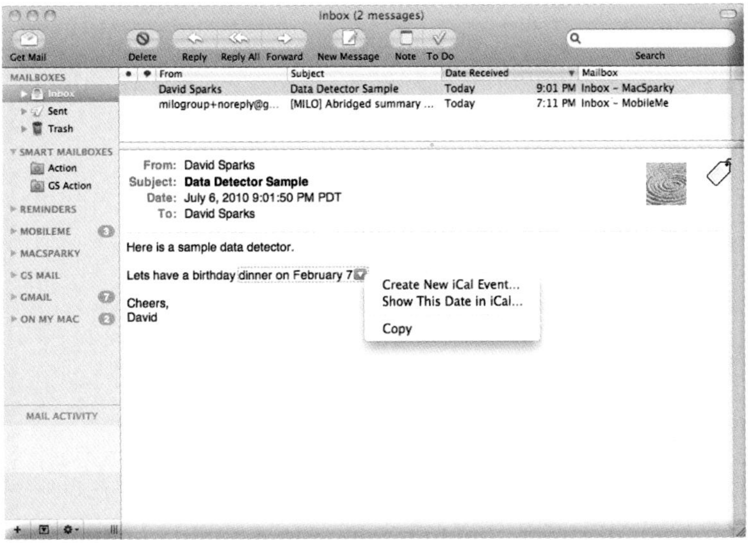

outgoing message box. This allows you to skip the step of shrinking large images to reduce file size before sending them; Mail does it for you.

Mail has tools to help you manage incoming e-mail. Mail incorporates the Mac OS X Quick Look feature that lets you preview a mail attachment by selecting it and pressing the spacebar. This works for most common data formats, including Microsoft Office, iWork, image, and PDF documents.

Mail's data detectors examine your incoming mail. If Mail detects the existence of contact information or a calendar event, you can add the contact to Address Book or the event to your iCal calendar by clicking the data detector disclosure triangle that appears next to the contact or event in the mail body, as shown in Figure 5-3.

Taking a page from iTunes, Mail allows you to create "smart" mailboxes where you can build a mailbox that automatically populates with messages based on the criteria you set. Note that the messages in a smart mailbox are actually aliases to the original messages, which remain in the inbox or in whatever folders Mail finds them. Thus, a smart mailbox is a virtual mailbox, which means you can have the same message in several smart mailboxes, even though the actual message resides in just one physical location. To create a new smart mailbox, choose Mailbox ▶ New Smart Mailbox or click the + (plus) iconic button in the lower left of the Mail window.

As an example, you could create a smart mailbox that looks for e-mail with the words "Smith account" in the subject line, dated in the last two months, and is flagged. Once you create that smart mailbox, it automatically fills with all e-mails matching your criteria, and keeps updating the smart mailbox as you receive more e-mail. So, if you unflag a message in the smart mailbox, that message is immediately removed from the smart mailbox, because it no longer satisfies the smart mailbox criteria. (The message isn't deleted from your mail database, of course.)

You can be very creative with smart mailboxes. For example, you can create a smart mailbox for messages from your supervisor, messages to your key clients, or messages that contain the words "new order." Smart mailboxes are easy to create and can be easily deleted when they are no longer needed. Because the process of manually sorting your mail into subfolders is usually a waste of time (as I explain later in this chapter), creating a smart mailbox when the need arises is the better approach.

Mail also includes a powerful search engine. When using its search bar, Mail searches as you type each letter. You can search your entire mail database, including all the information in every message, or limit your search to the sender, recipient, or subject fields. You can also limit your search to specified mailboxes. I have always found Mail search to be fast: My e-mail database contains about 50,000 messages and I'm able to quickly locate messages using Mail search. Some users report that Mail's search slows down with larger databases. In that case, there are third-party applications designed to streamline Mail's search, such as Rocketbox ($15; www.getrocketbox.com).

Mail has a useful rule system for automating your mail messages. In the Rules pane of the Preferences dialog box, you can create rules to automatically process incoming e-mail. For example, you can create a rule that takes any incoming message from your key client and turns the message red, forwards a copy to your assistant, and plays an alarm when it arrives (see Figure 5-4). You could also create a rule that takes any e-mail message from that one relative who enjoys forwarding e-mail about dancing cats (we all have at least one of those relatives) and moves it straight to the trash.

FIGURE 5-4

Creating a Mail rule

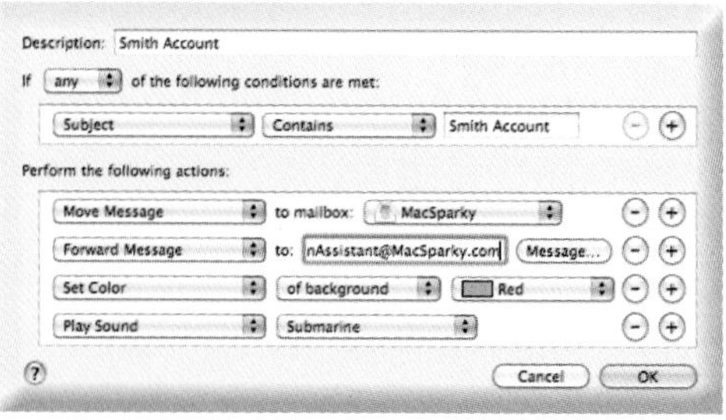

Rule-based e-mail management is limited only by your imagination. Mail's rules management even includes the ability to run AppleScripts (covered in Chapter 24) upon receipt of the message. Mail's native rule support applies to every incoming message. You cannot limit its application to specific messages or outgoing messages. Nor can you create rules that act on messages inside folders, such as to archive older mail from specific folders on a periodic basis to keep your server storage under control. The ability to apply rules to outgoing mail and specific messages is, however, available with the Mail Act-On plug-in covered later in this chapter.

Apple Mail add-ons

Like most Apple software applications, Apple Mail focuses on the user experience details but does not include a lot of extra features. Fortunately, Apple Mail is extensible. Several software developers have created add-ons for Apple Mail to enhance its capabilities. My favorite ones include the following.

Mail Act-On

Mail Act-On ($25; www.indev.ca/mailacton) allows you to file e-mail messages much quicker. Although the Apple Mail rule system provides a way to manage messages, everything is automatic. You do not have a choice of when, and when not, to activate rules. Mail Act-On gives you this ability. It allows you to create rules that are selectively activated on your keystrokes.

For example, in Apple Mail the only way to move a message to a folder is to click and drag it. This takes time. First you must take your hands off the keyboard and put them on the mouse. Then you must drag the message to a folder and drop it. In addition to the lost time, there is always the possibility that you will land on the wrong folder and misfile the message. If you process 50 messages a day, this lost time adds up. Using Mail Act-On, you can create a keyboard rule that automatically files messages in a designated mailbox when you press a keyboard shortcut. The rules are created in the Mail Act-On window of the Apple Mail Preferences dialog box, shown in Figure 5-5.

FIGURE 5-5

A Mail Act-On filing rule

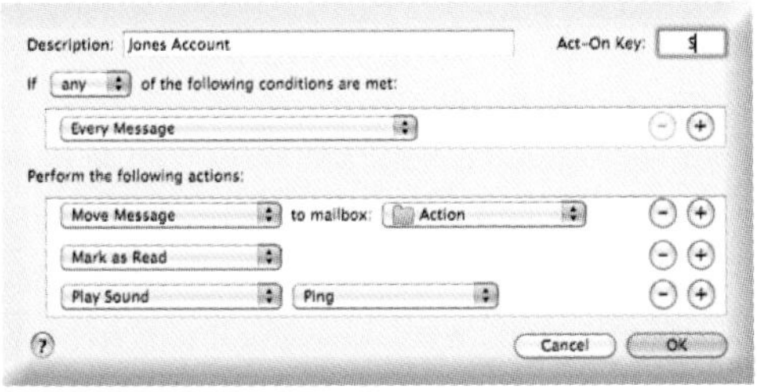

Let's break down the rule in Figure 5-5 to understand how it works. The rule name is listed in the rule description field so you can identify it later. The Act-On Key is the keyboard letter that is combined with the Control key to activate the rule. In this case, the keyboard combination is Control+S. Leave the default setting at Any, so any conditions satisfy the criteria; in this case, there is just one criterion: Every Message. Now that you've defined how the rule applies and what keyboard combination triggers it, you need to instruct Mail Act-On what to do with the messages when activated. You do that with the rule actions. In this case, I'm telling Mail Act-On to move the message to a specified mailbox and mark the message as read. Finally, I'm asking Mail to play the Ping sound to notify me the move is done. Using rules like this, you can file all your mail messages to different mailboxes with different key combinations.

Moving messages isn't the only use for Mail Act-On. You can also copy messages, set their color, and delete them. If you want to create rules to process mail, you can set actions to reply, forward, and redirect messages. You can also use Mail Act-On to trigger AppleScript code or apply additional Mail Act-On rules. With a little thought, you can automate much of your mail processing with this application.

In addition to allowing you to trigger rules upon keystrokes, Mail Act-On also gives you the ability to apply rules to your outbox. If, for example, you wanted to color every outgoing e-mail to a certain client green, you can create a rule to do that. You could also create a rule to copy any e-mail sent to a specified client to the account manager for the client. The outbox rules do not require a keyboard combination; they are applied automatically to every e-mail you send.

MailTags

MailTags ($30; www.indev.ca/mailtags.html) adds tagging to Mail messages. You can tag any e-mail message you send or receive with multiple tags, such as client and project. The interface, shown in Figure 5-6, appears on the right side of every Mail message.

Tags created by MailTags can be added as a smart mailbox criterion. For example, you can create a smart mailbox that includes all the messages you have tagged with a certain project name. Likewise, tags created with MailTags are searchable in Mail's search bar. The tags are also attached to the e-mail message's IMAP data, so if you sync your messages among multiple devices using an IMAP server, your tags will follow.

MailTags can be applied in Mail rules. You can, for example, create a rule that automatically adds a MailTag to each incoming message that includes specified terms, such as "Jones Proposal." You can also create rules based on people. If, for example, you receive e-mail from Hank Morgan only in relation to a medieval

FIGURE 5-6

The MailTags Mail plug-in

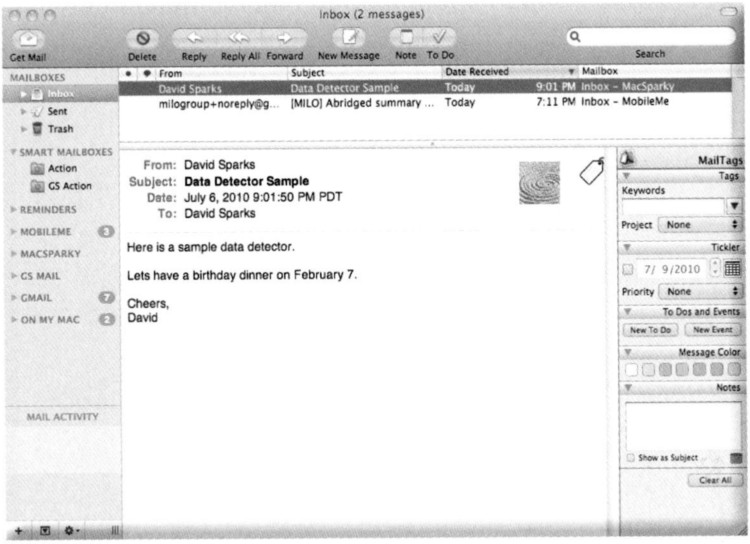

studies project, you can create a rule that automatically applies the Medieval Study MailTag to every e-mail from Morgan. The benefit of MailTags is increased control over indexing and searching.

MailSteward

MailSteward ($50; www.mailsteward.com) lets you create a searchable backup of your Mail message database. In addition to backing up your mail, MailSteward can also archive old messages to slim down Mail's message database. (There is also a $100 version that provides more flexibility and search tools.)

Gmail

Google Mail (free; www.gmail.com), known as Gmail, is a Web-based e-mail service. Several years ago, Google decided to start from scratch and do Web-based mail right. It largely succeeded. Gmail is not so much an e-mail client as it is an e-mail service. It supports POP and IMAP protocols (although Gmail IMAP is not the same as normal IMAP, as covered later in this section). You can sign up and get your own gmail.com e-mail account with an ever-increasing amount of free storage space. Gmail is shown in Figure 5-7.

Rather than install a client on your Mac, Google Mail is Web-based. You access your account at www.gmail.com. The Gmail site is a work in progress, and Google is constantly updating and adding features. The Gmail Web site looks and feels a lot like engineers designed it: It is efficient, but not very pretty.

FIGURE 5-7

The Gmail main window

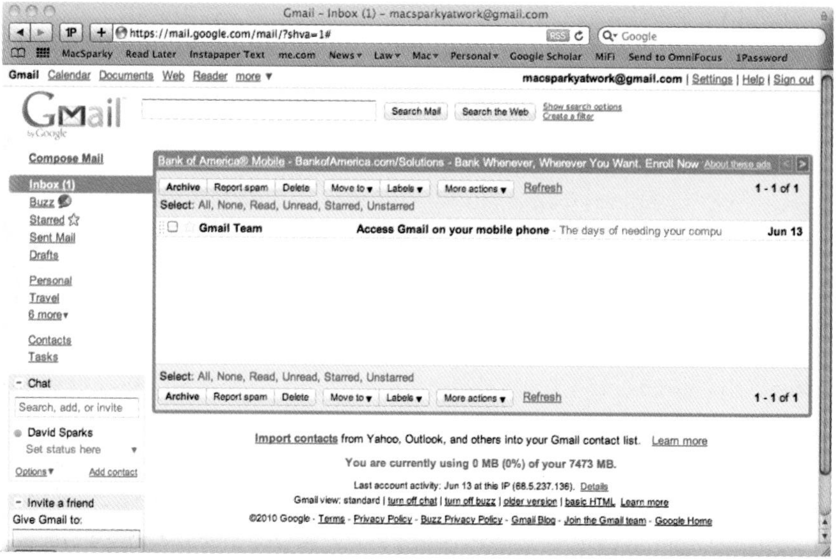

One of Gmail's best features is the ability to manage your e-mail using keyboard shortcuts. To move to the next message, press N. To compose a new message, press C. You can star a message (Gmail's version of flagging) by pressing S. These are just a taste of the shortcuts available. With a little practice, you can fly through a crowded e-mail inbox using Gmail's shortcuts — much faster, in fact, than anything you could do in Outlook/Entourage or Mail.

If you want Gmail but don't want to use the Web interface, you can also access your Gmail account using Apple Mail. There is a Gmail-only Mac OS X application, called MailPlane ($25; `mailplaneapp.com`), that includes multiple account support and is better at handling Gmail's pesky IMAP system.

Gmail supports e-mail message tagging similar to the MailTags plug-in covered earlier. You can tag your e-mail with multiple categories, and Gmail turns them into IMAP tags. Where IMAP normally identifies an e-mail with a single folder, Gmail IMAP identifies an e-mail with multiple tags. As a result, when you sync your Gmail account with a client looking for traditional IMAP, such as Apple Mail, things can get a bit wonky. It works, but sometimes Mail gets confused about where exactly a mail message belongs because each message has multiple IMAP tags.

In addition to setting up your own personal Gmail account, you can use Google mail for a company-wide e-mail system. This fee-based corporate e-mail service allows you to customize the domain and simply use Gmail as a cloud-based server. Google has a suite of Internet applications (including Gmail, Google

Docs, Google Calendar, and Google Tasks) that combine for a cloud-based computing lifestyle that a lot of Mac users are adopting. Google is fearless about adding new features, making usage of its applications always new and interesting.

Gmail's search capabilities are, naturally, outstanding. You can easily search your Gmail archive and locate long-forgotten e-mail with simple search terms. Gmail also pioneered threaded conversations, which link all e-mails together on a given subject, allowing you to view each in succession. Apple Mail and Outlook/Entourage have added this feature, but it still feels most natural with Gmail.

Another innovative feature in Gmail is the Priority Inbox. Gmail looks at all your incoming messages and compares them against your prior e-mails. Gmail then displays the messages it believes are the most important in the Priority Inbox. (Messages from people you've replied to in the past, for example, are considered to be priorities.) You can promote and demote specific correspondents to tell Priority Inbox your specific priorities.

There are downsides to switching to the Gmail. Sometimes, Google adds enhancements that aren't quite ready for prime time, leading to service problems. Also, Google makes its money selling advertisements. As a result, it uses all its applications to collect information about your preferences so it can do a better job of selling ads. If, for example, you send an e-mail to a friend asking about file server advice, there is a very good chance Gmail will simultaneously display to you an ad about file servers. I don't think there is any nefarious purpose behind

FIGURE 5-8

Microsoft Outlook for Mac

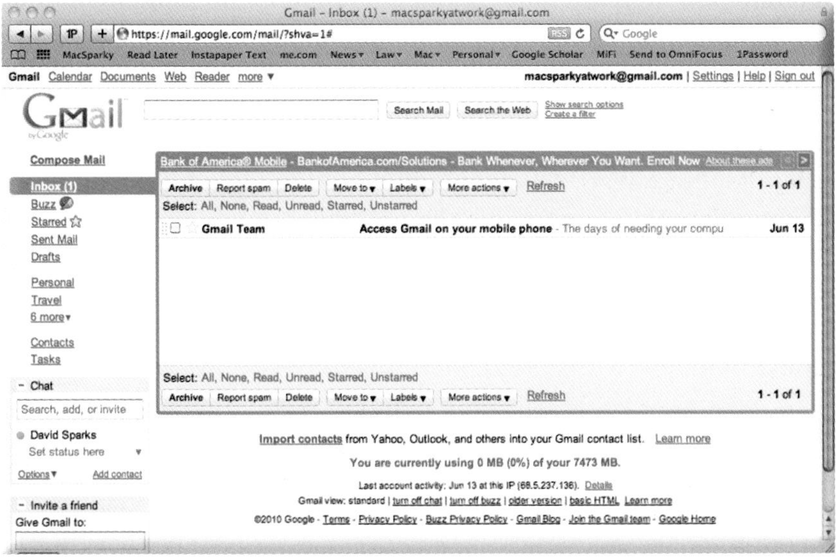

this data collection, but it still keeps some people — including me — from fully embracing the Google lifestyle.

Microsoft Outlook and Entourage

Outlook ($200; www.microsoft.com/mac) is a new addition to the Mac OS, coinciding with the release of Microsoft Office 2011. Outlook, shown in Figure 5-8, does not ship with the Office for Mac 2011 Home and Student edition; to get Outlook, you need to purchase the Home and Office edition. It supports POP, IMAP, and Exchange mail servers.

Outlook is a big improvement over its predecessor, Microsoft Entourage, which shipped with prior versions of Microsoft Office for Mac. Although Entourage had some benefits over the Mac OS X address, mail, and contact applications, it kept all its data in one single database file. If that database became corrupted, you lost all your e-mail, contacts, and calendars. In my own experience, this database corruption was not uncommon. Furthermore, because everything was in one large database, it threw Time Machine (covered in Chapter 2) into fits. Despite some interesting features, I recommend you avoid Entourage.

Unlike Entourage, Outlook uses a file-based database that is Spotlight-searchable and Time Machine-friendly. The new Outlook brings the familiar Windows Outlook experience to the Mac. If you like using Outlook on your Windows PC, you'll feel right at home with it on your Mac. It integrates easily with an Exchange server (covered later) and combines your calendar, contacts, and e-mail all in one place.

As an e-mail client, Outlook provides junk mail filtering, folders, and rule-based sorting. It doesn't, however, integrate with Mac OS X as well as Apple's Mail application does. For example, there are no data detectors. Outlook is best suited to Mac workers who are comfortable with Outlook on the PC or need its enhanced Exchange features covered next.

Microsoft Exchange and the Mac

Many workplaces use Microsoft Exchange data servers to keep track of e-mail, contact information, and calendars. As a Mac-based worker, you need to access the Exchange data. You can accomplish Exchange access and collaboration with varying degrees of success depending on your mail client and Exchange server version.

Microsoft Outlook and Entourage

Outlook is the easiest way to interact with Exchange, because Microsoft designed Outlook largely to work with Exchange. Outlook automatically detects your Exchange servers and makes account setup as easy as typing in your account credentials. Once authorized, you get immediate access to your company's e-mail system, contact database, and calendars. These can be reviewed, modified, and deleted depending to your Exchange permissions.

Microsoft Outlook also does the best job of working with the additional collaborative features available in Microsoft Exchange. It uses the Exchange Web services protocol, so you can make and accept invitations, create and view groups, access shared Exchange accounts, and use the other Exchange collaborative features. (Note that Microsoft Outlook works only with Exchange 2007 and later.)

Outlook's predecessor, Entourage, had more limited Exchange support. It did not include support for shared Exchange accounts and several other Microsoft server features, such as SharePoint support. Entourage remains the only application with built-in support for Exchange 2003, and working with an Exchange 2003 server is perhaps the only reason to use Entourage. If you decide to use Entourage, back up your database early and often.

Apple Mail, iCal, and Address Book

The ability to use the native Mac OS X Mail, iCal, and Address Book applications with an Exchange server depends on which versions of Mac OS X and Microsoft Exchange you are running.

USING LOTUS NOTES OR NOVELL GROUPWISE

Although Microsoft Exchange is the most popular corporate e-mail server, it's not the only one. IBM's Lotus Notes is widely used in large enterprises, while Novell's GroupWise is widely used in government agencies.

Both IBM and Novell have mail clients for the Mac. Just as Microsoft's Mac mail clients aren't quite as capable as their Windows counterparts, so too are IBM's and Novell's Mac clients not quite as capable as their Windows counterparts. For example, GroupWise for Mac doesn't let you subscribe to external calendars, import or export contacts, or support LDAP address books. Notes for Mac doesn't support left-reading languages such as Arabic and Hebrew, and doesn't integrate fully with Lotus collaboration tools such as Lotus Quikr. For both Lotus Notes and GroupWise, the more recent the client version, the more equal the Mac client is to the Windows client.

But, as with Microsoft Outlook and Entourage, the Mac clients for Lotus Notes and GroupWise support the capabilities most people use, so there's no reason if your company uses Lotus Notes or GroupWise that it can't support Mac users.

And like Microsoft Outlook and Exchange, both Lotus Notes and GroupWise support POP and IMAP servers in addition to their proprietary corporate servers, so you can use them for a mix of e-mail accounts.

Mac OS X 10.6 Snow Leopard includes native Microsoft Exchange support. If your workplace is running Microsoft Exchange 2007 or 2010 servers, setup is simply a matter of typing in your network domain, username, and password. At that point, Apple Mail, Address Book, and iCal do the rest: They interact with your Exchange server and begin sharing data. Mail has a separate account for your work Exchange e-mail and displays all the folders from your Exchange account. When you file an e-mail into an Apple Mail folder, the message is also filed in the corresponding folder on the Exchange server. (This works just like IMAP does, except Exchange allows mail folders on the server to have subfolders, while IMAP allows them only as subfolders to local folders, and Exchange can sync contacts and calendar data, whereas IMAP cannot.)

In essence, your Mac becomes pretty much just another client for the Exchange database of mail, contacts, and calendars. I say "pretty much" because Mail does not support shared Exchange mail accounts or out-of-office notifications, and it cannot integrate with other Microsoft server products such as SharePoint as Outlook can.

Unfortunately, neither Outlook nor Mac OS X 10.6 Snow Leopard Exchange support Microsoft Exchange 2003. (Microsoft Entourage does.) But you can get e-mail access from the older Exchange server if it is configured to use the Exchange IMAP protocol, in which case you would set up an Exchange IMAP account in Mail.

Syncing a calendar from a Microsoft Exchange 2003 server is difficult. There is an open source project called DavMail (`http://davmail.sourceforge. net`) that works for some users depending on how their Exchange is configured. Another possibility is to share your Outlook calendar data with Google calendar using Google's Outlook synchronization tool (`www.google.com/apps/intl/ en/business/outlook_sync.html`). Once your Outlook calendar is located on Google Calendar, you can access it there or sync it to your Mac using BusyCal, which I cover in Chapter 6.

E-mail Best Practices

No matter which e-mail client you decide to use, it is a good idea to form good e-mail habits. Too often, Mac workers face inboxes with hundreds (if not thousands) of unread e-mails. This becomes overwhelming. When the unread e-mail count begins accumulating, you feel powerless to keep up with it and eventually declare "e-mail bankruptcy" (a term coined by famed technology lawyer Lawrence Lessig) by deleting or archiving all the contents of your inbox without reviewing any of it. You can avoid e-mail bankruptcy by developing some new e-mail habits.

Inbox management

Think about the mailbox outside your front door for a moment. Has it ever been okay to just leave mail in your mailbox? Has it ever occurred to you to just let the mail pile up in the box as the mailman keeps stuffing mail in for weeks on end? How about taking some of the mail out of that overstuffed mailbox, looking at it for a few minutes, and then cramming it back in the mailbox before walking back in the house? Of course not. Nevertheless, it is common practice among many Mac workers to do exactly that with their e-mail.

Most of us treat our e-mail inboxes as some type of substandard to-do list. We open a few e-mails and we skip others. Regardless, we leave them all in the same place with the idea that we will somehow be able to go back and figure out what needs to be done and what can be ignored. I don't think we could design

FIGHTING SPAM

Although Mac OS X is much less susceptible to virus attacks than Windows PCs (see Chapter 23), there is no difference between Windows and Mac OS X when it comes to spam. According to some estimates, 80 percent of all e-mail sent is spam.

Your time is valuable. You should not have to spend it sorting through piles of spam to find important e-mail. Two ways to combat spam on your Mac are to use a mail server with its own spam filters and to install your own local spam filter to catch anything that still gets through.

Most mail servers (including Exchange, Gmail, MobileMe, and Mac OS X Server) have their own spam-fighting algorithms. So do most hosted e-mail services. These algorithms look at every arriving e-mail and discard most spam mail before you ever see it. Gmail is generally considered to have some of the best spam filtering available. In fact, some users direct all their e-mail to a Gmail account for the sole purpose of taking advantage of Google's spam filters.

You can also install your own local spam-fighting application on your Mac to catch any spam that makes it through your server's filters. The best spam-fighting Mac application is SpamSieve ($30; `http://c-command.com/spamsieve`). SpamSieve does its own search of all incoming e-mail and compares it against a database of known spam mail servers. SpamSieve works with most Mac e-mail clients. SpamSieve keeps its own "white list" of your previous correspondents so e-mail from your co-workers and clients never gets marked as spam. It also integrates with the Mac OS X Address Book. Additionally, SpamSieve looks inside attached images and documents to detect spam.

By combining mail server and local spam filters, you should be able to avoid most spam on your Mac.

a more inefficient and impractical system if we tried. So let's start over with the inbox.

Treat the inbox exactly like that mailbox outside your house. Let the mail be delivered there and collect it every day. Just like you sort the mail in your house, sort the mail in your inbox. It really is not that difficult. There aren't that many different kinds of e-mail. When you get right down to it, there are only four types of e-mail, and so four types of actions to take:

1. **Get rid of junk mail.** *"Dave, don't miss this once-in-a-lifetime offer to purchase Florida swamp land."* Trash your junk mail immediately. Junk mail doesn't just include the obvious spam and solicitations; it includes anything you are not interested in or don't need to keep. Be honest with yourself: Unless you are willing to archive or commit to take action in response to an e-mail, get rid of it. Keeping e-mail you are ambivalent about is the first step toward e-mail bankruptcy.

2. **If there is no response required, archive it.** *"Dave, it was great seeing you at the conference. Let me know if you need any further assistance in the future."* If the e-mail does not require a response, get it out of your inbox and into your archive. You can always seek it out again later if you need it.

3. **If the e-mail requires a quick response, quickly respond.** *"Dave, are we still on for lunch next Tuesday?"* A lot of e-mail from co-workers, clients, and friends just requires a brief answer and very little thinking to get there. We get these all the time. Don't waste time managing this e-mail. While it's still in your inbox, fire off your response, and file the original in your archive.

4. **Set aside the rest of your e-mail for later.** *"Dave, the supplier has let us down again. What should we do for a long-term solution?"* After getting rid of the junk mail, information-only e-mail, and quickie e-mail, you will inevitably have some e-mail that doesn't lend itself to a quick reply. The e-mail may require research, or you may need to spend some time thinking about your response. Either way, you don't deal with this type of e-mail while you're sorting your inbox. Instead you move it out of your inbox to some reliable place where you know you will come back to it later. I do this by copying the e-mail into OmniFocus (covered in Chapter 9). You could also put it in some other task application or you could create a folder in your mail client called Action where you keep e-mails requiring further contemplation and response.

This workflow is summarized in Figure 5-9.

FIGURE 5-9

A recommended e-mail workflow

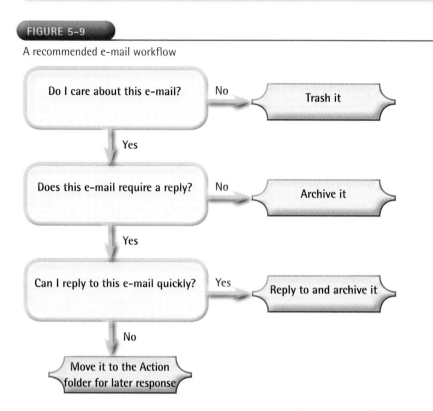

Folder management

If you were reading carefully my suggested e-mail strategies, you noticed that I referenced only three mail locations: the inbox, the Action folder, and the archive. Everything else went to the trash. I just use three folders. A lot of e-mail users rely upon a Byzantine jumble of nested mail folders including specific folders for every project, client, administrative function, and employee that have ever crossed their path. This system is completely unmanageable. You will spend literally days of your life maintaining such a system, and you will never get that time back. All the e-mail clients covered in this chapter include powerful search technologies that allow you to find any e-mail in your archive. It is important to note that the guy who never found that needle in the haystack did not have Google search or Spotlight on his side.

You will be fine dropping all your e-mail into a central archive and using search technologies to find them later. If the thought of getting rid of your e-mail folder hierarchy keeps you awake at night, you can add some additional search capabilities via plug-ins (like MailTags in Apple Mail) or tagging the e-mails with Gmail. The important thing is to put the nested folders in your past.

E-mail notification

How many times have you been working productively and suddenly heard that not-so-subtle "ding" from your Mac informing you there is new mail. As soon as you hear that sound, you have already lost. Your concentration is broken and it will take some effort to return to work. To add insult to injury, you find yourself powerless to resist leaving whatever you were doing and going to your e-mail client only to find that the subject of this urgent "ding" was an offer to attend a free seminar about the benefits of time-shares.

The default setting in Apple Mail is to check your e-mail every five minutes. That makes for 12 potential interruptions an hour, 96 interruptions a day, 480 interruptions in a 40-hour week, and 24,000 interruptions over the course of the year (assuming you keep your e-mail turned off during vacation). With this constant distraction, it's amazing anyone gets anything done. Break the chains of slavery to your e-mail notification system. Turn off the ding. Whatever e-mail client you use, disable the audio alert. It might be scary at first, but then it becomes liberating.

Next, decide how many times a day you need to check e-mail. This really depends on your work. I check my mail only twice a day. In some workplaces, that would not be enough. Either way, decide the absolute minimum number of times you need to check e-mail and stick to it. When it is time to check your e-mail, blitz through your inbox as I described earlier. Remember, four kinds of e-mail and three folders. Then, get back to work.

As you process mail over the course of your day, you will move several e-mails to the Action folder. Take some time and respond to the Action e-mail. I do this in the late afternoon. I can normally clear out most of the day's e-mail this way. There may be some items, however, that still require additional work and thought. I assign those items to be dealt with tomorrow or next month, as the case may be, in OmniFocus (covered in Chapter 9). Once I assign them to a future date, I can archive them and access them later from OmniFocus. By the end of the day, my inbox is empty and my Action folder is empty. I haven't necessarily responded to all my e-mail, but I have at least accounted for it.

Using the right applications and a little common sense, you can liberate yourself from you inbox and get real work done on your Mac.

Contacts and Calendars

s much as technology moves forward, everyone still needs a reliable address book and calendar. There are several tools for the Mac to help you manage this information. Some applications are dedicated to one task (like Apple's Address Book) while others seek to manage contacts, calendars, and more (like Microsoft Outlook). This chapter takes a look at the best tools for managing calendars and contacts on your Mac.

Contacts

Apple's built-in Address Book is a good tool for contact management. Shown in Figure 6-1, Address Book is a virtual version of that book of names and addresses everyone kept in a drawer a generation ago.

You can create a new contact in Address Book by clicking the + (plus) iconic button below the names column in the left pane of Address Book or by pressing ⌘+N. The new contact field is shown in Figure 6-2.

Address Book includes a default set of fields for each new contact but you can add fields by choosing Card ▶ Add Field. There are several additional useful fields. The Phonetic Last Name field, for example, is helpful if your contacts have unusual names. The URL field lets you add a contact's Web site to his or her contact card. You can add specific fields for individual cards or you can edit the default template (Choose Card ▶ Add Field and then the desired submenu option). If you have trouble remembering names, drag a picture of your contact on top of the picture placeholder, shown in Figure 6-2, and you can digitally keep a face with the name. The Company check box in the address card can be selected to convert a contact from an individual to a company, like from Steve Jobs to Apple, Inc. The contact will then be alphabetized by the company name instead of the individual's name.

The Birthday field in Address Book works directly with iCal. Any birthday you list in the Address Book can automatically synchronize to your iCal calendar. (iCal is covered in further detail later in this chapter.)

You should also create a contact for yourself. In it, list all your contact information and then make it your contact card by choosing Card ▶ Make This

FIGURE 6-1

Apple's Address Book

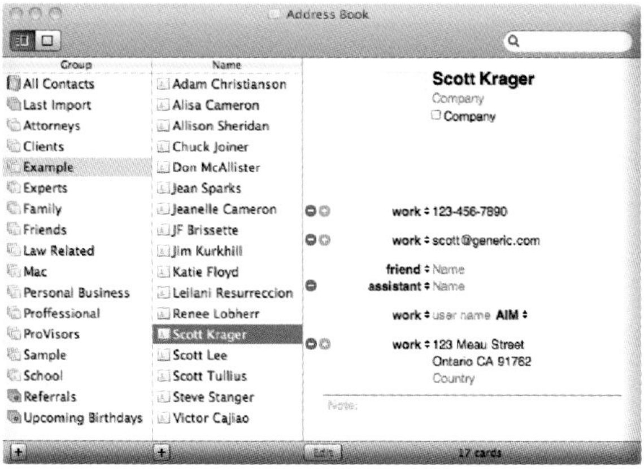

FIGURE 6-2

A new contact in Address Book

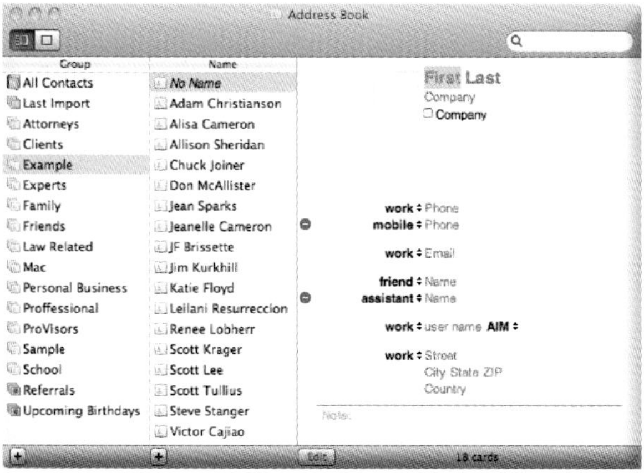

My Card. Once you do so, any component of Mac OS X that needs your contact data, such as a letter template in iWork Pages, will automatically fill in your contact information.

The Address Book window contains two panes. The right pane has the contact details. The left pane contains two columns: groups and individual contacts. You create groups by clicking the + (plus) iconic button at the bottom of the Groups column. You can create groups for any logical organization of your contacts, such as clients, vendors, and co-workers. Whenever I go on a trip, I create a group based on the trip. In it I put contact information for all the people I plan to meet as well as information on the hotels, restaurants, shuttle services, and other contacts I may need access to quickly.

An Address Book smart group

Address Book also lets you to create smart groups. Smart groups are similar to smart mailboxes in Apple Mail: You set up criteria and Address Book automatically populates the smart group with all contacts matching the criteria. A smart group could examine the notes section of every contact in your Address Book database and flag any contact containing the words Smith Proposal, for example. Smart groups lets you easily keep track of all your contacts on a big project. Another useful smart group is shown in Figure 6-3; it examines all the contacts in your Address Book database and selects any contact with a birthday in the next 30 days.

In addition to organizing your contacts, groups are useful for e-mail. You can type a group name in an Apple Mail recipient field to automatically populate it with all the individuals in that group.

Address Book is integrated throughout the operating system, letting you use your contact data in many places. For example, you can:

- Drag a contact (or group of contacts) into an address field of a new e-mail (covered in Chapter 5).
- Drag a contact onto a new Pages letter to automatically fill in the addressee's information (covered in Chapter 11).
- Drag a group of contacts on a Numbers spreadsheet to create a membership list (covered in Chapter 15).
- Extract contact data from e-mail messages using data detectors (covered in Chapter 5).

This integration throughout the operating system is Address Book's killer feature and the reason it has so few competitors.

Address Book provides several approaches for synchronizing your contact data. The easiest is with MobileMe. If you are a MobileMe subscriber ($100 per year), Address Book automatically synchronizes your contact database with the MobileMe service. You set this up through the Accounts pane of the Address Book Preferences dialog box, shown in Figure 6-4, or through the MobileMe system preference. Once your contacts are synced with MobileMe, you can access them through the MobileMe Web portal or, if you are an iPhone, iPod Touch, or iPad user, directly on your mobile iOS devices. So, if you're at lunch with a client and

FIGURE 6-4

The Address Book Accounts pane in the Preferences dialog box

she tells you her assistant's name, you can add it to the contact card on your iPhone and know it will also appear on your Mac.

You can also synchronize your contact database with Yahoo contacts or Google contacts in the Accounts pane of the Address Book Preferences dialog box, shown in Figure 6-4. If you use the Google or Yahoo services for e-mail, calendaring, and contacts, syncing provides an easy way to take advantage of Address Book's built-in Mac OS X integration and still use your Google or Yahoo contacts.

Finally, Address Book interfaces directly with Microsoft Exchange Server 2007 or later. Setting up synchronization with Microsoft Exchange is simply a matter of typing in your Exchange username and password (synchronization is covered in detail in Chapter 21). The Exchange contacts are synchronized separately from your other listed contacts, allowing you to keep your work and personal contacts separate. Depending on your network's Exchange settings, you can have a read-only access or a full synchronization of the Exchange contacts.

Calendars

Using a digital calendar is great. You can also print it, back it up, and even put it on your phone. Mac OS X has some fantastic desktop and online calendaring tools depending on how you work.

iCal

iCal, shown in Figure 6-5, is Mac OS X's built-in calendar application. iCal works much like Address Book. It has a left pane with a list of calendars and a right pane that shows the details. The right pane can display a daily, weekly, or

WEB CONTACT TOOLS

Web-based tools for managing contacts are on the rise. With an increasingly mobile workforce and the relatively small data size of contact databases, it makes sense to put your contacts on the Web. Using the Web, employees and co-workers can all have access to contact data from any computer or mobile device.

Google Contacts is one service for managing your contacts online. It synchronizes with your Google account and works particularly well if you use Google's Gmail (covered in Chapter 5) and Google Calendar (covered later in this chapter).

Because of the tight integration between Address Book in the operating system and the easy ability to synchronize with other contact applications, I recommend you use Address Book to manage the contacts on your Mac.

Some companies are taking online contact management one step further with CRM (customer relationship management) Web services. Salesforce.com (www.salesforce.com) and 37signals' Highrise (www.highrisehq.com) are two popular CRM services that work on the Mac.

These services track contacts, leads, and other tools to work with clients and synchronize with Microsoft Outlook and vCard (the format for Apple's Address Book). In addition to providing contact management, they provide tools to help you follow up on sales leads, track existing transactions, and better manage e-mail. Because they are Web-based, the software is updated "in the cloud" and does not require extensive IT support. Pricing for these CRM services depends on the size of your business and the tools you select. The customer relationship management industry is in its infancy and will no doubt expand in coming years.

monthly view of your calendar items. The iCal interface can also display to-do items (covered in Chapter 9).

Using iCal, you can create calendars for different aspects of your life. For example, you can create calendars for specific projects (which can be helpful for to-do items as covered in Chapter 9). To create a new calendar, click the + (plus) iconic button at the bottom of the left pane in iCal or choose File ▶ New Calendar.

To create a new iCal event, press ⌘+N or choose File ▶ New Event. Using the Inspector (accessed by selecting any iCal event and pressing ⌘+I), shown in Figure 6-6, you can modify the details of any calendar entry including adding alarms or sending out invitations to potential participants.

In addition to creating your own calendars, you can also subscribe to publicly available Internet calendars. Apple keeps a list of subscription calendars for iCal at www.apple.com/downloads/macosx/calendars. At the time of this writing, the list contained more than 200 calendars ranging from U.S. holidays to

FIGURE 6-5

iCal's week view

golf tour dates. You can also subscribe to third-party iCal calendars by choosing Calendar ▶ Subscribe and inserting the calendar's URL. URL calendar subscription also works with Google Calendar (covered later in this chapter).

iCal features tight integration with Mac OS X. You can create a birthday calendar by checking the Show Birthdays Calendar option in the General pane of iCal's Preferences dialog box; iCal creates a separate calendar with birthday events for every contact in your Address Book that has a birthday field entry.

FIGURE 6-6

iCal's event inspector

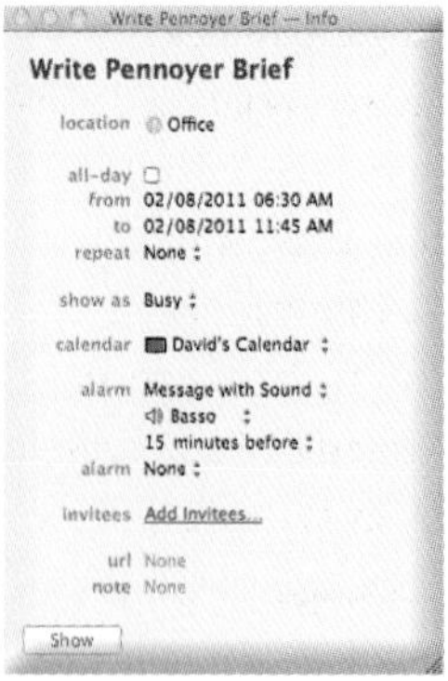

FIGURE 6-7

Mac OS X's data detectors at work to add an appointment from an e-mail to iCal

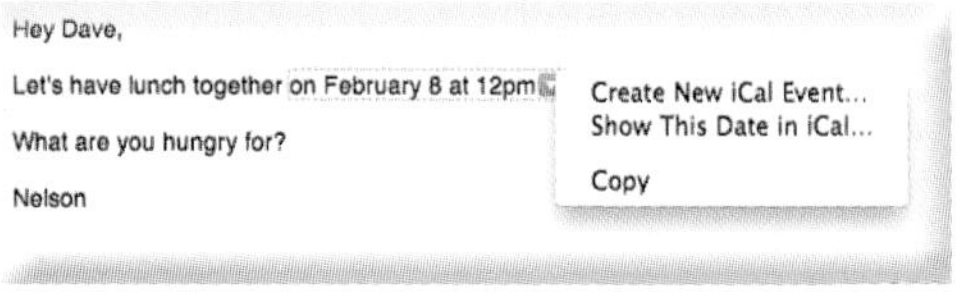

Apple Mail's data detectors (that read your e-mail and find contact information, covered in Chapter 5) also work with iCal. If you receive an e-mail with a request to meet for lunch tomorrow at noon, Mail sees the event in the e-mail text and lets you add it to iCal (demonstrated in Figure 6-7).

You can set up synchronization for your iCal calendar in the Accounts pane of the iCal Preferences dialog box. There are several options.

▶ CalDAV is an Internet standard that lets users access and modify scheduling data on a centralized remote server. It is similar to IMAP for e-mail (covered in Chapter 5). Because the calendaring data is on a server, multiple users can access it for planning and sharing calendar information. CalDAV was added to Mac OS X 10.5 Leopard. More recently, Apple embraced CalDAV further with the MobileMe service; the MobileMe CalDAV scheduling allows users to send invitations and share calendar data, two of the biggest complaints against iCal in years past.

▶ iCal also supports Microsoft Exchange 2007 and later. As explained in Chapter 21, you can enter your Exchange credentials in iCal and automatically synchronize with your Exchange server. Exchange calendars appear as a separate calendar in iCal, and you have access to view and modify the data as provided by your network administrator. The Exchange support in iCal, however, does not match that of Microsoft Outlook, covered later in this chapter.

▶ Like Address Book, you can also synchronize your calendar data with Google Calendar and the Yahoo calendar. Because so many companies are adopting the Google online applications and Google Calendar (covered later in this chapter), the ability to synchronize Google Calendar with your native Mac OS X calendar is important.

iCal is missing several features commonly found in other calendaring applications. These include the ability to set recurring to-do items and the ability to share calendars on the same network. iCal has been much maligned by calendar power users because of these missing features. Although Apple has answered some of these complaints with CalDAV integration and MobileMe synchronization, there are still unhappy iCal users. This, in part, led to the development of BusyCal.

BusyCal's week view

BusyCal

BusyCal ($50; www.busycal.com) bills itself as "iCal Pro." I can't disagree. BusyCal, shown in Figure 6-8, closely resembles iCal but provides several essential features. Most important, BusyCal can sync calendars with other users on your local area network without requiring a dedicated server such as Mac OS X Server (covered in Chapter 20). You can publish your BusyCal calendars on your network with read-only or read-and-write access. Using BusyCal, a small office can share calendars and avoid the expense of a dedicated server. BusyCal also syncs with Google Calendar (covered later).

BusyCal includes a number of features missing from iCal. BusyCal lets you create recurring to-do items. BusyCal also includes a list view, not available in iCal, that allows you to create a list of all events in your calendar and sort by type, calendar, and other criteria.

Mac OS X has a centralized calendar data file where iCal gets its data but BusyCal also saves to the same location. As a result, you can open and modify your calendar data in both iCal and BusyCal. MobileMe also looks at the same data set so your BusyCal data syncs automatically to MobileMe.

Google Calendar

Just like Google turned the world of e-mail on its head with Google Mail, it has done the same with Google Calendar (http://calendar.google.com).

Google Calendar's month view

Google Calendar, shown in Figure 6-9 is a simple to use and powerful free Web-based calendaring system.

You can register for the free Google Calendar as part of your Google account. The Google Calendar interface is noticeably Web-based. It does not have the typical Mac OS X feel but it is functional. The left side of the window includes a list of calendars. The right side includes the calendar data. The calendar can be displayed in day, week, month, four-day (showing the next four days), and agenda views. On the left side of the Google Calendar window, you can see a list of your calendars, and manage their setting and sharing preferences.

There are several ways to add a new event. One way is to click on the date in Google Calendar and insert the event details. Like Gmail, Google Calendar is keyboard-shortcut-friendly, so you can also create a new event by pressing N. (You can jump to today by pressing T.)

Like its other online applications, Google Calendar has fantastic sharing support. You can share your calendars with co-workers and friends, giving them read-only or read-and-write access. You can also make your calendars public. Alternatively, you can choose to share only the times that you're available for new events. With these controls, you can tailor your calendar sharing as liberally or conservatively as you want. Because it's a free service, your co-workers can do the same. Many progressive workplaces are switching their entire calendar system to the Google Calendar.

Google Calendar can also serve as the go-between for many calendaring systems. For example, as covered in Chapter 5, you can use Google Calendar as an intermediary between a Microsoft Exchange 2003 server and BusyCal. Google Calendar also associates a Web link with each calendar, making it easy to publish or import the calendar into another application, like iCal.

With the development of Internet protocols (such as CalDAV) the days of all work calendars being managed through a specific Exchange-like centralized server are over. Calendar sharing and modification are much easier now with these software tools. Over the next several years, it will be fascinating to see how calendars in the workplace change with the rise of CalDAV and Web-based calendaring.

Integrated Calendars and Contacts

Mac OS X also offers integrated tools for managing your calendar, contacts, and e-mail, but you may want to go beyond them. In that case, two of the best tools are Microsoft Outlook and Daylite.

Microsoft Outlook and Entourage

Microsoft Outlook ($200; www.microsoft.com/mac) is a welcome addition to Mac OS X. Outlook for the Mac, shown in Figure 6-10, was first

FIGURE 6-10

Microsoft Outlook's month view

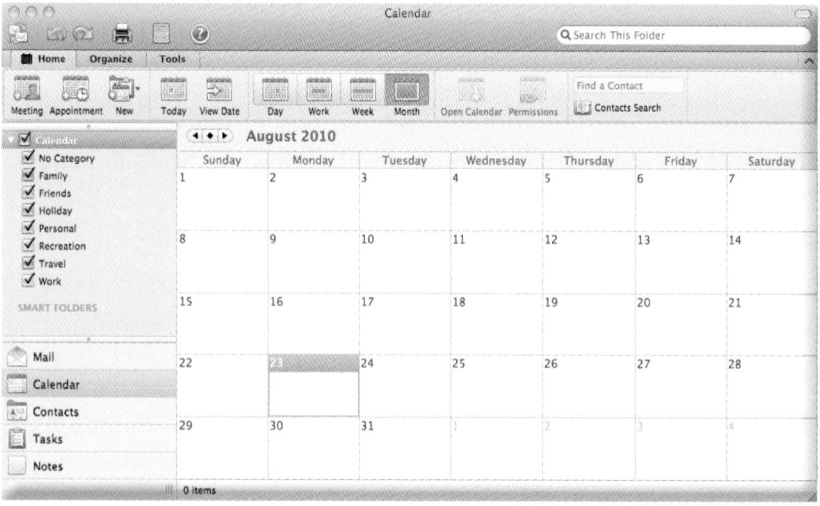

released with Microsoft Office 2011. (Microsoft Outlook replaces Microsoft Entourage software from previous versions of Office.)

As explained in Chapter 5, I am not a fan of Microsoft Entourage. It had, in my opinion, several fatal flaws, chief among them was how it stored data. The Microsoft Entourage database includes all your e-mail, contacts, and calendar items in one single database. The smallest corruption in the database can lead to a complete loss of your data. Entourage's large, constantly changing, database also caused trouble with Time Machine backups (covered in Chapter 2).

Microsoft Outlook fixes both of these problems by using an incremental database that easily backs up to Time Machine. Outlook brings many of the tools familiar to Outlook users on Windows computers to the Mac. Plus, Microsoft Outlook features the best Microsoft Exchange integration of any software application available on the Mac. Although Apple's built-in iCal and Address Book supports Exchange servers, Outlook supports more of Exchange's sharing and collaboration tools. For example, Outlook uses the Exchange Web services protocol and lets you use shared Exchange accounts; Mac OS X Mail does not. Outlook supports only Microsoft Exchange 2007 and later, so if your office runs on an Exchange 2003 server, you are out of luck.

The user interface in Outlook 2011 received a much-needed upgrade. Like the other applications in the Microsoft Office suite, Outlook now uses the ribbon-style interface which groups types of features together and allows you to transform the toolbar by clicking different portions of the ribbon. The ribbon is shown in Figure 6-10.

Creating and organizing calendar events is also easier with Outlook 2011. Shown in Figure 6-11, calendar event creation gives you several options to customize and share your calendar events.

Likewise, the user interface and contact windows received an overhaul. You can arrange contacts by group and update contact information easily. The best candidates for using Microsoft Outlook are those who are comfortable with Outlook on Windows. Although developed by separate teams, the applications

FIGURE 6-11

Creating a calendar event in Microsoft Outlook

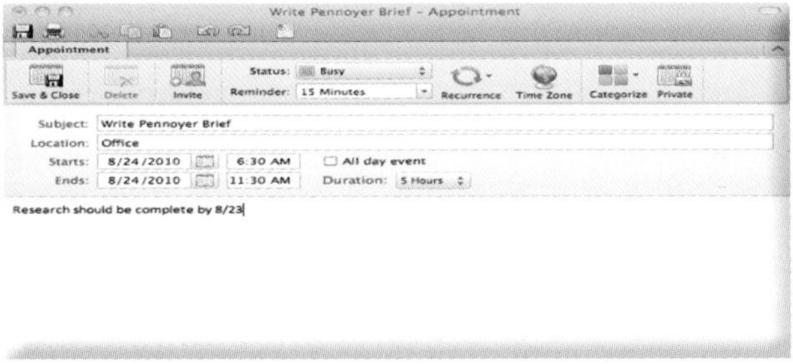

have similar functions and workflows. With the improvements and modifications in Outlook 2011, Microsoft now has a worthwhile alternative to the built-in calendar and contact management systems in Mac OS X.

Daylite

Daylite ($190 per user; `www.marketcircle.com/daylite`) is another integrated tool for managing your mail, contacts, calendar, and tasks. Shown in Figure 6-12, it is intended as a full-service business productivity application allowing you to manage a company's projects, sales, contacts, appointments, and e-mail. The Daylite system is fully networked, allowing users to access and modify data for other users. It can also be modified for particular industries. I've seen it used widely in the legal industry. It is also used in real estate, sales, manufacturing, and other businesses.

Team calendaring is easy in Daylite. To schedule a meeting, you pick the co-workers you would like at a meeting and the calendar shows you who's busy and when. The calendar in Daylite also includes project-planning components, allowing you to see key milestones for existing projects.

The contact database also works over your office network. Everyone on the Daylite network can add and modify contacts. Daylite color-codes contacts by their relationship to the business, such as customers, employees, and vendors. With color coding, it is easy to figure out who does what when looking through the contact list. Because the entire system is integrated, when you click on a contact, you can also see related appointments, tasks, e-mail, and notes to that contact.

FIGURE 6-12

Daylite

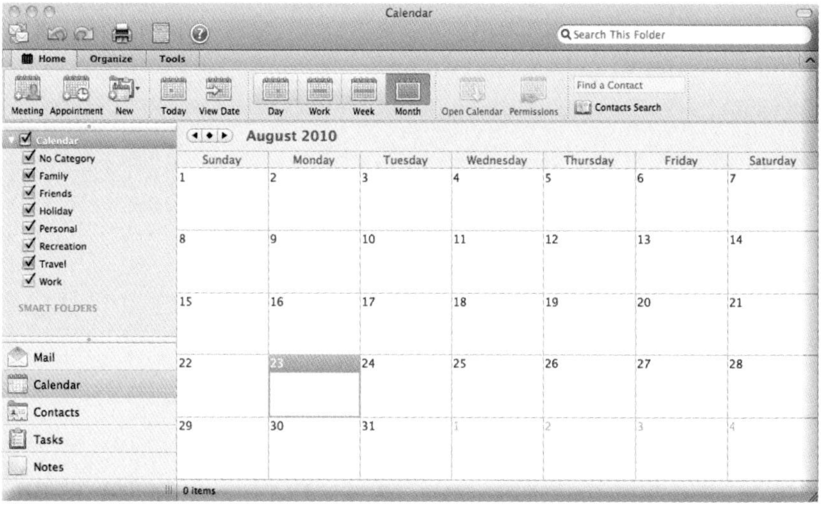

SHIPPING WITH YOUR MAC

What if your business requires shipping products to customers? You no longer need to spend your afternoons at the post office. Software exists to purchase postage, process, ship, and track your packages. Endicia (starts at $16 per month; www.endicia.com) is a reliable application for just this purpose.

It is an approved vendor of the United States Postal Service and accommodates domestic and international shipping. You can customize your postage with your company logo and change your plan depending on your shipping volume. It works directly with the Mac OS X Address Book and, unlike several of its competitors, does not require a long-term contract.

Daylite's project-management component allows you to define and manage projects and team members. There is also an iPhone application that lets you access your Daylite database on the go.

Both Daylite and Outlook go far beyond mere contact and calendar management. Both products focus on collaboration and are particularly useful with teams of employees working on a single project.

Macs and Mobile Devices

Mobile technology has improved to such an extent that we no longer talk about phones and personal digital assistants (PDAs). They've become pocket computers. Mobile devices do so much more for us now that some speculate they may end up replacing our desktop and laptop computers entirely. Apple played no small part in this quiet revolution with the release of the iPhone and iPad. Regardless, no matter which mobile device you use, there is a way to use it with your Mac.

iOS Devices

Not surprisingly, Apple makes the mobile devices easiest to use with Apple computers: The iPhone, iPad, and iPod Touch all run Apple's iOS mobile operating system. Although most synchronization between iOS devices and your Mac takes place through iTunes, there are limited wireless syncing options as well.

iTunes Sync

Originally designed to manage music libraries, iTunes has now expanded far beyond its original intention. Figure 7-1 shows the iTunes synchronization interface for an iPhone. The options work the same for the iPod Touch and iPad.

You can select a specific iOS device to manage in iTunes' left sidebar. Only iOS devices currently plugged into your Mac appear in the Devices list. Clicking on the iPhone (named *Trane* in Figure 7-1) brings up the device in iTunes' main window.

You manage your iOS device through a series of panes, accessed by clicking the names across the top of the window. The Summary pane, shown in Figure 7-1, provides details concerning the selected device, including software version number, capacity, free space, and serial number. The Summary pane also provides options for synchronizing your iOS device with your Mac.

- ▶ **Open iTunes when this iPhone is connected.** This option is self-explanatory: When you plug in your iOS device, iTunes starts.
- ▶ **Sync only checked songs and videos.** Every song and video file in iTunes has a check box next to it. Use this check box to manually synchronize music and video.

FIGURE 7-1

Synchronizing an iPhone with iTunes

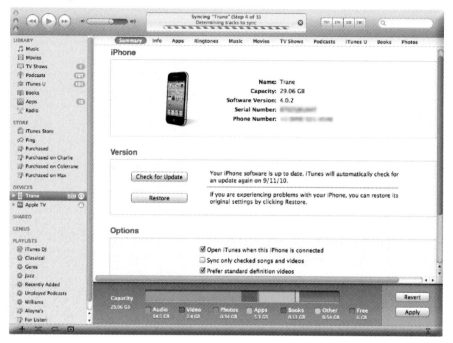

▶ **Prefer standard definition videos.** If your library contains both high-definition and standard-definition videos, checking this option ensures that the smaller file sized standard versions are synchronized to your device. This option is usually a good idea because you are not likely to see the benefit of high definition on those small screens.

▶ **Convert higher bit rate songs to 128 Kbps AAC.** The conversion option allows you to reduce the file size of your media files (this time, music) before being synchronized to your device and allows you to save space on your iOS device. Some users hear a big difference between 256 Kbps and smaller 128 Kbps audio files. Others don't. Decide for yourself.

▶ **Manually manage music videos.** This option allows you to avoid automatic synchronization entirely. Instead, you manually drag music and videos from your iTunes library to your iOS device.

▶ **Encrypt iPhone backup.** If you're concerned about the security of your iPhone data, you can encrypt the backup file. If this option is not checked, anyone with access to your Mac can open and inspect the contents of your iPhone backup file. Using an application such as iPhone Backup Extractor, covered later in this chapter, these users have access to all your backup files, including photographs, videos, media files, books, and other data stored on your iOS device.

FIGURE 7-2

Synchronizing iOS apps in iTunes

You can also use the Info pane to sync contacts, calendars, and e-mail between your Mac and your mobile device. If you're not a MobileMe subscriber, you can sync selected (or all) contacts, calendar, and e-mail account data directly to your iOS device using the Info pane. You can also sync your bookmarks to your iOS device. If you are a MobileMe subscriber, you do not need to sync through iTunes. Instead, you sync wirelessly via MobileMe (covered in Chapters 5 and 6). Finally, you use the Info pane to reset data on your iOS device, including its contacts, calendars, mail accounts, and notes.

Use the Apps pane, shown in Figure 7-2, to organize and install applications on your iOS device. This pane also has a graphical representation of the screen layout on your iOS device. Working in this pane, you can rearrange screens and individual icons by clicking and dragging them in the graphical representation of your iOS device screens. Interestingly, you cannot buy apps in the Apps pane; the Apps pane manages the iOS applications you have already purchased. Instead, you purchase Apps from the iTunes Store menu (located in the left sidebar).

Using the Apps pane, you can add and remove data from your iOS devices. If, for example, you use Pages on your iPad, you can copy Pages documents to or from the iPad and open them with Pages on your Mac. There are many useful iOS applications that take advantage of the ability to drag and drop files onto your mobile device.

FIGURE 7-3

Sharing data with iOS apps in iTunes

If, for example, you keep your records in PDF form (see Chapters 12 and 19), you could use a PDF-reading application to copy or remove PDF files on your iOS device. My favorite iPad application for this purpose is Air Sharing ($10; www.avatron.com/apps/air-sharing). To move files back and forth, simply click and drag data files from the Mac to the application's file window at the bottom of the Apps pane, shown in Figure 7-3. The applications that let you transfer files require that the files be in a particular format. Numbers for iPad, for example, requires that you transfer iWork Numbers (covered in Chapter 15) files to your iPad.

iTunes has several additional panes to let you customize the media on your iOS mobile device, including ringtones, music, movies, TV shows, podcasts, and photos. They all work the same. You can set iTunes to automatically synchronize unwatched or new media. You can also synchronize specific artists or albums.

An often-overlooked pane is iTunes U, which is a collection of university lectures available for free download to your iOS devices. Apple has partnered with universities all over the nation to make some remarkable lectures available for download.

The Books pane lets you load PDF and ePub (the electronic book format iOS uses) files directly to your mobile device as long as you have the iBooks application installed on the iOS device. Although the free Apple

> ## BACKING UP
>
> Every time you connect an iOS device to your Mac, iTunes makes a backup of all the data. This is really convenient if something goes wrong with your hardware. If you lose your phone, you can get a new one and restore your data from the backup.
>
> Once in a while, you may not want to restore an iOS device from a backup but still need some of the data from the backup file. There is a donation-supported application called iPhone Backup Extractor (`www. supercrazyawesome.com`) for just this purpose. iPhone Backup Extractor lets you open your iOS device backup file and extract individual files.

iBooks app is fine for reference materials, a dedicated PDF viewer (like Air Sharing) is better for viewing indexed, highlighted, and annotated PDF files. Dedicated PDF apps include additional features, such as the ability to view bookmarks and annotations, that you don't get with iBooks.

Wireless syncing with iOS devices

iOS does not make it easy to wirelessly sync documents from the mobile device to your Mac. Some applications get around this problem using Web-based services like Evernote and SimpleNote (covered in Chapter 10). Others include direct integration with Dropbox or Box.net (covered in Chapter 21), allowing you to open and save files directly from your cloud storage. All these applications rely on one trick or another to wirelessly sync documents. Although Apple has yet to provide a complete wireless syncing tool, it is moving in that direction. For example, you can synchronize Pages, Numbers, and Keynote files on an iPad directly with your MobileMe cloud storage.

Dangers of file-sharing

Whether you are sharing files directly through iTunes or e-mailing yourself copies, you always end up with multiple copies of the data. For example, copying a document from your iPad does not remove the document from your iPad.

Likewise, e-mailing a copy leaves the original on the iPad. Instead of syncing the file, you are copying it. You end up with two copies of the document: one on your Mac, and one on the iPad. If you continue to copy the same file, you will end up with a folder full of versions of the same document. If you're not careful, you can accidentally make changes to or delete the wrong version. When you have multiple copies, be careful.

The Missing Sync for iPhone

If you are using an iOS device, you're probably fine doing all your syncing through iTunes. There are, however, other options. Mark/Space is an application

FIGURE 7-4

The Missing Sync for iPhone

FIGURE 7-5

The Missing Sync for BlackBerry

developer that specializes in synchronizing mobile devices with computers. It has applications to help transfer data from most popular smartphones to a Mac. Several of its products are the best tools for syncing mobile devices to Macs.

The Missing Sync for iPhone ($40; www.markspace.com), shown in Figure 7-4, adds a few features not available with iTunes sync. It has its own ringtone editor, allowing you to make custom ringtones. You can sync notes from the Apple iOS Notes app directly to Entourage, Yojimbo, or Mark/Space's own Notes application. The Migration Assistant lets you transfer contacts, and other data from older smartphones to your new iPhone. You can also archive text messages and call history. You can even save visual voicemail messages to your Mac.

Other Devices

Not everyone uses Apple mobile devices, and for a long time, syncing phones and PDAs to a Mac was an odyssey of pain and suffering. Phone and PDA manufacturers treated Mac synchronization software as an afterthought (at best) — and it showed. But things are looking better for Mac workers these days: Hardware manufacturers are showing their respect for the Mac's increasing market share by releasing better syncing software for their devices and Mac OS X. Several application developers have also entered the fray, developing their own tools.

BlackBerry and the Mac

Research in Motion's free Mac syncing software (http://na.blackberry. com/eng/services/desktop/desktop_mac.jsp) for its BlackBerry devices is a lot better than it used to be. It allows you to back up your device and manage the installation and removal of applications. It syncs with Microsoft Entourage (Outlook 2011 support is in the works), iCal, and Address Book. It also syncs iTunes playlists.

If the BlackBerry application isn't enough, try The Missing Sync for BlackBerry ($45; www.markspace.com). Shown in Figure 7-5, The Missing Sync for BlackBerry lets you sync via a USB-to-MicroUSB cable or Bluetooth. In addition to syncing contacts, calendars, and tasks, you can sync music and movies. You can transfer (and view) Word and Excel documents from your Mac to your BlackBerry. The Missing Sync also lets you archive text messages and call history. You can synchronize BlackBerry notes with Entourage, Yojimbo, or The Missing Sync for Mark/Space's own Notes application.

Android and the Mac

Google's Android mobile platform is gaining popularity as several handset manufacturers adopt it. Because Android does most of its syncing through your

FIGURE 7-6

The Missing Sync for Android

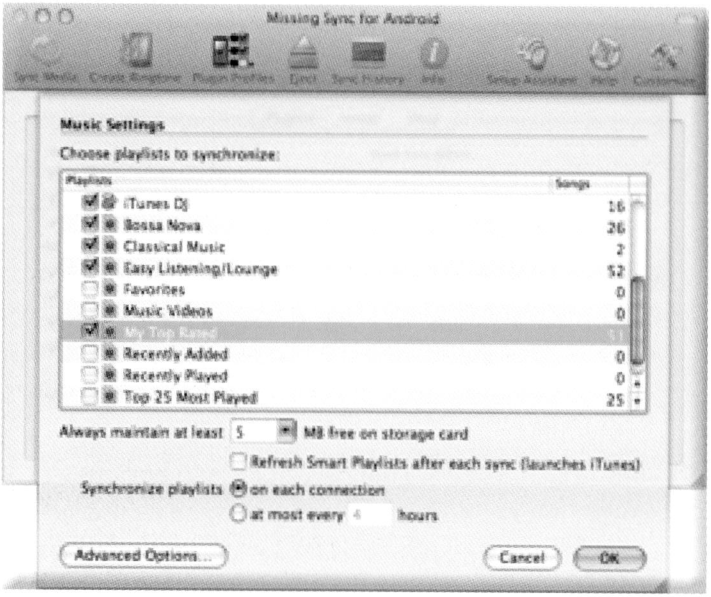

Google account, many of the traditional syncing problems are already solved. Google Android relies on Gmail (covered in Chapter 5), Google Contacts, and Google Calendar (both covered in Chapter 6) to keep your data in sync. Once you enter your Google account name and password on your Android device, Google does all the heavy lifting for your e-mail, contacts, and calendars. Google Android even pushes software updates to the handset. As a result, many Android owners never sync their handsets to their computers.

For the Android owners who want to sync their devices, getting music and media files on your handset takes a little more work. Salling Media Sync for Mac ($22; www.salling.com/mediasync/mac) lets you copy music, podcasts, and photos from your Mac to your Android device. Salling Media Sync shows the remaining capacity of your device and lets you sync all media or selected playlists (including iTunes Genius mixes). If you make smart playlists in iTunes, Salling Media Sync syncs them as well.

If you just want to sync music, videos, and photos, Salling Media Sync is probably all you need. If you need to sync more data, use The Missing Sync for Android ($40; www.markspace.com). Shown in Figure 7-6, it works over USB, Wi-Fi, and Bluetooth, although for large file transfers using a USB-to-MicroUSB cable is still much faster. The Proximity Sync feature automatically (and wirelessly) syncs your Android device when you are near your computer.

In addition to syncing music, podcasts, and pictures, The Missing Sync also downloads your other personal data. Calendars can be synced with Outlook,

Entourage, and iCal. Likewise, your contact database can be synced with Outlook and Apple Address Book. If you want to back up your call history, text messages, or Android Notes, The Missing Sync does that too.

Windows Mobile, Windows Phone 7, and the Mac

Microsoft has released a beta tool for Mac users that lets them synchronize some data from its Windows Phone 7 mobile devices. Mark/Space also plans to release a version of The Missing Sync that supports Windows Phone 7 on the Mac.

Some Mac workers still carry around Windows Mobile (the predecessor to Windows Phone 7) devices, of which many models are in use. If your Windows Mobile smartphone does not have native support for Mac syncing, try The Missing Sync for Windows Mobile ($40; www.markspace.com). It supports most Windows Mobile phones, including the HTC Touch, Samsung Omnia, Sony Ericsson Xperia, and Palm Treo W series.

The Missing Sync for Windows Mobile syncs calendars, contacts, music, pictures, and video. It works with Entourage, the Mac OS X Address Book, and iCal. It also lets you sync Word and Excel documents to your Windows Mobile phone. The Missing Sync for Windows Mobile lets you synchronize via Bluetooth or USB.

WebOS and the Mac

There was a running battle between Palm and Apple over how to sync the WebOS-based Palm Pre and Palm Pixi smartphones: Palm's engineers figured out how to sync directly with iTunes, even though Apple didn't permit such direct syncing — so Apple changed iTunes to block such syncing, Palm figured out how to get around it, and Apple found a way to block that end run.

Things have calmed down, especially since Hewlett-Packard purchased Palm, but if you are using a Palm Pre or Pixi, look into The Missing Sync for Palm Pre ($40; www.markspace.com). Using it, you can sync music, photos, ringtones, and your contact and calendar data to your Mac.

Other devices

There are several other mobile devices still in use. If your device doesn't have acceptable software for the Mac, look at Mark/Space's offerings. In addition to the applications mentioned earlier, Mark/Space also has Mac-based The Missing Sync software for Palm OS, Nokia's Symbian OS, and the Sony PSP.

With Mac OS X's recent success and corresponding growth in market share, just about any mobile device that fits in your pocket can now talk to your Mac.

Talking to Your Mac

have used speech recognition software for nearly 10 years. I started with Dragon Dictate version 1, which required me to pause … between … every … word. Speech recognition has come a long way since those days. Unfortunately, the advances were primarily on the Windows platform. Until recently, the best way to get speech recognition was by loading Windows on your Mac (see Chapter 22) and running Nuance's Dragon NaturallySpeaking for Windows. Fortunately, that has changed.

Mac OS X Speech Tools

Mac OS X has its own speech tools in the Speech system preference, shown in Figure 8-1. Using the Speech Recognition settings, you can set your Mac to accept basic verbal commands to control your Mac. You can also set your Mac to speak commands when you mouse over them, which is helpful for users with visual impairment. Although these tools are not a dictation solution, they do give you some voice control. However, even for voice control, the native speech command support in the Speech system preference is not as extensive as the Command Mode in Dragon Dictate, covered later in this chapter.

The Speech system preference's Text to Speech tab lets you choose a voice and speaking rate for the Mac OS X system voice, which can be a useful tool for proofreading. The default voice, Alex, sounds the most natural. In all applications that allow access to Mac OS X services (the Microsoft Office Suite does not support Mac OS X services), you can select a block of text and, by Control+clicking or right-clicking it, play back the text as speech, as shown in Figure 8-2.

Dragon Dictate

Dragon Dictate for Mac ($199; www.macspeech.com), shown in Figure 8-3, is published by Nuance, the same people who pioneered speech dictation on Windows PCs. With Dragon Dictate for Mac, Nuance brings its 10 years of dictation experience to the Mac, finally giving Mac users a legitimate speech-recognition tool.

Repetitive stress injuries such as carpal tunnel syndrome are a real danger for computer users, so many users are attracted to voice dictation to help avoid injury: Talking into your Mac is much easier on your fingers and wrists than typing for extended periods.

FIGURE 8-1

The Mac OS X Speech system preference

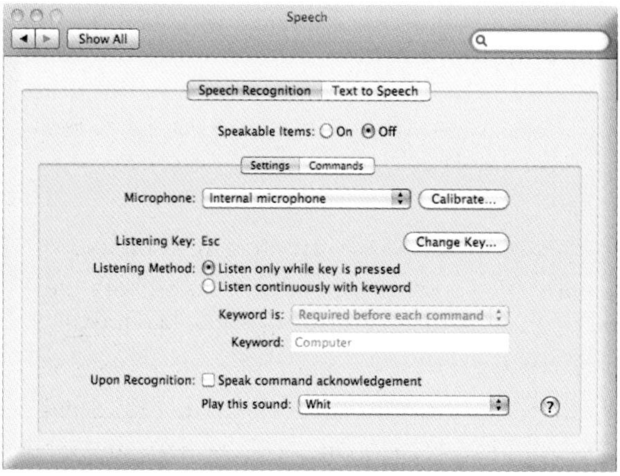

FIGURE 8-2

The Text to Speech service in Mac OS X

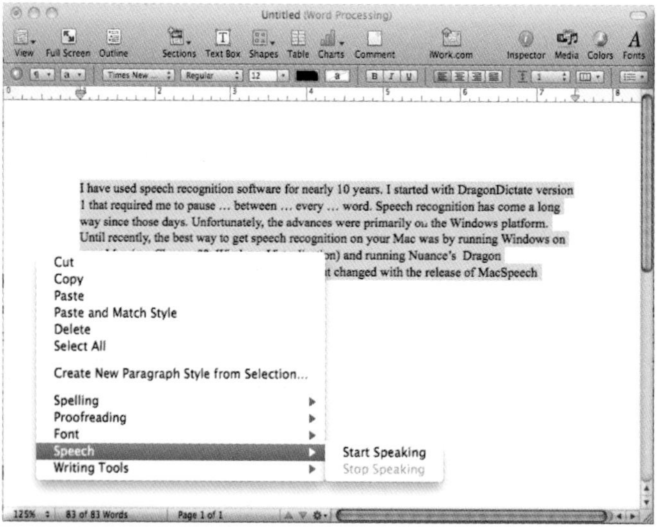

FIGURE 8-3

Dragon Dictate for Mac

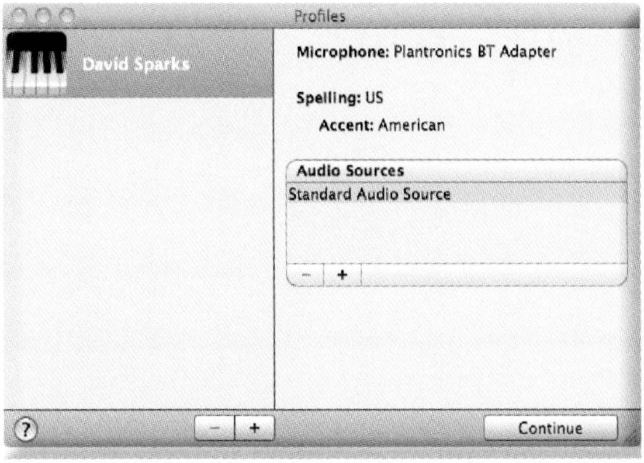

Profiles

David Sparks

Microphone: Plantronics BT Adapter

Spelling: US
Accent: American

Audio Sources
Standard Audio Source

− +

? − + Continue

An additional benefit is speed: If you spend time learning to dictate to your computer, you will be surprised how fast you can enter text. I'm a touch typist and still dictate much faster than I type.

Dragon Dictate includes a speech-friendly noise-canceling microphone. Although the software's installation takes a while (you need to install both the application and vocabulary files), it is not difficult. Once installed, the initial training takes about 15 minutes: Dragon Dictate sets your microphone volume and walks you through a short dictation training session where you read aloud an explanation of how to dictate. This helps you understand the basics and at the same time gives your Mac the voice samples required to create your voice profile, the file Dragon Dictate creates based on your voice and dictation style.

After the initial training, the speech recognition accuracy is surprisingly good. To further refine your voice profile, there are additional training modules you can use once you get more comfortable with Dragon Dictate.

Dictating to your Mac

The Dragon Dictate interface consists of a series of information panes that you can turn off or on in the application's window settings. The Status window, shown in Figure 8-4, indicates when the microphone is on, the application's interpretation of your most recently dictated text, and indicators for dictation, command, and other modes.

FIGURE 8-4

Dragon Dictate's Status window

FIGURE 8-5

Dragon Dictate's Available Commands window

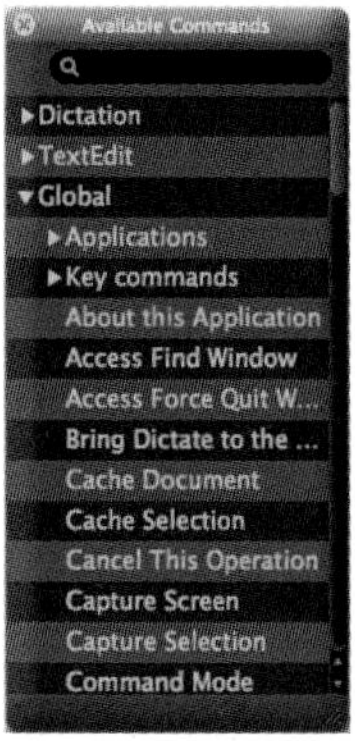

The Available Commands window, shown in Figure 8-5, provides a list of commands you can use. The application has global commands (meaning that they available throughout the operating system), dictation commands (relating to the dictation of text), and application-specific commands for the current application. For example, when working in TextEdit, Dragon Dictate provides a list of possible TextEdit commands. (I find TextEdit the best application for dictating text.) The application-specific commands must be built specifically for the application; although Dragon Dictate does not have application specific commands for every application, it does cover several of the most common Mac OS X applications.

The Recognition window, shown in Figure 8-6, is opened in the Dragon Dictate Preferences dialog box or via the voice command "Open recognition window." This window takes your most recently dictated text and provides a list of alternative transcriptions of your dictation. You can select one of the alternative transcriptions when MacSpeech makes a mistake. If you select an alternative transcription, Dragon Dictate will make note of the change and adjust your voice profile accordingly.

Although you can dictate text into any word processing application, it is best to use Mac OS X's built-in TextEdit for your first draft because Dragon Dictate's support for TextEdit is superb. You can easily make any text dictated in TextEdit into plain text (choose Format ▶ Make Plain Text) and copy and paste it into your application of choice.

When editing text with Dragon Dictate for Mac, you can select words with your voice. You just say "Select" then say the words you want to select. You can then dictate the words you want to replace the selected text. You can also say things like "Put parentheses around" and "Capitalize that" for selected text. Alternatively, you can say "Correct" and add the words you need to correct.

Dragon Dictate's Recognition window

Dragon Dictate then gives you correction options. Every time you correct your text, Dragon Dictate remembers what you did and gets smarter for the next time. The more you use Dragon Dictate for Mac, the better the dictation gets.

Because Dragon Dictate keeps track of the words typed and where the cursor should be, if you move the cursor with the keyboard while editing with your voice, Dragon Dictate gets confused. To avoid this, speak the "Cache document" command; Dragon Dictate reviews the entire text of your dictated document and refreshes its memory as to where all your words fit. Because you will inevitably make changes using your keyboard, the Dragon Dictate memory buffer becomes confused again until you again speak the "Cache document" command. This is another reason to use TextEdit: Dragon Dictate automatically caches text you have in TextEdit so you don't have to keep repeating the "Cache document" command.

Although Dragon Dictate works well out of the box with minimal training, the application really finds its legs when you complete the additional training modules and learn the voice commands. For example, instead of fumbling with your scroll wheel in a document, just say, "Go to beginning." The "Train the word" voice command lets you add words to the Dragon Dictate library. If you change your mind halfway through a sentence, just stop and say "Scratch that." MacSpeech then erases your last dictation, and you can start over.

Dictating dates, deleting words, and changing capitalization all can be accomplished with specific voice commands. Dragon Dictate gives you a lot of power over your text, but you must know the proper commands to wield it. When first learning Dragon Dictate, keep the Available Commands window open to display the available commands for the applications you are using. Once you memorize the commands, your dictation will go faster. Spending a few hours learning Dragon Dictate significantly increases its usefulness.

In addition to learning the Dragon Dictate commands, you also need to train yourself. Don't mumble or skip words; Dragon Dictate relies on the context of your words to work.

Starting a sentence without an idea of how it is going to end doesn't work, either; all dictation engines work best when you give some thought to what you are going to say before speaking. When doing extended dictation, first create an outline. I use OmniOutliner. Looking at an outline helps keep the dictation clear and on point.

Once you have your thoughts composed, sit up straight and dictate as if you were Walter Cronkite. Using a deliberate, steady dictation voice goes a long way in improving dictation accuracy.

A common mistake is speaking too slowly. When you dictate too slowly, Dragon Dictate may break individual syllables into separate words. If you want to take your time, pause between sentences while composing.

I also upgraded my dictation microphone. I use a Plantronics Calisto Pro Bluetooth microphone ($90; www.plantronics.com). Although the audio quality is not as good as with a wired microphone, the freedom from a cord is liberating. If you decide to upgrade your microphone, make certain Dragon Dictate supports it — not all microphones are compatible.

Another important bit of advice when dictating: Proofread. Don't just read it back once. Print the draft and get out your trusty red pen. As fantastic as dictation technology is, it sometimes makes mistakes, and those mistakes are difficult to catch. "Relevant" may be transcribed as "Irrelevant." "He" might become "She." Save yourself some embarrassment and keep a sharp eye out when proofreading dictated text.

Using voice commands

Using the Command mode, Dragon Dictate can also operate your Mac. You can do just about anything on your Mac, including launching applications, opening new files, and saving documents. With practice, the Command mode can take the place of several mouse clicks and key presses and is particularly helpful for users with disabilities.

In addition to using Dragon Dictate to command your Mac, you can also use it to search the Web. For example, you could say, "Search the Web for MacSparky" to make Dragon Dictate open your default Web browser and perform a Google search.

Again, this functionality is slightly more rough around the edges than its Windows counterpart. Dragon Dictate is not yet at the point where you can simply sit back and drive your Mac without any keyboard and mouse interaction.

Vocabulary Editor

Dragon Dictate's Vocabulary Editor, shown in Figure 8-7, allows you to customize the Dragon Dictate dictionary by adding frequently used words and phrases. When adding specific words or phrases to the vocabulary editor, be certain to repeat them several times for increased accuracy. Also, you don't have

Dragon Dictate's Vocabulary Editor

to add just individual words as dictionary entries. For example, you could add the name "Mr. Hank Morgan" as a single vocabulary entry. After you train Dragon Dictate with a longer phrase, it is unlikely Dragon Dictate will get it wrong.

In addition to adding particular phrases, you can also have Dragon Dictate scan documents you specify on your Mac to pull out new words. This significantly increases recognition.

Speech recognition also increases with usage. Once you get comfortable with the application and have refined your voice file, you will get better accuracy. This improved accuracy is most noticeable with the little things, like plurals and possessives.

The processing power required to recognize and transcribe spoken words is significant. Dragon Dictate can use more than 1GB of active memory. On an older Mac or one without sufficient memory, the program can hang or even crash. However, if your work requires lots of writing, you will appreciate Dragon Dictate. Sitting back in your chair and dictating while the words appear on screen feels like something out of the future.

There is no competition to Dragon Dictate on Mac OS X. The only other viable alternative is to load Windows through a virtual machine and run Dragon NaturallySpeaking, which has the same dictation engine but a slightly better editing interface and more features. Because running Windows is a significant burden on your system memory and processor, it is not worth the trouble. I've used Dragon Dictate and its MacSpeech Dictate predecessor on my Mac as my only dictation tool for more than a year without regret.

In addition to the basic version of Dragon Dictate, which is sufficient for most users, there are vocabulary-enhanced, higher-priced editions for doctors and lawyers, as well as an international edition. The legal and medical editions cost $600 each, and the international edition costs $300. Whether you need one of the professional editions depends on how much you need their specialized dictionaries. The basic application can learn new words and already has a good dictionary of basic medical and legal jargon.

MacSpeech Scribe

Although Dragon Dictate is great for dictating while sitting at your Mac, what if you want to dictate when you are not at your computer? Nuance, the maker of Dragon Dictate, has a separate product for translating previously recorded

FIGURE 8-8

Training MacSpeech Scribe

FIGURE 8-9

MacSpeech Scribe's Dictation window

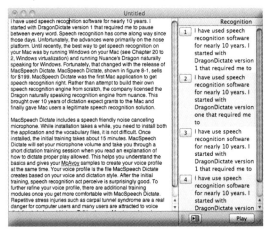

dictation called MacSpeech Scribe ($149; www.macspeech.com/scribe). Using MacSpeech Scribe, you can turn recorded audio into text.

Training MacSpeech Scribe involves making a recording (at least two minutes long) of your voice reading text and loading the resulting audio file. MacSpeech Scribe transcribes the first 15 seconds of the recording and displays its transcription in a window where you can compare the recording to the transcribed words and make corrections, as shown in Figure 8-8. Learning from its mistakes, the program starts over. The initial training takes about 20 minutes. Once you are finished, MacSpeech Scribe can transcribe future recordings.

The supported audio formats are AIFF, WAV, M4V, MP4, and M4A. Strangely, MacSpeech Scribe does not support the widely used MP3 format. You can use any electronic recorder that saves in an approved format, but the better quality recorders provide better transcription. Interestingly, the iPhone's Voice Memo recorder application makes a clear recording that is a good starting point for MacSpeech Scribe.

MacSpeech Scribe's interface is simple, as Figure 8-9 shows. Because MacSpeech Scribe does not have to work inside other Mac OS X applications as Dragon Dictate does, it does not require as many tools. You can review the text and make corrections. When done, copy and paste the completed text wherever it belongs.

MacSpeech Scribe frees you from your computer and is well suited to longer dictation projects. Although not having the immediate feedback of seeing your words appear on the screen can be disconcerting, it also removes the distraction. Again, there are enhanced versions for the legal and medical professionals for an additional $99 each.

If you want to dictate to your Mac, I recommend you try Dragon Dictate first. Having the on-screen feedback helps refine your dictation skills. Once you master Dragon Dictate, moving to MacSpeech Scribe should not be difficult.

PART

III

Basic Business

Task Management

I am a believer in keeping task lists. I would like to say this arises from some inherent sense of order and organization. In truth, however, it arises from my realization that I am scatterbrained and often have the attention span of a goldfish. As a result, if I cannot do something immediately, I write it down. Dumping tasks into a list is liberating. When my tasks are on a list, I don't forget them. When I was a student, I had a really simple task-management system. Every morning I'd eat my cereal and write on a napkin the three things I needed to accomplish that day and then put it in my pocket. It worked brilliantly.

Today my responsibilities have expanded, exponentially. I have personal and professional commitments that affect many people. At any time, I have many plates in the air and if any of them crash to the ground, it is a problem. As I write this sentence, I have 1,713 tasks stored in 257 projects. Although this sounds completely insane, I have it under control thanks to the tools I cover in this chapter.

This chapter gets into the nitty-gritty of the best available tools for task management on the Mac. The focus is managing your *tasks*; managing your *team* is covered in Chapter 17.

Task-Management Fundamentals

Before diving in, let's cover some fundamentals of how a task-management system should work. There are four pieces to serious task management: capture, organize, process, and review. Putting these ideas in perspective will help later when I explain the task management options on the Mac.

Capture

The purpose of a task-management system is to avoid having tasks fall through the cracks. As the number of tasks increases, the ability to keep them in your head becomes increasingly difficult. A task-management system needs to make it easy to record new tasks as they occur to you. If you are working on a report and remember you need to buy spicy carrots, you should be able to capture that task and return your attention to your report. Getting from brain to paper should require a minimum of fuss. Otherwise, you wait to capture that task and, quite often, forget entirely about it until something goes wrong. All the tools covered in this chapter have capture capabilities.

But capture doesn't need to happen on your Mac. Of all the task-management fundamentals, capture is the one that can be accomplished without digital assistance. Many people use a notebook or a pocket recorder, for example, to capture tasks and later add them to their Mac's task-management software.

Organize

Once you've captured your tasks, you next need to organize them and your Mac can be a big help. Traditionally, task lists are organized by date or project. Modern task management strategies expand these criteria to also include priority (using a grading system, flags, or other mechanism) and context (for example, differentiating tasks that can be completed on the phone versus those that can be completed on the computer). A Mac and task-management software can make organization much easier.

Process

The big payoff with a task list is completing the tasks. Working through the list and checking off items is the purpose of the exercise. Software tools again can be helpful for sorting and presenting your task list and then getting out of the way so you can get work done.

Review

The best task-management tools have a system to allow you to audit your tasks and make sure you are not missing anything. An audit system is that one last safety net keeping those plates from hitting the floor.

The trick with setting up a task-management system is to make it as complex as you need it to be and not a single bit more complex than that. When in law school, my napkin task list was perfect: I captured and organized every morning, I processed the tasks throughout the day, and I audited my list every night when I emptied my pockets. Now I have many more responsibilities, so the napkin no longer cuts it.

It is easy to let a task-management system take over. For some people, it becomes a form of procrastination, where they spend hours a day making their list and accomplishing very little work. When looking at the options in this chapter, think about your needs and find the system that gives you as much complexity as you require but doesn't get in the way of completing your work. After all, the point of task management is task completion.

Task-Management Software

Until the last few years, the state of task-management software on the Mac was dismal. Fortunately, however, there has been an explosion of task management tools for Mac OS X. This chapter covers some of the most useful tools in their order of complexity, starting with the simplest, iCal.

iCal tasks

iCal, the free calendar application that ships on every new Mac, includes a built-in task manager. iCal calls tasks *to-do items*, and they can be added to the right pane in the iCal window, as shown in Figure 9-1. (If that To-Do Lists pane is not displayed, choose View ▶ Show To-Do List or press Option+⌘+T to display it.)

You create a new to-do item in iCal by double-clicking the To-Do List pane or pressing ⌘+K. Adding to-do items to the list just requires that you type in the name of the to-do task, such as "Call Smith Client." You can add further data to

FIGURE 9-1

iCal's To-Do List pane (at right)

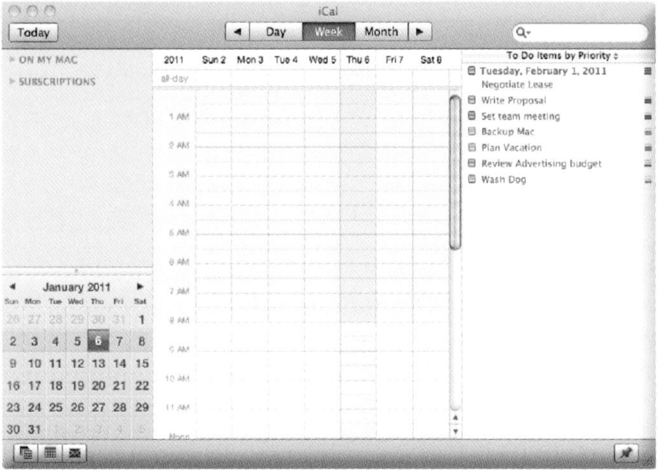

FIGURE 9-2

iCal's to-do info window

your to-do item by double-clicking on the to-do item (or selecting it and pressing ⌘+I). This calls up the to-do info window shown in Figure 9-2.

In the to-do info window, you can rename a task and mark it as completed. You can set a task's priority level choosing low, medium, high, or no priority. You can optionally set a due date or alarm for your to-do item. If you have more information about your to-do item, you can use the Note field. There is also a URL field into which you can copy a Web site's address.

iCal lets you attach a to-do item to a specific calendar. You assign to-do's to calendars in the info window or by Control+clicking or right-clicking the to-do item in the To-Do List pane. Assigning to-dos to calendars can be useful if you have separate iCal calendars for different areas of responsibility. You may have distinct calendars for work and personal items. By attaching your to-do items to the appropriate calendars, you can turn off the display of certain tasks by hiding the affiliated calendar. For example, you could, upon arriving in the office deselect your personal calendar (by unchecking the box for your personal calendar in iCal's left pane) to hide your personal to-do items. You can take this method to another level by making custom calendars for each work project. If you have a separate calendar for each major client, you can filter your to-do list by selecting (and deselecting) calendars.

You can display your to-do items in order of priority, due date, title (alphabetically), or calendar. You can also organize them manually dragging tasks into your own pecking order.

Adding to-do items to iCal requires loading iCal and adding them directly to the application. If you use an Exchange server, you can sync to-do items to iCal. Strangely, Apple does not have an iOS to-do app and there is no way to sync to-do items to your iPhone, iPad, or iPod Touch using iTunes. Using MobileMe, you can save the To-Do items to an IMAP mail account, which then syncs to the Mail iOS application on your mobile device in the Apple To Do mailbox. The whole process is unintuitive and un-Apple. If you want to sync to-do items to an iOS device, move on to one of the other options in this chapter.

Likewise, organizing your tasks by calendar can become tedious, requiring multiple mouse clicks for each item. iCal to-do lists also do not allow you to create recurring tasks. If you want to prepare a staff meeting agenda every Monday morning, you need to create a new to-do item; you cannot simply create one and set it to repeat every week. Organizing your tasks from one big list is fine if you only have a few dozen to-dos, but if you have hundreds, it is unworkable.

It is easy to poke holes in Apple's to-do management. However, if your task management needs are small, iCal may work for you. It would have been a fine replacement for my napkin 20 years ago in school. Remember: The point is not to spend your time managing your task list but instead completing tasks.

FIGURE 9-3

Remember the Milk's Web interface

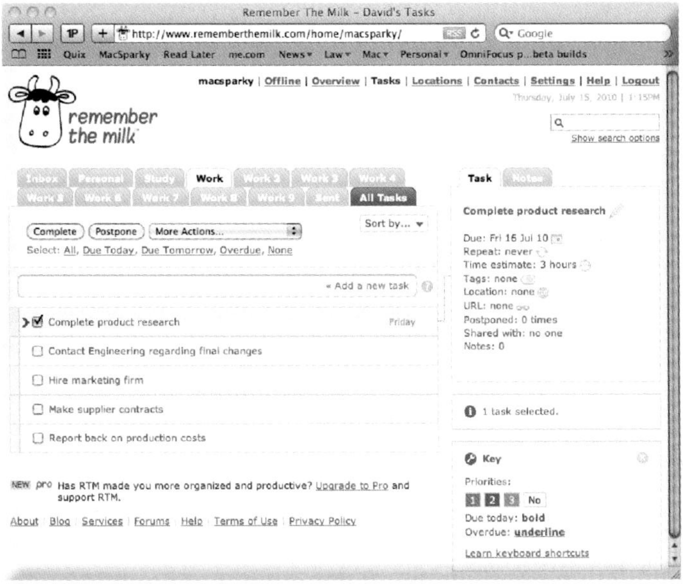

Remember the Milk

There is a growing crop of Web-based task-management services. These allow you to create your task lists in the Internet cloud and access them from connected computers and mobile devices. A Web-based tool is convenient for mobile Mac workers because it allows access to task lists from iPhones, Macs, PCs, and other Internet-connected devices.

One of the leaders in this space is Remember the Milk (free; www.rememberthemilk.com). Shown in Figure 9-3, Remember the Milk allows you to create and manage tasks through your Web browser. In addition to creating tasks, you can set due dates, priorities, and time estimates.

Remember the Milk uses intelligent data recognition to make entering dates easier. For example, if you want an item to be due in three weeks, you type 3 weeks in the Due field and Remember the Milk calculates the date for you. It also interprets days of the week, like "Next Tuesday." Remember the Milk supports recurring tasks; if you want a task to repeat every three days, type 3 days in the Repeat field. Remember the Milk also lets you tag your task items with keywords to make searching easier.

The interface uses a tab system to keep tasks in different projects. You can create tabs for each project. This works well if your project list isn't too large. After you have nine projects entered, the Interface starts adding additional rows of tabs. After you have about 20 projects, the interface gets noisy.

Because it is Web-based, Remember the Milk can send reminders to your Internet-connected devices with e-mail, SMS, and instant message accounts. Remember the Milk gives you an e-mail address with every new account. You can e-mail tasks to this address to have them automatically added to your task list. Although this gives you a way to capture tasks from your mobile device, stopping to write an e-mail every time you think of a new task isn't efficient. There are mobile Remember the Milk applications for iPhone, Android, BlackBerry, and Windows Mobile devices to put your list in your pocket.

The basic Remember the Milk service is free, but for $25 per year you can get a Pro account that gives priority e-mail support and has better syncing and push notifications with the mobile device applications.

The big advantage of a Web-based tool occurs when you are working on both Macs and Windows PCs. Because everything is browser-based, you can access and modify your task lists from either operating system using a Web-based service like Remember the Milk.

This marriage to the browser is also Remember the Milk's biggest disadvantage. It does not have the polish that you get with a native Mac OS X application. Remember the Milk has tried to compensate with extensive keyboard shortcuts to streamline the service, but it still feels uniquely un-Mac-like compared to other task management applications. Regardless, Web-based task management applications are only going to become more sophisticated and polished over time. This is one to watch.

Things

Things ($50; `http://culturedcode.com/things`) is one of the most widely adopted task-management applications on the Mac. Things, shown in Figure 9-4, excels at the software design principles Mac users love. It has a simple interface but includes sufficient features to handle the task-management needs of many Mac workers.

The Things application window uses the familiar Mac OS X left-and-right-pane format, where the left pane includes a source list of projects and search criteria and the right pane holds the task list. There is also a toolbar on the bottom of the task window.

The interface is clean, and you can immediately start using the application. All the information for each task is included in each task entry. There is no inspector.

There are several ways to create tasks in Things. Perhaps the easiest is by clicking the New Task iconic button in the lower-left section of the toolbar. You are then presented the screen view shown in Figure 9-4. The top line holds the name of your new task. The check box to the left of the name allows you to mark

FIGURE 9-4

Things' task-management interface

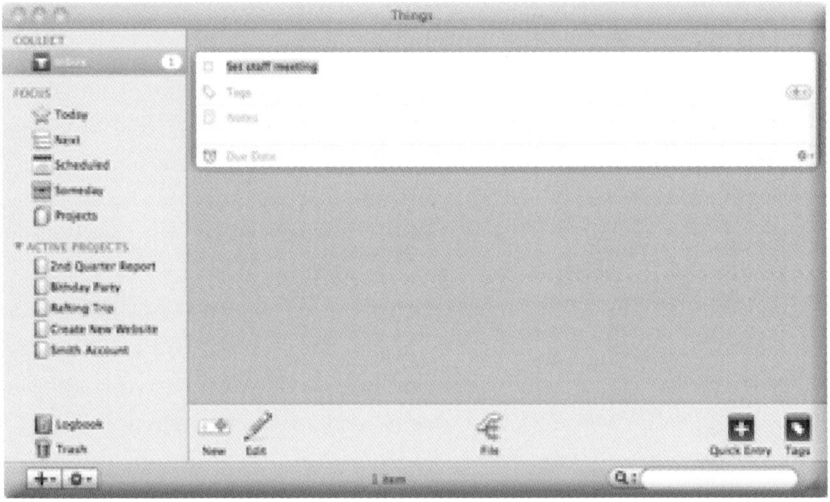

the task as completed. You can optionally assign tags in the second line and add notes to your task item in the Notes field. The bottom line lets you assign a due date to the task. If you assign a due date, you are given the option to assign a start date relative to the due date. For example, you can have a task not appear until three days before the due date.

Things also has a Quick Entry panel that is activated with a keyboard shortcut (the default is Control+spacebar), shown in Figure 9-5. The Quick Entry panel opens in the middle of the screen without requiring you to exit your current application and enter Things, although Things must be running in the background. You type in your new task and any tags, notes, and due dates, then press Return. The task is automatically added to Things. You can also add Web pages, e-mails, and files to the tasks by dragging them into the Quick Entry panel.

Once you start building your list of task items, you'll need to organize them. Things' primary means of organization is the use of descriptive tags. To edit a task's tags, reopen it (by double-clicking it, by selecting it and clicking the Edit iconic button in the toolbar, or by selecting it and pressing Return) and add

FIGURE 9-5

The Things Quick Entry panel

descriptions in the Tags field. Things includes a set of pre-defined tags accessed by clicking the + iconic button at the right side of the Tags field. The predefined tags include contexts (work, home, and errand), priority (low, medium, and high), duration (15 minutes and one hour), and difficulty (easy and challenge). You can add your own custom tags to this list. You can also create new tags by typing them in the tag field of any task item.

Because you can apply multiple tags to a task, you can create as many indices as you can handle. For example, a task item to write a contract can include tags with the name of the client, the name of the project, the project priority, the people involved, and the estimated time. It is important when you start using Things that you structure your tags to be manageable. If you start creating different tags for every task item, the tags become useless as an indexing tool. Once you have a tag system in place, you can quickly drill into your task list by selecting specific tags. So long as you spend time thinking about the tag descriptions, tagging is an effective way to manage tasks.

Whatever task-management system you embrace, you do not want to start every day facing a list of all your future uncompleted tasks. For some people (myself included), the whole list could number in the thousands. To keep your task list from including all your future task items every day, Things has a Scheduled list. When you drag a task into the Scheduled list, Things prompts you to choose a date. That task then disappears from your task list until the scheduled date. Things also has a Someday list where you can drag tasks that you are not ready to start but want to review again in the future.

Tasks in Things can also be organized into projects by dragging a task into the Projects list. You can then input additional tasks for a specific project, as shown in Figure 9-6. Projects in Things can be flagged as active or inactive. All active

FIGURE 9-6

The Things Project list

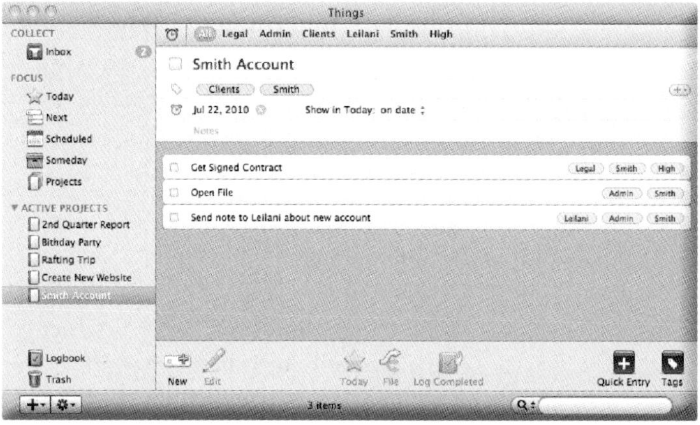

projects are displayed in the left pane. Keeping the Project list on screen works great if you have 10 to 15 projects. But if you have 200 projects, it becomes a mess.

The Next list shows you the next few tasks available for every project. As you check off those items, additional tasks from the project will appear. You can then scroll through the list of projects, pick the tasks you want to complete, and get to work. You can also type in some task tags to further narrow the available task list for easier management in the Next list.

One of the easiest ways to prioritize tasks with Things is to drag the tasks you want to complete onto the Today list. The Today list holds all the tasks you drag onto it and automatically adds any tasks with an active start date or from the Scheduled list set for the current day. You can then spend the rest of the day completing the Today list tasks. Once you complete a task, it is sent to the Logbook, found on the lower portion of the left pane. You can open the Logbook and view your completed tasks. While in the Logbook, you can mark a task as uncompleted and it will return to its project.

Things also has dedicated iPhone and iPad applications. But syncing requires that your mobile devices be on the same wireless network as your Mac. You cannot, for example, update your iPhone's tasks while at the coffee shop using its Wi-Fi hot spot.

There is no review mechanism built into Things. Although you can review your tasks in total, there is no way to set different review periods for each project.

You will know within 30 minutes if Things is right for you. The application works straight out of the box with little need for customization. In my opinion, it is the best "install and go" task-management system on the Mac. I've set up Things for many Mac workers who are efficiently keeping up with their task list. But for the most comprehensive task-management system, look at OmniFocus.

OmniFocus

OmniFocus ($80; www.omnigroup.com/omnifocus), is the most powerful task manager covered in this chapter. Where most task-management applications are built with a planned workflow in mind for users, OmniFocus, shown in Figure 9-7, includes numerous task-management tools so you can make the application as simple (or complex) as you choose.

Collecting tasks and sorting your Inbox

As you go about your day, new task items might occur. You want to quickly enter those items into OmniFocus so you can clear your mind of that item and get back to work. With OmniFocus, you enter tasks in the inbox, shown in Figure 9-7. Accessed from within OmniFocus by clicking the Inbox iconic button in the

FIGURE 9-7

OmniFocus's task-management interface

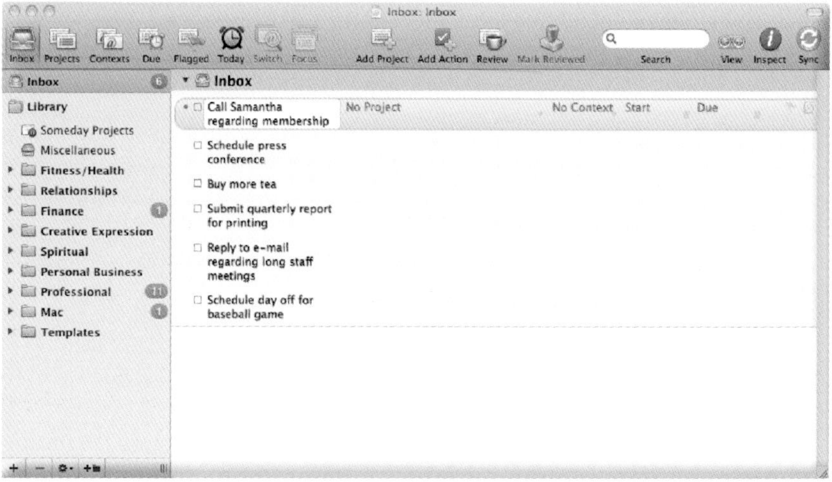

toolbar or pressing Option+⌘+1, the inbox presents a list of all your new and unassigned tasks. If you are brainstorming about a project, the inbox is a great place to quickly get your tasks into the system. You enter new tasks by typing the task description and pressing Return.

The inbox is not the only way to collect tasks. OmniFocus has a Quick Entry panel that can be activated from anywhere in Mac OS X with a key combination; the default is Control+Option+spacebar. The Quick Entry panel, shown in Figure 9-8, then appears on your screen and you can type in a new task. For this panel to work, OmniFocus needs to be running in the background. Like Things, the Quick Entry panel lets you add new tasks quickly and return to your work. There is no need to switch applications or break your concentration. You can configure the Quick Entry panel so you just enter a task's description or you can add additional details such as start and end dates, context, project, and flag status.

OmniFocus also lets you automate task collection with clippings. Using the Preferences dialog box's Clipping pane, you can define a keyboard shortcut (I use Control+Option+⌘+C) that, when activated, takes any selected text and creates a new task. For example, you could select text on a Web page and activate the clipping shortcut to automatically save that selected text to OmniFocus.

The Clipping pane also lets you install a clipping service in Apple Mail, called the Clip-o-Tron 3000, that automates clipping e-mails. You can click any e-mail message (or group of e-mail messages) and, by activating your clipping keyboard shortcut, drop the e-mail into OmniFocus as a new task. The task will include the entire text of the e-mail and a link that you can later click to reopen the e-mail in Apple Mail. This is a great solution for dealing with e-mail that requires later

FIGURE 9-8

OmniFocus's Quick Entry panel

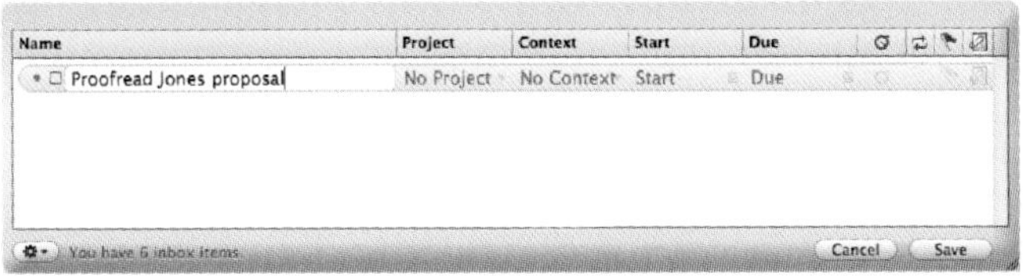

action: It gives you a reliable way to track the e-mail and lets you file the original out of your e-mail inbox. (For more information on integrating tasks with e-mail, see Chapter 5.) OmniFocus can also use Apple Mail rules to add tasks from incoming e-mail to the OmniFocus Inbox. You can, for example, send yourself an e-mail about taking the dog to the vet and it will appear in OmniFocus.

When you are on the road, you can add tasks to OmniFocus with the iPhone and iPad applications. Both mobile apps have an easily accessed inbox that sync to your Mac.

Once your tasks are collected in the OmniFocus inbox, you can add notes and attachments to the tasks. I scan most important documents that come my way and drop them into OmniFocus as an attachment to their corresponding tasks so, I don't have to go searching for the related documents when it comes time to get to work.

The two primary view modes in OmniFocus are projects and contexts. Processing your inbox requires you to identify a project and context for each new task. A project is a goal that requires one or more tasks. A project can be lofty, like creating a foundation, or mundane, like washing the dog. It doesn't matter: The tools for managing all projects are the same in OmniFocus.

A context is the location, people, or tools necessary to accomplish a task. For example responding to e-mail requires that you are sitting at your computer and are connected to the Internet. E-mail is, therefore, a context. You can assign a task (such as responding to a client e-mail) the context of E-mail. Later, you'll see how OmniFocus can use that information to give you a list of all tasks with the E-mail context, making it easy for you deal with all outstanding e-mail tasks at once. Contexts can also be a specific location or a person. I have a context for several of my co-workers. That way, when we get together, I can select their context in OmniFocus and immediately have a list of all tasks I need their assistance on.

OmniFocus does an intelligent job of sorting your projects and contexts. For example, when adding tasks to my project for this book, I would type maw and OmniFocus figured out I was using the Mac at Work project. You can also add new projects and contexts in the inbox by typing the name and pressing ⌘+Return. When processing inbox items, you can add start and due dates, estimated time, and flag status. Once an item has a project and a context, it disappears from the inbox. After you are done with the inbox, you can further manage your tasks in the Projects and Context views.

Organizing and processing tasks

The Project view, shown in Figure 9-9, is a list of all the projects you are working on. You create new projects in OmniFocus by clicking the New Project iconic button in the toolbar or pressing Shift+⌘+N. You can create projects for all aspects of your work and personal life. I have projects for specific clients, articles I want to write, and upgrading my backyard vegetable garden. Each chapter of this book was, at one point, a project in OmniFocus.

Anything that merits your time and attention can have its own place in OmniFocus. You can have one long list of all your projects or create hierarchical folders to organize your projects. For example, in my Work folder I have a subfolder called Clients where I keep a separate folder for each client. This way I can keep all projects related to each client in a single folder.

When using Project view (activated by pressing ⌘+1 or clicking the Projects iconic button in the toolbar), you are presented a list of all your projects in the left pane. When you click a project, all the related tasks appear in the right pane, as Figure 9-9 shows.

In the Project view, you can also choose whether a specific project's tasks are shown in sequential or parallel order. A sequential project is one where tasks need to be performed in order. For example, if you want to wash the dog, you first need to get the tub, then fill it with water and soap, and then put Rover in the tub. This is true for work projects, too: Quite often, pitching an account or writing a report are sequential projects. If you mark a project in OmniFocus as sequential

---

FIGURE 9-9

The OmniFocus Project view

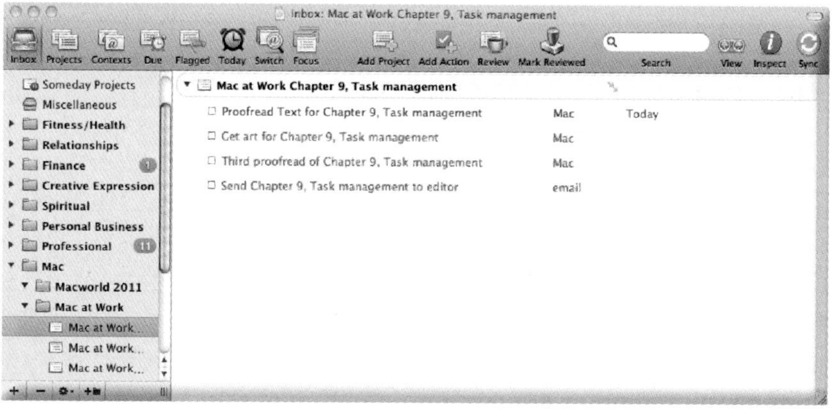

FIGURE 9-10

The Sequential/Parallel iconic button (highlighted here via the yellow circle)

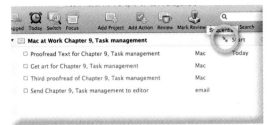

(by clicking the Sequential/Parallel iconic button shown in Figure 9-10), it shows the tasks in order, making only the next task available. Using the dog-washing project as an example, you won't see a task to fill the tub with water until after you've checked off that you have a tub. Marking a project as sequential is useful to remove extra noise from your daily task list.

Tasks in parallel projects can be completed in any order. Checking in with clients, for example, is a parallel project. The order in which you call clients doesn't matter. If you have a project that involves a series of parallel tasks, all available tasks are shown; all the parallel tasks can be accomplished independently of one another.

The Project view is also a good place to manage start and due dates for your tasks. There are several ways to enter dates in OmniFocus. You can enter a date by writing the month and date, such as 11/12 for November 12. You can also set dates relative to the current date. If, for example, on October 11, you typed 3d in a date field, OmniFocus would fill in the field with the date in three days, or October 14. If you want to push the start date of a task to begin two weeks from Monday, type 2w Mon and OmniFocus will fill in the right date.

When using OmniFocus, you should be aggressive with the use of start dates and conservative with the use of due dates. Start dates are a great way to keep your task list manageable. If you are going to write the Smith proposal in two weeks, set the start date in two weeks. Otherwise, it will appear as available on your task list every day between now and then. The idea is to only have items on your task list that you intend to complete on any given day.

Due dates are the exact opposite. Most tasks don't require a due date. When you give every task a due date, the list becomes unwieldy because OmniFocus puts a red badge on its icon telling you the number of overdue items. If every item has a due date, every morning you will be swamped with many artificial due dates (on items that don't require a due date) and the few true due dates will get lost in the noise. Only enter due dates on tasks that truly need them. Then when you see that red badge, you can make sure to take care of it.

FIGURE 9-11

The OmniFocus Context view

Contexts: Errands

The Context view organizes all tasks by context, as shown in Figure 9-11. If you entered contexts for your tasks in the inbox, you now have a simple way to organize your tasks by where you are sitting. For example, my office e-mail server crashed a few weeks ago. Everyone in the office completely freaked. I turned off my e-mail context and switched over to other contexts where I had the necessary tools and people available and got back to work.

Both the Context and Project views allow you to filter the tasks displayed. There are several filters, including project name, flag status, and duration. OmniFocus lets you customize the filters to create custom views of your tasks, called *perspectives*. You can then save the perspectives for later use. I have created several custom perspectives to help me manage tasks. One, called Today, just shows tasks that are active today. Another, called Clear, lets me quickly audit uncompleted tasks at the end of the day.

Once the planning is over, you need to get to work. I usually spend about 20 minutes every morning planning and prioritizing as necessary in the Today perspective. Although I keep OmniFocus running in the background the rest of the day, I rarely open its window except to check off items and add new tasks. Remember: The point is to get work done and not fiddle with task lists. In the evening, I go back into OmniFocus and clear out the day's tasks and process any new items in the inbox so the following day I can hit the ground running.

Reviewing tasks

The last piece of OmniFocus is its review capability. You can set a review period for every project. The review period could be once a week for an important project or once every six months for a not-so-important project. You can then activate the Review pane, shown in Figure 9-12, by clicking the Review iconic button in the toolbar. The Review pane presents all projects that are due for review. You can make sure the tasks are still necessary and the project is still

FIGURE 9-12

The OmniFocus Review pane

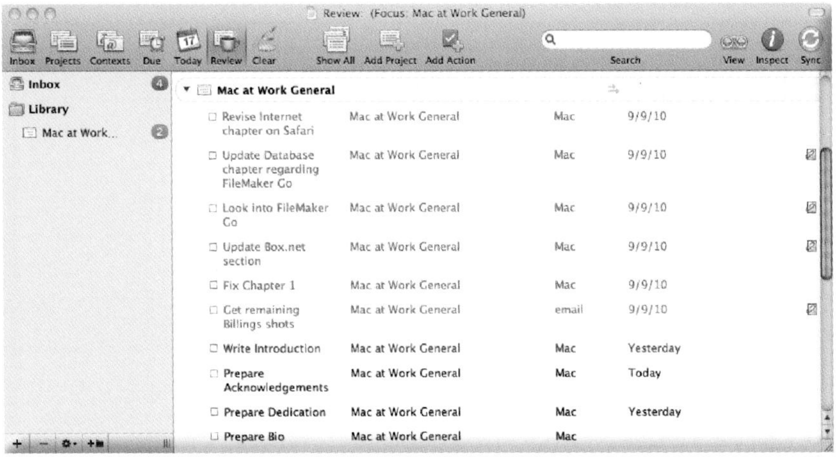

relevant. After you mark the project as reviewed, you can set the new review period and OmniFocus will reset the review timer on that project and the project will disappear from the Review pane. A methodical review process is another way to make sure no project or task gets overlooked.

Among productivity nerds, there is a running dispute between OmniFocus and Things. Both applications are good, but they are also different. Things has an accessible simplicity at the cost of some additional OmniFocus features that I find useful, such as better implementation of start and due dates, sequential versus parallel tasks, and a project review process.

In the last few years, the task-management support on the Mac has matured from a barren wasteland to a rich spectrum of applications covering all Mac worker's task-management needs.

Notes and Outlines

lthough there was a time where bringing a computer to a meeting was frowned upon, laptops at the conference table have since become commonplace. Whether at weekly staff meetings or client sales calls, there are several opportunities to take notes using your Mac.

Of course, not everyone takes notes the same way. Some users want a linear outline while others prefer the fluid style of a mind map. This chapter looks at some of the best note-taking and outlining tools available for Mac OS X. No matter how you manage notes and information, at least one of the applications in this chapter should work for you.

OmniOutliner

The Omni Group's OmniOutliner ($40; www.omnigroup.com/products/omnioutliner), shown in Figure 10-1, is the best outlining application on the Mac. OmniOutliner's interface presents a basic outline that you can expand on during meetings or planning projects. You can promote and demote outline entries using Tab and Shift+Tab and insert a new row using Shift+Return. You can also move and adjust outline entries using the mouse. After just a few minutes, you will be structuring and building outlines in OmniOutliner. If you are in a meeting or an interview that jumps around among several topics, you can easily keep up with an outline by adding and expanding outline branches as you go.

OmniOutliner is much more than a traditional outliner. You can add multiple columns with different data types such as pop-up menus, check boxes, numerical values, dates, durations, and even plain text, as shown in Figure 10-2. Often, following a meeting, I add columns to my outline. For example, I include a column for the person responsible for an item, the estimated time to complete, costs, and deadlines. The columns can be shown or hidden. What starts out as an outline becomes a project management tool.

If you keep numbers in a column, you can instruct OmniOutliner to calculate sums and averages. Another good use for columns is to embed links to Web sites and files. If, for example, you have a PDF document that relates to an outline entry, drag the document to your outline, and OmniOutliner creates a link. You

The Omni Group's OmniOutliner

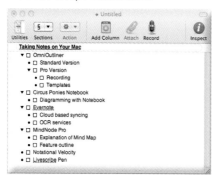

can then access that PDF while in OmniOutliner by clicking the link. This also works for the built-in Mac OS X Address Book. You can make a separate column for contacts and drag names from your Address Book straight into the outline. OmniOutliner also holds larger media such as images, audio files, and movies.

Each OmniOutliner entry supports inline notes. This feature lets you attach a writing pad to every outline entry. The inline notes can collapse or open as needed, as shown in Figure 10-3. Some writers use this feature to outline a document in OmniOutliner and then write the full text in the inline notes. You can then adjust the document by re-arranging the outline. Later the outline, including the inline notes, can be exported to a word processor.

OmniOutliner's styles capability allows you to customize the look of your outline. For example, if you want every Level 1 outline item to have a blue background and every Level 3 item to use italicized text, you can make that happen. Your entire OmniOutliner outline is also searchable. All the search results appear in a Utility drawer that slides out the side of your outline window.

There are two versions of OmniOutliner: Standard and Professional. The $70 Professional version includes clipping, recording, and template features. The

OmniOutliner's column data types

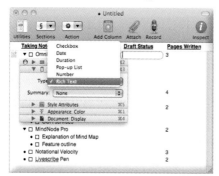

OmniOutliner's inline notes feature

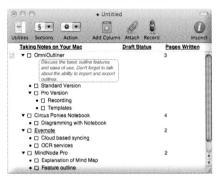

clipping service adds text from other applications with a keystroke. OmniOutliner Professional can additionally record audio. Using the recording feature, you can capture the audio from a meeting while making an outline. You can later go back and update your outline while listening to the recording. The Professional version's custom template support gives you a starting point for repeating outlines. For example, if you have a weekly staff meeting, a custom template with the repeating agenda items will save you time.

If you want to work on your outline in a different application, OmniOutliner provides several export options. You can export your outline to Microsoft Word, HTML, RTF, and several other text formats. OmniOutliner also supports the OPML (Outline Processor Markup Language), which allows you to open the outline in other applications and preserve your outline formatting. OPML export works particularly well with Scrivener, covered in Chapter 11.

Moreover, OmniOutliner exports directly to Apple's Keynote. Many of my best presentations started life in OmniOutliner. When exporting slides to Keynote, OmniOutliner creates a new Keynote slide for every Level 1 outline entry.

I use OmniOutliner often. Anytime I have a collection of random thoughts, sorting and organizing them in an outline helps. In fact, this book started in OmniOutliner.

Circus Ponies NoteBook

Circus Ponies' NoteBook ($50; `www.circusponies.com`) allows you to create virtual three-ring binders on your Mac. Just like the binders you carried in school, NoteBook allows you to remove pages, cut and paste pictures or articles of interest, and add tabs to give you quick access to key information, as shown in Figure 10-4.

The NoteBook interface is immediately useful. You can customize your pages with several ruled and grid options, including a Cornell-style note-taking format.

FIGURE 10-4

Circus Ponies NoteBook

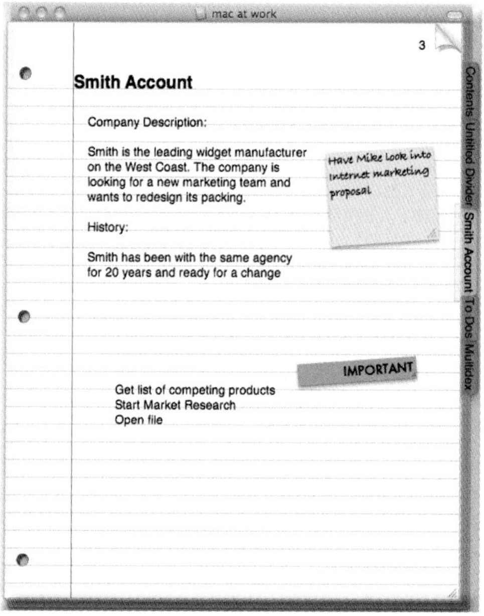

You can also customize the binding to make it look as modern (or as old-school) as you prefer. Once you set the look of your notebook, you can start adding data. To add text, click on the page and start typing. You can write the next great novel or a series of notes from customer telephone calls. Once you've entered your text, you can flag it with sticky notes or clip art.

NoteBook also supports to-do lists that you can append to a page. The NoteBook index, covered later, tracks unchecked items so you can find them quickly. (Although NoteBook is great for tracking tasks for a particular project, it doesn't provide the global task management tools found in the applications covered in Chapter 9.)

If you think visually, you can create diagrams. NoteBook includes an assortment of shapes and connectors that you can size and move around the page. As an example, you could create an organizational chart for your client to help remember who fits where in the organization, as shown in Figure 10-5. (Again, the diagramming tools in NoteBook are not as capable as those in a dedicated diagramming application such as OmniGraffle, covered in Chapter 13.)

NoteBook accepts just about any media you throw at it, including image files, video, and sound. It also imports and displays PDF files, giving you the ability to annotate them. These components can be mixed on a page, allowing you to customize the pages for your projects.

FIGURE 10-5

NoteBook diagramming tools

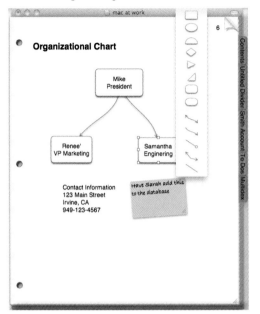

Normally, copying information to NoteBook involves selecting the text, e-mails, or Web pages in a separate application, opening NoteBook, finding the page where you want to save the information, and pasting it in. Using NoteBook's Clipping feature, you can bypass those steps. To enable Clippings in NoteBook, open your notebook to the page you want to receive clippings and choose Page ▶ Add a Clipping Service. After that, you can select text, e-mails, or Web pages in a separate application and invoke the Clipping Service, by Control+clicking or right-clicking the selected item, and sending the selection to the designated notebook page. This is all done in the background, saving you the trouble of jumping between applications. In addition to copying in the text, e-mail, or Web clipping, NoteBook adds additional information to the clippings, including the name of the application and (in the case of Web clippings) the Web URL the clipping came from.

Like OmniOutliner, NoteBook can record audio. You can later reference your voice-annotated NoteBook pages. You can also password-encrypt notebooks containing sensitive data.

NoteBook's Multidex search engine prepares a live index of everything in your notebook. The index pages are automatically added to the end of your notebook. To locate any information in your notebook, turn to the index pages and find it in the alphabetized list. Clicking on an entry takes you directly to that page.

You can export your notebook in PDF format. NoteBook also provides the option of exporting to a Web-ready HTML file. In addition to publishing your notebook on the Internet, you can install it on your iPad by choosing File ▶ Export as a Web Site ▶ To Disk. Create a folder on your Mac with the name of your notebook and save the HTML file to that folder. Then move the HTML folder to your iPad using the iPad applications Air Sharing HD (www.avatron.com/apps/air-sharing-hd) or GoodReader (www.goodiware.com). You can then view and navigate the hyperlinked HTML file on your iPad.

NoteBook is a great project management tool, giving you one place to keep every scrap of data concerning a project. Although there are better alternatives for many of its components, there are few applications with the same expansive feature set. Because NoteBook is so flexible, it is greater than the sum of its parts.

Evernote

Evernote (www.evernote.com), which has a free and a premium, $50-per-year option, is a virtual notebook application with a wrinkle: It stores all your data on Evernote's Internet-based servers. Evernote is ideal for Mac workers who use multiple computers or must switch between Windows and Mac OS X. The Evernote client application that runs on your Mac includes a text editor for taking notes. The completed text files are automatically indexed so you can later search for words contained in the file. You can add tags to the text files with keywords. You can also organize the text files by putting them in folders.

Because the Evernote application links to your Evernote cloud storage, your notes are automatically synced to the Evernote Internet servers and shared back to other computers and mobile devices with your Evernote account.

Using Evernote, you can take notes in a meeting using your Mac laptop and access those notes on your desktop Windows PC when you return to the office. You can limit access to the Evernote data to just yourself or you can share the login with co-workers, giving everyone access to the Evernote data and notes.

Evernote accepts more than just text. Using the Evernote Mac OS X client, shown in Figure 10-6, you can upload notes, documents, pictures, audio files, and other data to the Evernote servers. You can set Evernote to sync your records to its cloud servers automatically or manually. All the records you upload to Evernote (whether they be text files, pictures, or audio) can be tagged with keywords or stored in folders you create on your Evernote account.

As an example, let's say you are going to Chicago for a sales presentation. Using your Evernote account, you can upload PDF images of your plane tickets and hotel confirmation, a text file with your shuttle reservation number, your sales estimates and reports, selected Web pages from your potential customer's

FIGURE 10-6

Evernote's Mac OS X client

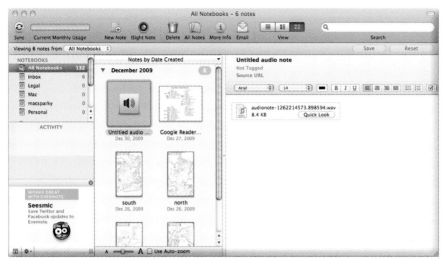

Web site, a text file with the contact information for everyone you will meet, the schedule for the Art Institute (just in case you have free time), and the text for a half-written letter to your sister. Because your data is then in the cloud and Evernote has applications for all the major desktop and mobile platforms (including Mac OS X, Windows, iPhone, iPad, BlackBerry, and Android), you can view, append, and modify your Evernote data from any device. Some companies run their entire business through the Evernote database. If you lose your Mac on the way, you can log in to your account from any Internet-connected computer and access the stored information.

The mobile applications, particularly the iPhone application, are engineered to quickly capture information. It is easy to dictate a voice note, snap a picture, or simply enter some text on the go and have it immediately synchronized to your Evernote database.

An added benefit of cloud-based data storage is that the Evernote servers can work on your data for you. With the free account, Evernote runs a text-recognition algorithm that extracts the text from uploaded pictures. With a paid account, it also does this for PDF files. So, if while in Chicago you find a particularly good oolong tea and have the foresight to take a picture of the label, you can sync it to Evernote, which searches and indexes the text from the picture. If, two months later, you want to see that label again, just type `oolong` in the search field and find the picture. This becomes very powerful if you have a paid account and keep your work-related PDFs in your Evernote database.

Many Evernote users make a practice of taking a picture of people's business cards and letting Evernote pull the text out so it may easily search for that information in the future. Another good use for this feature is to take pictures of the whiteboard at the end of your meetings. You can then go back and search for the text on the board.

There are some limits to cloud-based data. The first is a concern for security. Because your data is on Internet servers, anyone with your user name and password can access it. Also, although Evernote makes it easy to put data into your account, it is not as easy to pull data back out; it does not offer the drag-and-drop export functionality that you get with many native Mac OS X applications. But if you work on multiple platforms and don't mind keeping your data in the cloud, Evernote is a good tool for taking notes and tracking information.

MindNode Pro

A recent addition to the arsenal of digital note-taking is *mind-mapping*. As computers have advanced, people have moved beyond mere text input and now use graphical mind-mapping applications to take notes and develop ideas more visually. A mind map is a diagram arranged around a central idea. It allows you to visualize a project and the necessary branches or components that grow out of it. A mind map consists of a page (often called a *canvas*) upon which there are a series of connected ideas, called *nodes*. For example, in Figure 10-7, there is a node for Basic Business. That node has a parent node called Mac at Work. The line between Basic Business and Mac at Work is a connection. The Basic Business node has children nodes called Fundamentals, Backing Up, and Useful Utilities and sibling nodes called Advanced Business, Mac Basics, Communications and Connections, and Advanced Topics.

Because a mind map is in diagram format, it is easy to draw lines between connected ideas and find connections that you may not otherwise realize exist. Mind maps are useful both when working alone and when brainstorming in a meeting. There are several mind-mapping applications available for Mac OS X. One of the most useful apps is MindNode Pro ($25; www.mindnode.com), shown in Figure 10-7.

Using MindNode Pro requires no learning curve. To make a new node, you click the + (plus) iconic button on any existing note and drag. The application can also be operated with keyboard shortcuts for quicker entry. The Return key, for example, opens a new node. You can set a constrained width for the nodes and even combine multiple mind maps on one canvas. (The page or canvas automatically grows to fit your mind map.)

MindNode Pro allows you to create secondary connections, called *cross-connections*, between otherwise unrelated branches. You can expand and collapse

FIGURE 10-7

MindNode Pro

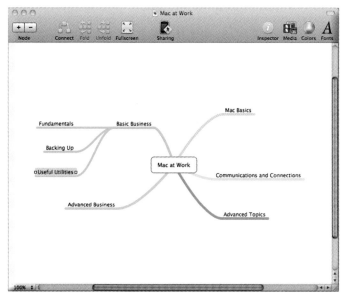

branches of your mind map. You can add images by dragging them on top of the node.

You can export MindNode files to several formats, including OPML (which works with the OmniOutliner application covered earlier in this chapter), FreeMind, RTF, HTML, and several image types, including PDF, PNG, and TIFF. There is an iPhone version that works on both the iPhone and iPad. MindNode Pro's simplicity and clean interface make it a great tool for creating mind maps in meetings or while planning strategy.

Notational Velocity

Notational Velocity (free; www.notational.net) is an interesting contrast to Evernote. Where you can put just about anything in an Evernote database, Notational Velocity just holds text. However, if you want a place to manage text, this application is pretty spectacular.

Notational Velocity has no interface to speak of, just a search bar and a list of text files, as shown in Figure 10-8. The search bar and new note creation are all tied to one line. Creating a new note does not require pressing any key combination or clicking a button; you just type the name of your new note and press Return.

If you start typing in the name field and already have a similarly titled note, just press Tab and then Return to start editing that note. No dialog boxes. No

Notational Velocity

mouse clicks. Just enter a few keystrokes and you are working. Notational Velocity also searches the text note contents.

The trick with Notational Velocity is to use smart naming conventions so you can quickly search your notes. For example, you could start all work related notes with the letters WK followed by the client name, followed by a date string and the event. As an example, for a note you took while talking to Mike on the Smith account on October 11, 2010, the name would be WK-Smith-2010-10-05 Phone call from Mike. Using this naming convention, you could type WK-Smith-2010 in the search bar and get all your notes on the Smith account from 2010. By putting a little thought into how you name your notes, you can get even faster access in a large Notational Velocity database. If you have trouble remembering how to name your Notational Velocity notes, create a note called Naming Conventions.

This application has one of the simplest user interfaces I have ever experienced. For example, there is no Save button; Notational Velocity saves everything as you type. The first time I used it I thought I was doing something wrong. Once you get the hang of it, you can fly through your notes. This application quickly moves from being a way to capture notes in a meeting or a phone call to becoming a text bank with snippets of reference information and frequently used text at your fingertips.

There aren't many additional features in Notational Velocity. You can choose to keep your database as one single file or a series of individual text files. You can also encrypt your data. If you use multiple Macs, you can relocate your

Notational Velocity data to a cloud-based storage location, such as Dropbox (covered in Chapter 21) and have your Notational Velocity data sync among every Mac you own.

If you use an iPhone or iPad, the free application SimpleNote (`www.simplenoteapp.com`) also synchronizes with the Notational Velocity database. Using SimpleNote, you can have all your Notational Velocity notes in your pocket ready to review or edit. SimpleNote has an optional $9-per-year paid service that allows you to access your SimpleNote database from the Web. This is useful for accessing your data from a Windows PC. Quite often, I start writing bits of text for correspondence, reports, and even pieces of this book, on SimpleNote on my iPad that gets finished in Notational Velocity on my Mac.

Notational Velocity is one of my favorite Mac applications and my Notational Velocity database is bursting with snippets of text, code, and random thoughts.

Livescribe Pulse Smartpen

The Livescribe Pulse Smartpen ($150 and up; `www.livescribe.com`) offers a different approach to taking notes. This device, shown in Figure 10-9, is a computer in a pen. It has an infrared camera and audio recorder built in. In a meeting, you just take out your Smartpen and take notes on its special microdot paper just as if you were using normal pen and paper. However, the Smartpen records every pen stroke; when you synchronize your Smartpen to your Mac, the Livescribe software re-creates the pen strokes on the screen. It looks as if you

FIGURE 10-9

Livescribe's Pulse Smartpen

scanned in your notes. You can then save your notes as a PDF file or e-mail them to a co-worker. Livescribe also has a Web service for sharing your notes over the Internet. If your business frowns upon bringing laptops into meetings, this pen is the perfect digital solution.

Even more useful, during a meeting you can — after getting permission of all the people in attendance, of course — record audio from the meeting with your Smartpen. Its computer synchronizes the recording with the pen strokes as you take notes. You can later go back and touch the Smartpen to any portion of your notes; the pen plays back the audio from the exact moment you wrote those pen strokes through its internal speaker. These audio files are also synchronized to your Mac, so you can play back the audio on your computer. The Smartpen's ability to synchronize audio with written notes has proven to be a real game-changer in my work.

Because the Smartpen is a computer, it also has several additional functions, including time-value-money calculations and a limited capability of translating written words. Livescribe has its own App Store where you can buy additional applications for your Smartpen such as optical character recognition for your hand-writing, conversion applications, or, for boring meetings, Hangman.

Word Processing

Word processing is probably the most common work task we all do on our computers. No matter what your business, at some point you will find yourself pushing the curser slowly across the screen. Not long after personal computers first landed on our desks, word processors gravitated toward a standard interface that hasn't changed much in the last 20 years — until recently.

Today, there are more software developers creating word processing applications than ever before, with some interesting new innovations. There is a rich field of word processors available on the Mac, with feature sets ranging from sparse to intricate. This chapter covers the word processing veterans (Microsoft Word and iWork Pages) and some of the newer, promising rookies that may change the way you write.

Microsoft Word

Microsoft Word is the *de facto* word processor of many workplaces. Microsoft was an early supporter of the Mac platform; the first version of Word for the Mac shipped in 1985, the year after the Mac was first released. Despite its long history on the Mac, there have been several issues with the last few releases of Word on the Mac. When Apple switched to Intel processors in 2006, Microsoft was one of the last major software companies to ship an Intel version of its application: Microsoft Office 2008 didn't ship until January 2009. In the interim, Word had to run on Intel Macs through the use of an interpreter, which made Word nearly unusably slow; there was a noticeable delay between the time you pressed a key and the letter appeared on the screen.

When Office 2008 was released, it felt rushed. The user interface was cluttered with buttons and switches, and support for Visual Basic, a macro language many Office power users rely on, had been removed because Microsoft said converting it to the Intel-based Mac OS X would take too long. Finally, with the recent release of Office 2011, Microsoft appears to have recovered from the Intel switch and once again has a useful version of Word on the Mac.

Word (www.microsoft.com/mac) is part of the $200 Microsoft Office Home & Business suite, which also includes Excel, PowerPoint, and Outlook. (The $120 Home & Student edition does not include Outlook.) Starting with Office 2011, Microsoft switched to a per-installation licensing system: Each copy can be installed on only one Mac. So if you own a laptop and desktop Mac, you'll need to purchase two copies. Fortunately, there are multiple-install discounts: You can get two install codes for the Home & Business edition for $280, and three install codes for the Home & Student edition for $150.

When you open Word 2011, you are given an opportunity to open a new document from one of the many included templates or a previously opened document, as shown in Figure 11-1. You can access and download additional templates directly from Microsoft in the same window. Your previously opened documents are indexed by the last day you worked on them; for example, you could choose from the seven documents you opened yesterday.

Word improves the user interface over prior versions, and it adopts the ribbon toolbar paradigm used in Microsoft Office for Windows, as shown in Figure 11-2. The Mac Word ribbon isn't identical to the Windows version, but it does use many of the same labels and tools to make cross-platform use easier.

Improvements to the interface with Microsoft Office 2011 are significant, and they go beyond the ribbon.

FIGURE 11-1

Opening Word 2011

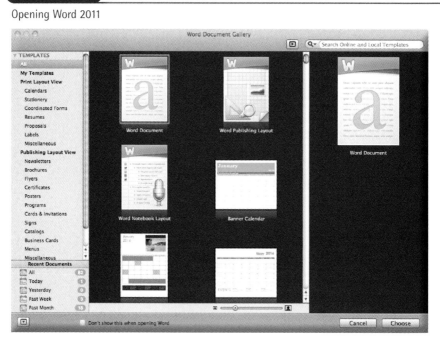

For example, Word's style tools simplify document formatting, and Word 2011 has improved styles. For 20 years, Word's styles have let you designate exactly how you want headings, paragraphs, footnotes, and other common document elements to look. By applying styles, you can automatically set that formatting. If, later, you decide to change some element of any particular style, it is automatically corrected throughout the document. For example, you may decide to increase the line spacing of your body text formatting from 14 to 18 points; adjusting the style applies this change throughout your document anywhere the body text style is applied. The problem with styles in Microsoft Word before version 2011 was that they were difficult to access and modify. That has now changed: The styles are listed in the Home ribbon bar, shown in Figure 11-2. Word even puts the most commonly used styles right in the ribbon bar so you can access them with one click.

In previous versions, changing formatting required navigation of complex inspector windows, but in Word 2011 you can now format your document much easier using the Layout ribbon. It has easily identifiable iconic buttons for orientation, size, page break, and margins. It also gives you a specific measurement for your top, bottom, left, and right margins. You can also create columns, watermarks, and borders using iconic buttons in the Layout ribbon.

FIGURE 11-2

Word 2011 and the ribbon toolbar

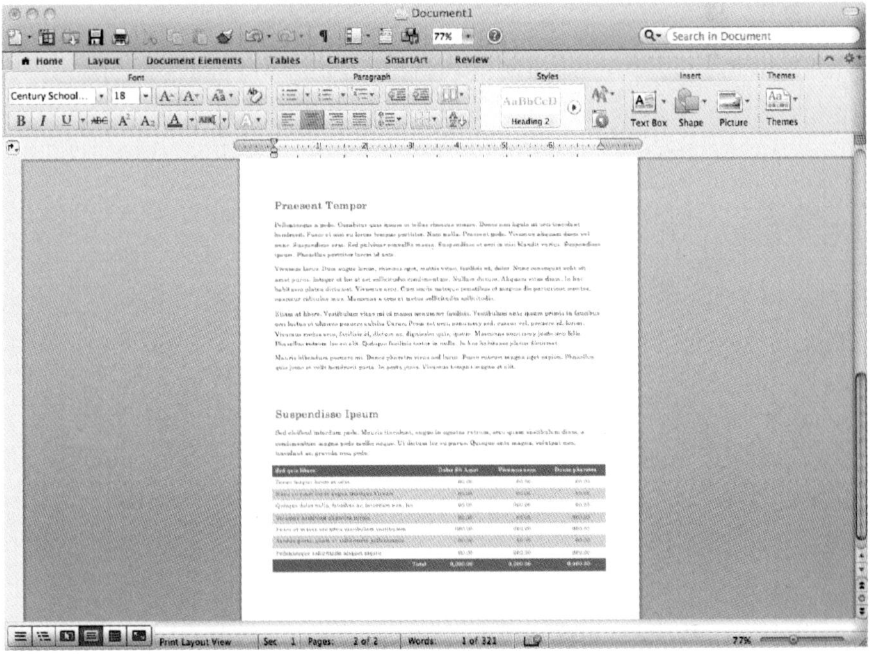

FIGURE 11-3

The Word 2011 review tools

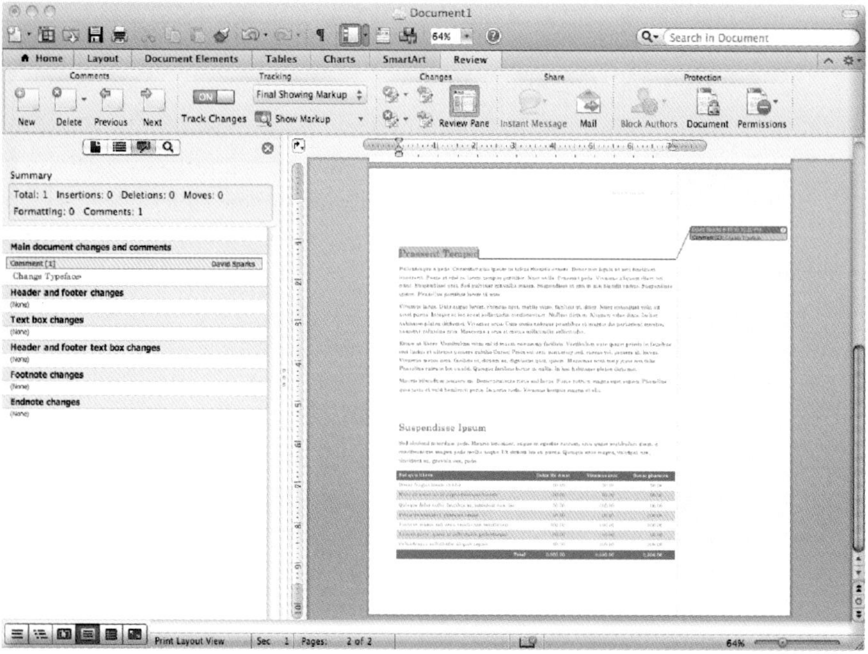

The Document Elements ribbon lets you customize the header and footer settings. The Document Elements ribbon also simplifies creation of tables of contents, bibliographies, text boxes, Word Art illustrations, and equations boxes. Although none of these tools is remarkable, all were tedious to use in prior versions of Word for Mac. By including them in the ribbons, Microsoft has made them more intuitive and easier for Windows switchers.

In addition to its ability to import Excel spreadsheets, Word has its own chart support, allowing you to input your own data for simple charts directly in the word processor. The Chart ribbon makes it easy to adjust colors and styles with predefined color schemes. The application previews the predefined formats in your document as you mouse over them so you can get a look at the final product before selecting a format.

Word 2011 also tweaks the user interface for tracking changes and review. Until Word 2011, tracking changes was clumsy in Mac Word. That is no longer the case: Using the Review ribbon, shown in Figure 11-3, you can add and delete comments, turn on change tracking (with an easily understood slider switch), set which changes to display, and accept or reject changes. You can manage all this from the Review ribbon without having to open and navigate inspectors or the menu bar as before.

Thankfully, Word 2011 supports Visual Basic. This scripting language lets you automatically format documents and share Word data with Excel, PowerPoint, and Outlook. If you are interested in automating your word processing using Word, Visual Basic (along with Word's additional support for AppleScript and Automator) is where you can go nuts.

Word 2011 supports the traditional .doc and controversial Office Open XML (.docx) formats. (Some people argue the Office Open XML standard is overly complicated and, ironically, not open.) Regardless, Mac workers need access to both formats, and Word provides it. Documents can be exported to several other text formats as well as to Microsoft's version of the Web's HTML format. But note that Microsoft's HTML export is considered very messy (it is legendary for adding excess HTML code) and thus difficult to use on Web sites. All the special code Microsoft adds to make the final result look just like what's on your Word screen is formatting you usually don't want to carry over to the Web, ironically.

With decades of development behind it, Word has the most features of any word processor on the Mac. No matter how obscure your feature request, Word is the most likely word processor to support it. If the feature isn't available, there is probably a way to add it using Visual Basic, AppleScript, or Automator.

This abundance of features comes at a cost. The user interface is crowded with controls. So many controls in fact that, despite the ribbon toolbars improvement, it can be baffling trying to find the two or three features you really need. Somewhere along the way in Word's development (I would argue the trouble started with version 6), it stopped being a word processor and became a processor-killing feature list. Microsoft has improved the performance but every new version of Word adds still more features that take up screen real estate and your Mac's resources.

Despite its improvements, Word still does not fully adopt Apple's programming frameworks. Word 2011 uses some of the Apple Cocoa programming frameworks (the ribbon bar, for example, is programmed with Cocoa, taking advantage of Mac OS X's built-in graphics acceleration), but it still has not fully adopted Mac OS X technologies. As a result, Office 2011 runs only in 32-bit mode and so cannot take advantage of Mac OS X's latest 64-bit technology, such as accessing significant amounts of memory. Although this probably won't be an issue for word processing documents, it can be a problem with larger Excel and PowerPoint files.

It has been some time since there has been a reliable version of Word on Mac OS X, so Word 2011 is a welcome upgrade. You can now certainly get your word processing done with Word for Mac 2011. But do you *have* to get your word processing done in Word? The time when Word was your only option is long gone. There are good reasons (price and feature glut, to name two) to avoid Word, and today there are several alternatives available.

Apple iWork Pages

Pages is the word processing component of the iWork Suite ($79; `www.apple.com/iwork`) that also includes Numbers and Keynote. Pages premiered in 2005 but the initial versions were much more about page layout than word processing. It wasn't until version 3 in 2007 that Pages came into its own as a word processor. Pages, shown in Figure 11-4, does not try to match Word in terms of features. Instead, Pages included the features Apple considered to be the most important and then polished the heck out of them.

In addition to its own format, Pages can open Microsoft Word, plain text (ASCII), RTF (Rich Text Format), and AppleWorks files. When Pages imports a different format, it creates a new instance of the document, leaving the original untouched in case anything goes wrong. When importing documents, Pages does a passable job of converting the formatting. Word styles are imported and converted to Pages styles, for example. For documents with complex formatting, Pages provides a notification of any conversion problems with the Document Warnings dialog box that explains what parts of the document Pages had trouble with.

FIGURE 11-4

iWork Pages

It's no surprise that Pages (developed by Apple) is the best word processor in terms of integrating with Mac OS X. If, for example, you open a letter template in Pages and then go to the Mac OS X Address Book and drag a person's contact on top of the letter template, Pages automatically fills in the letter with the relevant contact information. Likewise, Pages fills in your address and contact information on the letter using the contact information you used when you registered your Mac.

The Pages toolbar demonstrates the key difference between Pages and Word: There is no ribbon or crowded buttons. The Pages toolbar includes just the most commonly used tools — and no more. You can customize the toolbar: Choose View ◗ Customize Toolbar or Control+click or right-click the toolbar and choose Customize Toolbar from the contextual menu. When you choose to customize the toolbar, Pages provides the settings sheet shown in Figure 11-5 from which you can add or remove tools by clicking and dragging them onto or off of the toolbar — the same method Apple uses to customize the toolbars in Mac OS X and its other applications.

Below the toolbar is the format bar, which holds context-sensitive tools specific to whatever task you are working on. If you are working with text, you get text tools. If you are working on images, you see image tools. This is a clean alternative to other word processors' cluttered controls that quickly turn the user

FIGURE 11-5

Customizing the Pages toolbar

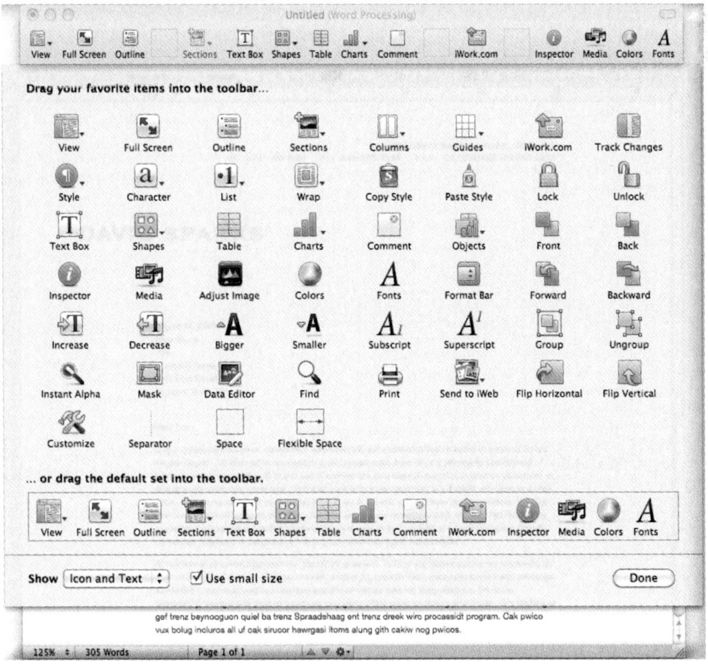

interface into something that more closely resembles a NASA control panel than a place to write.

Writing in Pages is friction-free. Pages is snappy and melts out of the way, letting you focus on the work of getting your words on the screen. Pages taps into the built-in Mac OS X dictionary and thesaurus tools. It also provides spell-check and proofreading support. The distraction-free writing mode (see the sidebar "Writing sans Distraction") in Pages is well-designed and especially useful for proofreading.

Pages includes several view modes. You can put two pages on the screen at once (called Two Up) or zoom the page width to match the screen. One of the most innovative views is the thumbnail view, which puts a thumbnail-size strip of images down the left side of the page showing all the pages in the document.

If you work with Microsoft Office users, you can track changes in Word documents. I've traded documents with tracked changes several times with Word users without them ever knowing I was working in Pages. The only exception I've encountered is documents with unusually complex formatting, such as legal pleadings. The tracked-changes view in Pages, shown in Figure 11-6, is also attractive.

FIGURE 11-6

Tracking changes in Pages

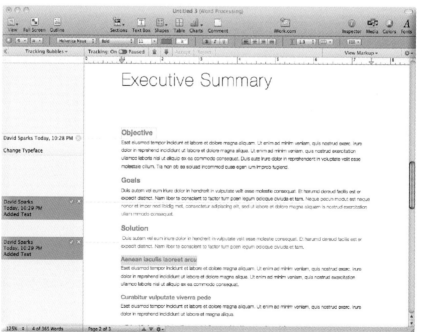

Pages' Save dialog box lets you save a copy of your document in Microsoft Word format. You can also export Pages documents to text, HTML, and RTF formats. The RTF standard is supposed to act as the *lingua franca* across word processors, allowing you to copy text with formatting from one word processor to another. Unfortunately, Pages does not support all the RTF formatting functions, so exporting a document to RTF from Pages does not always retain all the formatting you would expect. Specifically, Pages does not export style formatting: If you need to convert a Pages document to RTF with styles retained, you must first export it as a Word (.doc) file and then open it in Word, where you can export it as a proper RTF document.

One glaring omission in the entire iWork Suite is the lack of an automatic save feature, a standard feature on most word processors for the past 20 years. If you work on a document in Pages for 10 hours without saving and the power goes out, consider those 10 hours lost because you'll be starting from scratch. So,

WRITING SANS DISTRACTION

Something we've lost as writers with the advent of word processing is simplicity. Not so long ago, you sat down with a pen and a blank sheet of paper. Then you wrote. Writers didn't have the marvelous distractions we get these days with dinging e-mail reminders, chiming RSS feeds, and chirping Twitter updates to interrupt our writing with important information about our friends' tastes in fizzy cola.

When you consider all the diversions available on our Macs, it is remarkable anything gets written at all. Distractions have become such a problem that some Mac workers use applications like Freedom ($10; www. macfreedom.com) to disable their Internet connection when they need to grind that grindstone.

Word processors are starting to help. Microsoft Word has a full-screen mode that places your page on a black background. Likewise, Pages' Full-Screen View helps you avoid distractions and get back to work. Once activated, Pages turns your entire screen black except for the page you are working on. It is a great way to focus on your writing and avoid the distractions. And Scrivener's distraction-free mode lets you customize it to also display your research.

However, the champion of distraction-free writing on the Mac by far is WriteRoom ($25; www.hogbaysoftware.com/products/writeroom). This application displays green type on a flat black screen. If you are old enough to remember using an Apple II, WriteRoom will take you back. Although simple in execution, WriteRoom gets the details right. For example, rather than push your active text line to the bottom of the screen, WriteRoom keeps the line where you enter text in the center of the screen.

when you're writing with Pages, train yourself to save often. The universal keyboard shortcut to save in Mac OS X is ⌘+S, and it works in Pages, too.

Another save feature, accessed in Pages' General Preferences dialog box (press ⌘+, [comma] or choose Pages ▶ Preferences), allows you to back up previous versions of documents. This way, every time you save a file, the new version is saved in the same directory as the prior version. Doing so is a good idea: Disk space is much cheaper than your time.

There are also third-party applications that automatically save your documents for you. One of the best is ForeverSave ($15; www.tool-forcesw. com/foreversave), which can auto-save and back up files from most Mac OS X applications, including iWork.

One place that Pages clearly outshines Word is page layout. Pages makes it easy to create newsletters, flyers, and other graphics-intensive documents. Importing and placing graphics is as simple as dragging and dropping them. Pages does the rest. You can easily create your own layout using Pages or use one of its built-in templates (there are more than 160). The page layout tools go far beyond anything offered by Word 2011 — or any competing word processor, for that matter. Although the Pages layout tools don't rival a professional layout application, such as Adobe InDesign, they are sufficient for most users.

Although the usability disparity between Word and Pages is not nearly as large now as it was before Word 2011, I still find Pages to be the superior writing environment. But this is now legitimately a matter open to debate, and Mac workers more familiar with Microsoft Word will not go wrong electing to use Word on the Mac.

Scrivener

There has been a renaissance of sorts for word processing on the Mac. Not so long ago, everyone used Microsoft Word. It was, practically speaking, the only word processor on the Mac (and Windows too). That is no longer the case. Apple built many text-management tools into the Mac OS X development software. As a result, application developers can tap into the Apple code and design their own word processors more easily. With this lower barrier of entry, small developers are rethinking the word processor. This has resulted in some truly revolutionary writing software. One of the best in this class is Scrivener.

Scrivener ($40; www.literatureandlatte.com), shown in Figure 11-7, is a word processor with extensive research tools baked in. The developer created Scrivener to help him write his own novel, and the application has the kind of subtle touches you find when a developer creates software for his own use.

FIGURE 11-7

Scrivener

Scrivener is as much about planning and organizing your writing project as it is about getting your words on the screen. Using Scrivener, you can capture all your research in the same space you use for writing. Although developed as a novel-writing tool, it works equally well for other kinds of serious writing. I use it to write legal briefs, research projects, and this book.

Quite often, your writing project includes source materials. These can be bits of text, Web pages, videos, pictures, and any other digital scrap of information. Traditionally, these reference materials are kept in a folder or some other application on your Mac. But Scrivener holds them for you and makes them accessible next to your writing space. Scrivener takes just about anything you throw at it and organizes it in a research tab.

Scrivener holds research in a series of nested icons on the left side of the screen. Adding research just requires you to drag and drop it there. For text, you can open a research tab and start typing. You can then arrange Scrivener to display your research next to your typing window. With everything nicely organized, Scrivener is an efficient way to make progress on writing projects.

You may remember the day when you pinned index cards to a piece of corkboard to organize large writing projects. It was a great way to summarize important points and work out the flow. Following this paradigm, Scrivener has a virtual corkboard, shown in Figure 11-8, and an endless supply of virtual note cards. All your research notes and related documents are given their own index cards, which you can then shuffle and sort on the virtual corkboard. Scrivener keeps an eye on how you move the cards around and sorts the underlying

FIGURE 11-8

The Scrivener corkboard

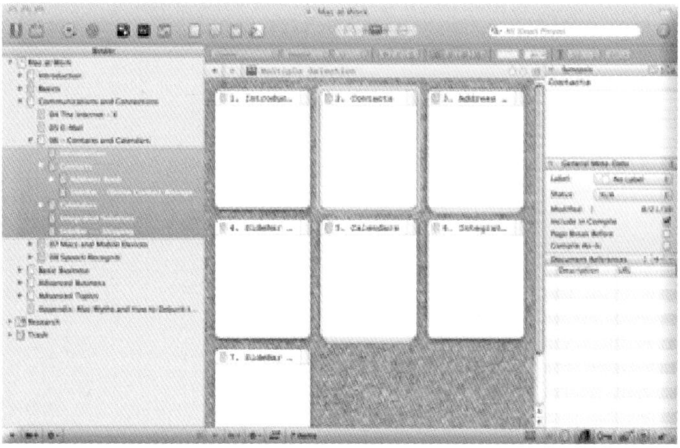

FIGURE 11-9

Scrivener's full-screen mode

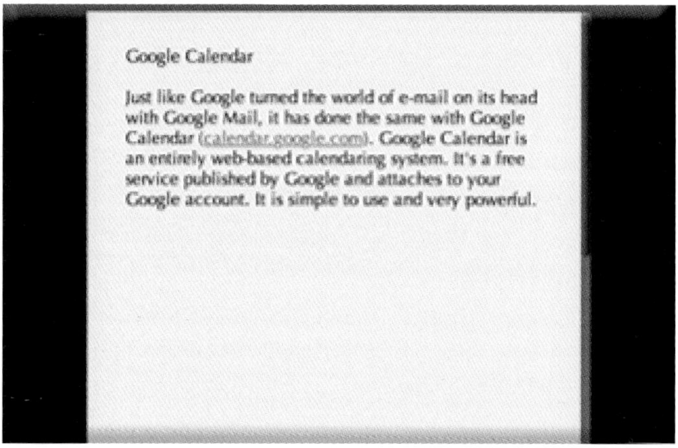

documents accordingly. It also lets you to tie keywords to your note cards to make organization and retrieval easier in large projects.

If you need to reduce your note cards to an outline, Scrivener can handle that as well. Although Scrivener is not as powerful an outliner as OmniOutliner (covered in Chapter 10), it is enough for most writing projects and has the added bonus of being attached to your research and drafts. Because Scrivener can import files in the OPML format, you can use OmniOutliner with Scrivener. I often start a large project as an OmniOutliner document and then export it to OPML format. Then I import the OPML outline into Scrivener, which converts the outline to an organized writing project. Scrivener also syncs with SimpleNote, a Web-syncing text service covered in Chapter 10, so you can work on bits and pieces of your Scrivener project using your iPhone and iPad.

Scrivener understands that sometimes editing can go a bit astray, so it has a "snapshot" feature that allows you to capture versions of a document during the editing process. You can then go back and retrieve that discarded treasure when you come to your senses. It is a bit like Time Machine for words.

Scrivener makes the process of writing as simple and distraction-free as possible. It has a very clean full-screen mode, shown in Figure 11-9, that clears all the usual diversions off your screen and provides easy access to your research.

Part of Scrivener's charm is how it breaks the old paradigm of what a word processor does. Although you can mark text as bold, underline, and italic, Scrivener has no page-formatting support. Instead, you get your text and research displayed in a way conducive to making the words better. Using a construction

CLEANING DIRTY TEXT

No matter which word processor you use, you will occasionally bump into text that has an overabundance of carriage returns or apostrophes turned into dollar signs. You then end up spending valuable time moving your cursor around the screen and fixing the offending text. The good news is there is an app for that.

TextSoap ($40; www.unmarked.com) cleans your dirty text. TextSoap is loaded with tools that address all the common text problems that anyone who writes on a regular basis has come to dread. It includes more than 100 built-in cleaners and allows you to make your own custom cleaners.

TextSoap's Scrub filter, shown in the figure below, handles the most common cleaning tasks, like removing extra spaces, fixing broken paragraphs, and removing those e-mail forwarding marks (>) that look like they want to stab every line of text. Using TextSoap, you can eliminate the tedious act of manually cleaning text and get back to work.

analogy, Scrivener lets you set the foundation and erect the walls but painting is done elsewhere. The application lets you focus on the words and leaves the formatting for later.

Once you are done writing, you can print your document or export it to one of several formats, including Microsoft Word, plain text, and HTML. Scrivener supports *multimarkdown* (a writing syntax that lets you embed codes for footnotes, emphasis, and other text effects in plain text documents), which lets you easily publish to multimarkdown-supported Web services. Although I write most of my large projects in Scrivener, I ultimately export the document to Pages or Word for the final formatting. Scrivener is substance over style, and a gem for all Mac writers.

Web-Based Word Processing

Word processing is no longer just in the domain of local applications. There are several Internet-based tools available now. One of the best is Notational Velocity when combined with SimpleNote (both covered in Chapter 10). There are also Web-based, full-featured word processors being developed to run from your browser. The two biggest are the Microsoft Office Web Apps version of Word and Google Docs.

FIGURE 11-10

Microsoft Office Web Apps' version of Word

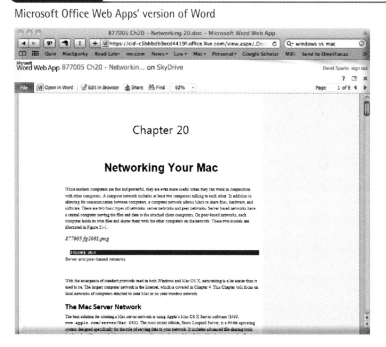

Microsoft Office Web Apps, shown in Figure 11-10, is a Web-based version of Microsoft Office. To use it on an office network, you need Microsoft SharePoint (a set of network sharing tools) installed on your server and a license for the Microsoft Home & Business edition. Consumers can use the Microsoft Web Apps for free using a Microsoft SkyDrive account (`www.windowslive.com/online/ skydrive`). This new iteration of Microsoft Office was first released in 2010 as a competitor to Google Docs. Microsoft Office Web Apps is the best online tool for uploading and modifying intricate Word, Excel, and PowerPoint documents. Although not a replacement for Microsoft Office on your Mac, Microsoft Office Web Apps does a creditable job viewing and editing Office documents with complex formatting. Although it doesn't have most of the features available in Word for Mac 2011, in a pinch Office Web Apps will do.

Google Docs, shown in Figure 11-11, is several years old and more mature in some respects than Microsoft Office Web Apps. Although not as seamless with Word formatting as Office Web Apps, Google Docs shines at collaboration. Google Docs lets multiple users edit the same document at once and is rock-solid at keeping the document in one piece. (Many text editors, including Pages, go into fits if multiple people edit a document at once.) Collaboration is the best use of Google Docs: It is a great way for colleagues to work on the same document from multiple locations. Once the collaboration is completed, the text can be moved to Word or Pages for final formatting and editing. Microsoft announced

FIGURE 11-11

Google Docs

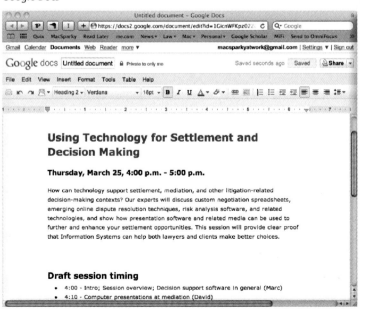

its intention to add multiuser file access and collaboration to Office for Mac 2011 and the Microsoft Office Web Apps but it was not available as this book went to press.

Google Docs takes advantage of Google's other products. It has great search tools, for example. Google Docs also feels more responsive when typing compared to Office Web Apps; you don't think about the fact you are typing onto the Web with Google Docs whereas Microsoft Office Web Apps' Word has just enough of a delay to remind you it is a browser and not a local application when you are typing.

It is not surprising that while this new class of word processors is still in its infancy. Microsoft is marching toward lots of features and Google is marching toward simplicity. The user interfaces of both Office Web Apps and Google Docs are unmistakably Web-based. Neither one is very pretty, but the color coding and organization of Google Docs is more utilitarian and easier to understand.

Although the idea of cloud-based, available-everywhere word processing has a certain appeal, I still prefer a locally installed word processor. I've tried to work exclusively in both Google Docs and Microsoft Office Web Apps and in both instances happily came back to Scrivener, Notational Velocity, and Pages. Still, like other Web services, I suspect cloud-based word processing will become more appealing as the technology improves, and we may one day look back on the locally installed word processor and data files with the same nostalgia we now have for floppy disks.

Ernest Hemingway wrote amazing fiction on a napkin, while I often write complete drivel on my expensive Mac. No matter what software you use to write, at the end of the day it is your words, and not some arbitrary feature set, that determines the quality of the final product. Find the word processor that suits your needs and start writing.

Managing PDF Files

Adobe's Portable Document Format (PDF) is the *lingua franca* of the Internet for document-sharing. Because PDF-formatted documents embed the layout and fonts of the original document, they can be shared with others who don't have the same application, or even the same operating system. Spreadsheets, timelines, contracts, and sales proposals often end up in PDF format before being released to the world. Mac OS X includes built-in PDF support. There are also several useful third-party PDF applications.

Creating PDFs

In Mac OS X, you can create a PDF document from any application that can print. The standard Mac OS X Print dialog box has a pop-up menu in the lower-left corner labeled PDF. Figure 12-1 shows a Print dialog box with the PDF pop-up menu open.

This menu provides several PDF options:

- **Open PDF in Preview:** This option creates a PDF file in Preview, the basic PDF management and annotation tool that comes with Mac OS X. (Preview is covered in detail later.)
- **Save as PDF:** The Save as PDF option enables you to create PDF documents from any file you could otherwise print, including spreadsheets, Keynote presentations, and diagrams. The PDF files can then be sent to your Windows co-workers without any further processing.
- **Save as PostScript:** This setting saves your document to a PostScript file. The Postscript file format contains codes and instructions for a PostScript interpreter, used by some printers.
- **Fax PDF:** If you have a facsimile (fax) modem attached to your Mac, you can encode your document to PDF and send the facsimile in one step.
- **Mail PDF:** The Mail PDF option lets you to share PDF files in one step: A new mail message is created in your default e-mail application and the freshly minted PDF is attached.
- **Save as PDF-X:** PDF-X is a customized PDF format used in the printing industry.

FIGURE 12-1

The Mac OS X Print dialog box PDF creation options

- ▌ **Save to application:** Depending on the applications you install, you will find additional options to save PDF files directly to installed applications. Independent developers can also add entries to this menu.
- ▌ **Save to custom location:** You can add your own destinations for PDF files by choosing the Edit With menu option and pressing the + (plus) iconic button, to select a folder. That folder then becomes a new entry with the selected folder as a PDF target. This feature is useful for making custom PDF file locations for clients, expenses, and other categories.
- ▌ **Security settings:** The PDF Save dialog box also include the Security Settings button that leads to a second dialog box, shown in Figure 12-2, where you set access and passwords for your PDF files. The security settings allow you to set passwords for opening, copying text from, and printing your newly created PDF document.

PDF Applications

In addition to creating PDF files, there are several applications that allow you to edit and modify PDF files, starting with Mac OS X's Preview.

Preview

Mac OS X ships with the Preview application that, among other things, you can use to edit PDF files. In Mac OS X 10.5 Leopard and 10.6 Snow Leopard, Apple has added several PDF management tools to Preview that were previously

FIGURE 12-2

Security options when creating a PDF file in the Mac OS X Print dialog box

only available by purchasing additional software. For basic PDF document editing and management, Preview may be all you need.

Because PDF documents are more like printed documents then application files, you need tools to mark them up electronically in a fashion similar to using your highlighter and red pen for printed documents. In Mac OS X 10.5 Leopard, Apple added annotation tools to Preview for this purpose.

Preview has tools for highlighting and annotating PDF files, as shown in Figure 12-3. For deleting text, there is the Strike Through Text tool. You can draw attention to specific sections of a PDF document with the Oval and Rectangle tools. All the Preview PDF annotations save to the PDF file and are viewable in other PDF applications on Windows and Mac OS X, including Adobe Acrobat.

To add text annotation to your PDF document, choose Tools ▶ Annotate ▶ Add Note. Then click the location in your PDF document where you want the note to appear, and Preview will insert a small yellow icon. You can move the icon to any location in your document. When you click the icon, a yellow text box opens and you can add notes. Unlike the more advanced PDF applications PDFpen and Adobe Acrobat Pro, you cannot hide Preview comments when printing or sharing.

To apply other text revisions, choose Tools ▶ Annotate. You can pick among several markup tools — including Highlight Text, Strike Through Text, and Underline Text — and go to town. For the text-markup tools to work, however, Preview must recognize there is text in the PDF file. It doesn't always do so: Some scanned documents do not have embedded text, so the annotation tools are unavailable. PDFpen and Acrobat Pro, covered later, can fix this problem.

Preview's Link tool lets you include links to a different page in the same PDF file or to an external Web site. To do this, choose Tools ▶ Annotate ▶ Add Link. Then use the mouse to click and drag a link box over the relevant portion of your PDF document. Once you have created the link box, Preview prompts you to either create a link within the PDF document or to an external Web page. The link is not active, however, until you save, close, and reopen the file.

FIGURE 12-3

Preview's PDF annotation tools at work

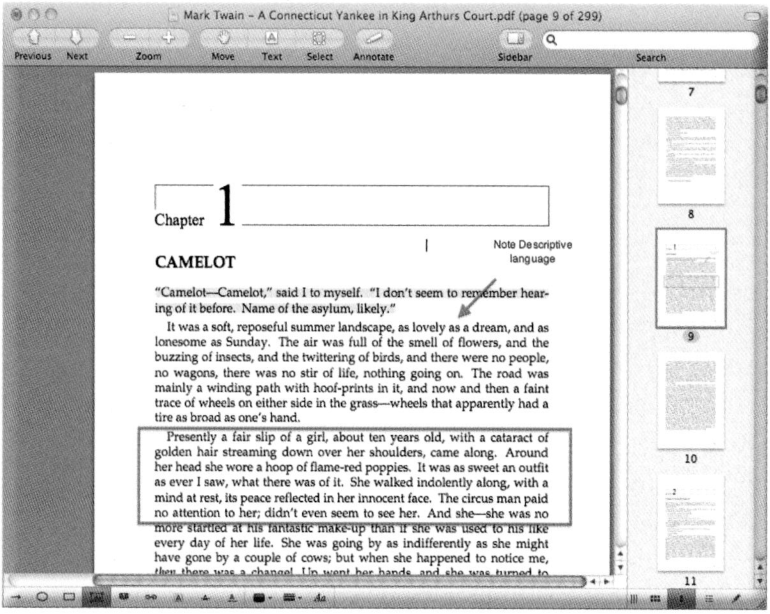

Quite often, multipage PDF documents may be out of order or contain extra, unwanted pages. Using the Preview sidebar, shown in Figure 12-3 and accessed by clicking the Sidebar button in the Preview toolbar or pressing Shift+⌘+D, you can view all the pages of a PDF document. Working in the Preview sidebar, you can click and drag to rearrange pages or delete pages by selecting them with the mouse and pressing the Delete key.

You can combine two PDF documents in Preview by dragging pages to and from the sidebars. You can also merge an entire PDF file by dragging the PDF file icon into the Preview sidebar of another PDF file. After you merge, you can then rearrange or delete pages further from the Preview sidebar. Once saved, all the pages will be combined into a single PDF file.

Preview makes it easy to export pages from a PDF file. If you have a large PDF file and need to send a few pages to a colleague, select the pages in the sidebar and then drag them onto the desktop. Preview makes a copy of the pages as a separate PDF file. When selecting pages in the sidebar, Shift+clicking selects consecutive pages, whereas ⌘+clicking selects pages out of sequence.

Considering that Preview comes free on every new Mac, it has a surprising number of PDF management and annotation features. However, Preview is still missing several tools useful for working with PDF files. If Preview isn't enough for you, consider using one of the dedicated PDF applications.

PDFpen

Smile Software's PDFpen ($50; www.smilesoftware.com), shown in Figure 12-4, includes all the tools found in Preview and adds more PDF management and editing features.

PDFpen has several text-annotation tools, including ones to highlight (in multiple colors), strike-through, underline, and squiggle-underline. To apply annotations, first select the text, then apply the desired effect from the toolbar. PDFpen has a redaction tool that can block out or blur those portions of your PDF documents you want to keep private.

PDFpen gives you the ability to select text embedded in a PDF document and change it using the Correct Text tool, activated by Control+clicking or right-clicking the highlighted text. Once you complete correcting the text, you can save the file and the corrected text is embedded in the PDF document. Although the Correct Text tool works great for correcting a few words or typos, if you intend to make significant changes to an article, I recommend going back to the original document, making the changes, and then resaving the PDF file.

Scanning software often saves scanned documents as an image without recognizing the text; as a result, you cannot edit or annotate the text in the PDF document. If your PDF document is just an image without embedded

FIGURE 12-4

Smile Software's PDFpen

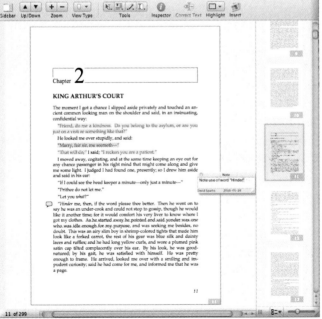

FIGURE 12-5

Electronic signatures in PDFpen

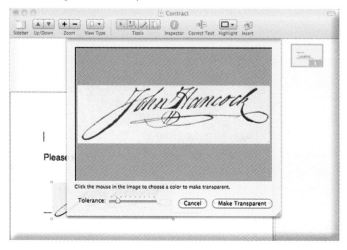

text, PDFpen can perform optical character recognition (OCR) on the scanned image to reconstruct the text and add it to the PDF document file so you can later annotate, edit, and search it. The PDFpen OCR engine does a good job of recognizing printed text, but it cannot recognize handwriting.

If you receive electronic documents requiring your signature, PDFpen has tools for digitally signing the document on screen with a mouse, pen tablet, or a saved digital version of your signature. You can use a scanned version of your signature and PDFpen can make the image transparent, as shown in Figure 12-5. First, choose Edit ▶ Make Transparent Image; then you can move the signature image in your document and proportionally resize it by holding down the Shift key and moving the resizing handles.

PDFpen features more annotation shapes than Preview, including polygons, rounded-corner boxes, and a free-form scribble in addition to rectangles and ovals. You can further customize the shapes fills, line color and thickness, and opacity settings. Except for the Rectangle and Oval annotation tools, Preview does not allow you to insert graphics and images in your PDF documents. PDFpen does. In addition to adding and manipulating graphics, PDFpen allows you to move, resize, copy, and delete images in the original PDF file. This is convenient for business use. For example, I use PDFpen to insert an image as a semitransparent watermark on important documents.

PDFpen works with interactive PDF forms. When you click in a field, a blue border appears, and you can type in the form. For noninteractive forms (forms with spaces but no built-in fields), choose Tools ▶ Text Tool (similar to Adobe Acrobat's Typewriter tool) to create a field and type in the blank space. If your

PDFpen's Library Panel

form requires several entries, double-clicking the Text tool in the toolbar keeps it active so you can quickly move through the PDF document.

The PDFpen Library Panel allows you to collect commonly used graphics such as watermarks, diagrams, and company logos for repeated use. (Choose Window ▶ Library to open it.) Assuming you are comfortable with the security risks, you can save your signature to your image library. The Library panel also includes proofreading marks, shown in Figure 12-6, with more than 100 standard editing marks, for use in your PDF document.

Finally, PDFpen includes automation support, allowing you to customize repeated PDF management tasks using AppleScript, which is covered in Chapter 24.

PDFpenPro

PDFpenPro, ($100; www.smilesoftware.com) includes all the PDFpen features plus the ability to add tables of contents and create fillable forms.

The Table of Contents feature, shown in Figure 12-7, is PDFpenPro's version of bookmarks in Adobe Acrobat Pro. It allows you to set jump points in long PDF documents, making them easier to navigate. The table-of-contents entries can be nested, so you can, for example, have one group of content entries called Contract and another group of content entries in a group called Attachments. If you are sharing PDF documents with Adobe Acrobat Pro (Windows or Mac OS X versions), everything works: PDFpenPro reads Acrobat Pro bookmark entries as table-of-contents entries and Acrobat Pro reads the PDFpenPro entries as bookmarks.

Using PDFpenPro you can also build cross-platform PDF forms. You can add text fields, check boxes, and buttons and save the PDF document as a fillable form usable on both Mac OS X and Windows. To prepare a fillable PDF form in PDFpenPro, use the Text Field pop-up menu in the toolbar to insert a text field, check box, or radio button. If you are adding a text field, click and drag the tool over the blank area of your PDF document. Check boxes and radio buttons can likewise be dropped on your document and sized and labeled appropriately. You can set default values for your fields where appropriate and limit the number of characters in text boxes.

FIGURE 12-7

PDFpenPro's Table of Contents view

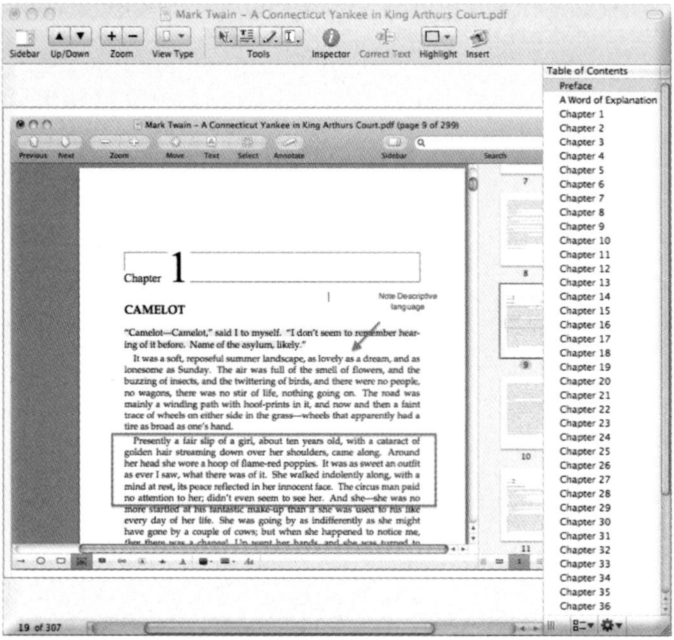

Adobe Acrobat Pro

Adobe Acrobat Pro ($449; www.adobe.com/products/acrobatpro), shown in Figure 12-8, is the most feature-rich PDF editor on the Mac. (Adobe does not sell its $299 Acrobat Standard application for Mac OS X.) Adobe is the originator of the PDF format and, as a result, Acrobat has a lot of features for managing and altering PDF files.

In addition to reading PDF files, Acrobat Pro accepts Web pages and image files. Like PDFpen, Acrobat Pro can perform optical character recognition. Adobe didn't stop there, however: Acrobat Pro also allows you to insert 3D animations and video in your PDF documents.

Acrobat Pro has a rich tool set for PDF markup. You can highlight, underline, and cross out text. You can also insert many graphic forms, including callouts, text boxes, arrows, rectangles, ovals, lines, polygons, and a useful cloud tool. You can even attach files and audio notes as comments.

Acrobat Pro also features advanced security tools. You can encrypt your PDF files with 256-bit encryption. As with PDFpen, if your PDF file contains confidential information, you can use Acrobat Pro's Redaction tools to strike out portions and permanently delete information, including text and images, from the PDF file. Adobe Acrobat Pro also allows you to use a digital ID to verify your documents came from a trusted source.

FIGURE 12-8

Adobe's Acrobat Pro

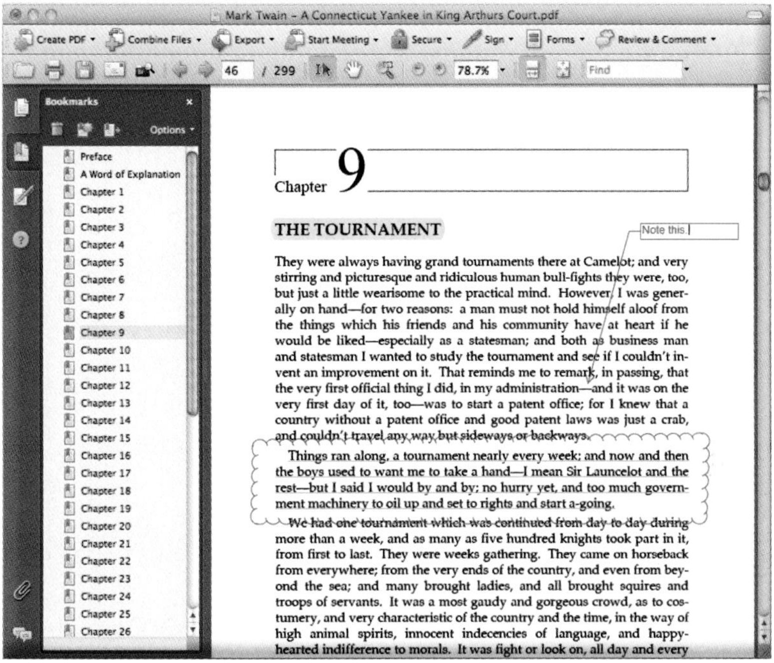

Another Acrobat Pro feature is the ability to create PDF portfolios that combine multiple documents in a single PDF package. You can customize your PDF portfolio with headers, footers, and watermarks. A portfolio is not limited to just PDF files. It can also hold Microsoft Office documents and image files. The documents are kept in their native format, so you can open them in the appropriate applications. Although you could largely duplicate this feature by creating a Zip archive, a capability built into Mac OS X, PDF portfolios are more presentation-friendly: You can open a portfolio as part of a presentation and jump between the portfolio documents.

The collaboration tools in Acrobat Pro are impressive. Comments for individual team members are all tracked. Users can also comment on a PDF document using Adobe's free Reader application, covered later. Because Acrobat Pro allows you to embed video in PDF files, the markup and annotation tools additionally provide frame-specific feedback.

The Acrobat Pro PDF form tools go beyond anything else available on Mac OS X. In addition to the ability to create fillable forms, Acrobat Pro can assist with form distribution and collection. Once you distribute an Acrobat Pro created form, Acrobat Pro can track which users have submitted completed forms and send reminders to users who still have incomplete forms.

TABLE 12-1

Feature	Preview	PDFpen	PDFpen Pro	Adobe Acrobat Pro	Adobe Reader
Price	free	$50	$100	$449	free
Insert text	✔	✔	✔	✔	–
Modify existing text	–	✔	✔	✔	–
Add notes	✔	✔	✔	✔	–
Add comments	–	✔	✔	✔	✔
Selectively print comments	–	✔	✔	✔	✔
Comment tracking and history	–	–	–	✔	–
Add highlights, underscore, and strikethrough	✔	✔	✔	✔	–
Add hyperlinks	✔	✔	✔	✔	–
View bookmarks/tables of contents	✔	✔	✔	✔	✔
Create bookmarks/tables of contents	–		✔	✔	–
Optical character recognition (OCR)	–	✔	✔	✔	–
Add ovals and rectangles	✔	✔	✔	✔	–
Add additional geometric shapes	–	✔	✔	✔	–
Adjust images in original PDF	–	✔	✔	–	–
Add images to PDF	–	✔	✔	✔	–
Built-in image library	–	✔	✔	–	–
Add video and audio to PDF	–	–	–	✔	–
Import Microsoft Word files	–	✔	✔	✔	–
Import Microsoft Excel and PowerPoint files	–	–	–	✔	–
Import HTML	–	–	–	✔	–
Insert, remove, and reorder pages	✔	✔	✔	✔	–
Fill out PDF forms	✔	✔	✔	✔	✔
Create fillable PDF forms	–	–	✔	✔	–
Distribute PDF form	–	–	–	✔	–
Track PDF form responses	–	–	–	✔	–
PDF digital identification	–	–	–	✔	–

CONVERTING PDF DOCUMENTS

Although there are several tools to convert your documents to PDF format, what about the other way around? The PDF format has become so universal that sometimes you receive PDF documents that you want to open in a word processor or spreadsheet application.

PDF2Office ($129; www.recosoft.com) converts PDF files to Microsoft Office format. For Word, the conversion doesn't just extract the text file, it tries to re-create the PDF formatting as Word formatting — and it does a credible (but rarely perfect) job of it: It creates frames, headers, footers, footnotes, and columns. PDF2Office also converts PDF documents to Excel, PowerPoint, Rich Text Format (RTF), and the Web HTML formats.

Recosoft also publishes the $59 PDF2Office for iWork, which converts PDF documents to Apple's Pages and Keynote formats. The PDF file's formatting is replicated in the converted paragraphs and graphic elements in iWork.

In addition to Acrobat Pro, Adobe publishes Reader. This free application allows users to view and fill in PDF forms. Because every new Mac ships with Preview already installed, Reader is largely unnecessary in Mac OS X. Preview is faster, is more stable, and includes more features than Adobe Reader. Also, several security flaws have been discovered in Reader. The only reason to install Reader is if you work on a team that uses the collaborative features of Acrobat Pro. (Acrobat Pro can track comments made in Reader.)

Which PDF Document Application?

With varying prices and features, summarized in Table 12-1, deciding which PDF document application to use can quickly become overwhelming.

If you are not sure what is best for you, start with Preview. It is free and already on your Mac. If you need more PDF tools, move up to PDFpen. At $50, this application has many features comparable to Adobe Acrobat Pro at a fraction of the price. If you know you need form creation or the table of contents features, try PDFpenPro; it is still significantly less expensive than Adobe Acrobat Pro. (PDFpen and PDFpenPro both offer a free 30-day trial.) If you still need more features, get Adobe Acrobat Pro. But note that the extensive features available in Acrobat Pro come at a cost, and not just price: Acrobat is slow to load and generally more sluggish than Preview and PDFpen.

Graphics for Business

No matter what your business, at some point you are likely to show a product, concept, or idea visually. This used to be possible only by hiring an artist or graphics designer. Graphics are not nearly so hard as they used to be. From its very inception, graphics designers embraced the Mac. As Macs have become more powerful and software more sophisticated, all Mac workers now have the ability to create compelling diagrams and graphics with very little time and effort. This chapter presents easy-to-use applications for business graphics. Although Adobe Photoshop and Illustrator are impressive, their expense and complexity don't lend them to business graphics and so I do not cover them in this chapter.

OmniGraffle

 OmniGraffle ($100; www.omnigroup.com/products/omnigraffle) is the premier diagramming tool on the Mac. As shown in Figure 13-1, when you first open OmniGraffle, it gives you a choice of 16 template forms. The templates include organizational charts, hierarchical structures, and mind-mapping. You can also create custom templates.

Once you start a new project, OmniGraffle opens the main window, shown in Figure 13-2. The toolbar includes the most frequently used tools. With OmniGraffle, you can create multipage diagrams. Each page is called a *canvas*. You can display or hide the canvases using the Canvases iconic button in the toolbar.

The drawing tools

The toolbar also has several basic drawing tools, including the Selection tool, Shape tool, Line tool, and Text tool. Each tool has a small triangle icon in the lower-right corner; clicking the triangle displays additional options for each tool.

Clicking on the tool divider (to the immediate right of the Text tool in Figure 13-2) opens the remaining drawing tools in the toolbar. The expanded toolbar is shown in Figure 13-2. (You can also customize which tools appear in the toolbar in the Drawing Tools pane in the Preferences dialog box.)

FIGURE 13-1

Opening a new document in OmniGraffle

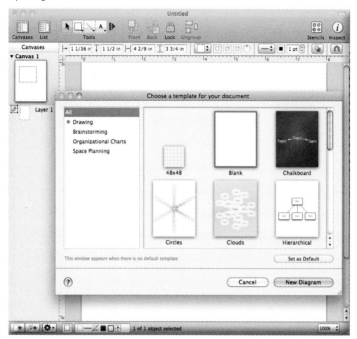

FIGURE 13-2

The OmniGraffle Main Window

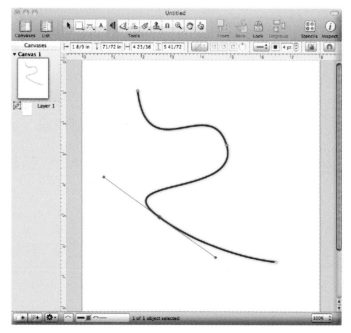

The Selection tool

This tool looks like the standard Mac OS X mouse pointer. Using this tool, you can select and move objects around the screen. You can also select multiple objects (by clicking the objects while holding the Shift key or clicking and dragging a selection box around the desired objects) and move them as a group.

If your object is resizable, it will sprout eight selection handles when you click on it with the Selection tool. You can then resize the object by grabbing a handle and dragging it with the mouse or trackpad. If you Shift+drag the handle, the object is resized proportionally. If you ⌘+drag a handle, you can rotate an object.

When resizing or moving objects, you can take advantage of OmniGraffle's smart guides. To activate smart guides in OmniGraffle, choose Arrange ▶ Guides ▶ Smart Alignment Guides and then choose Arrange ▶ Guides ▶ Smart Distance Guides. Smart guides automatically generate measurement guides that show the spacing and sizing of objects as you move objects around your OmniGraffle canvas, similar to the guides in Keynote (covered in Chapter 14).

The Shape tool

You create shapes with the Shape tool. To do so, pick a shape, then click and drag on the canvas. There are several shapes available. More can be added using the Stencil tool, covered later in this chapter.

By default, if you choose the Shape tool, it remains selected so you can draw multiple objects. If you just want to draw one shape, click the Shape tool; a small blue circle with the numeral 1 appears, which indicates the Shape tool will work only once and then OmniGraffle will revert to the Selection tool.

The Line tool

There are several styles of lines you can draw with the Line tool, including straight, curved, orthogonal (perpendicular), and Bézier (highly customizable curves). A Bézier curve is shown in Figure 13-2.

When drawing a line in OmniGraffle, you can constrain the line to 45-degree increments by holding down the Shift key. (When the line is at the length and at the location you want, release the mouse button and then the Shift key.) You can also add labels to lines by creating a text item (with the Text tool explained on the next page) and dragging it onto the line until the line becomes highlighted.

If you want to connect two shapes with a line, select the Line tool and then, rather than drawing a line, click the two shapes you want to connect; OmniGraffle creates a line between the two shapes. Afterward, when you move the shape with the Selection tool, the line follows.

The Text tool

Clicking the Text tool turns the pointer into a cursor-insertion point. You can click anywhere on your canvas and start typing text. That is not the only way to add text in OmniGraffle: You can also add text to a shape by double-clicking inside it. You can make adjustments to the text using the Text inspector (covered later). Interestingly, OmniGraffle adds all text inside your canvas to the file's Spotlight index, so you can then search your OmniGraffle documents using Spotlight (covered in Chapter 1).

The Pen tool

You use the Pen tool to create custom shapes in OmniGraffle. To create a custom shape, click anywhere on the canvas. Then continue clicking to add points to your shape. When you double-click (or press Return), the shape is completed. You can drag and adjust your shape points or use the Bézier handles to customize the shape.

The Diagramming tool

This tool is helpful when quickly assembling a diagram (such as during a meeting). With the Diagramming tool is selected, click on any empty space on the canvas to create a generic shape that is automatically selected. With that first shape selected, click any empty spot and a new shape is connected to the original. If you leave the second shape selected and Option+click another empty space, OmniGraffle creates a sibling shape (connected to the same parent). Holding the Shift key instead of Option creates an aunt (connected as a sibling to the parent). Holding the ⌘ key creates a separate, disconnected shape. Once you master the modifier keys, you can assemble professional-looking diagrams quickly, as shown in Figure 13-3.

The Style Brush tool

Say you just created a diagram using the Diagramming tool, with seven different shapes that are all plain white boxes. You then use inspectors to give one of the boxes just the right shading, shadow, and other graphic elements. You don't want to repeat that task for each of the other six boxes. Using the Style Brush tool, you can copy the styling of your customized box and paste it to each of the remaining six. Select the Style Brush tool, click the source shape that has the styling you want to copy, and then click on each of the remaining shapes to paste that formatting.

In addition to the Style Brush tool, the lower-left corner of the main OmniGraffle window holds the Styles tray, shown in Figure 13-2. The Styles tray also lets you copy and paste styles.

FIGURE 13-3

A diagram created with OmniGraffle

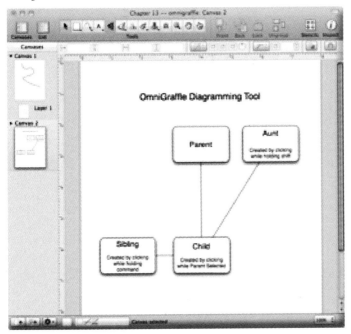

The Rubber Stamp tool

This tool lets you take any existing object and duplicate it, multiple times. Select the tool and click any object. Once selected, the dot on the Rubber Stamp tool icon changes from white to dark. The dark dot indicates the Rubber Stamp tool has an image and is ready to duplicate it. In other words, when the dot is dark, the stamp has ink. After that, every click on the canvas with this tool creates an exact copy of the original object.

The Magnet tool

When attaching lines to different shapes, the default connection point is the center of the shape. The Magnet tool allows you to adjust the point. If, for example, you want all your lines to be attached to the lower-right corner of a box, select the Magnet tool and move the magnet to the lower-right corner and you are in business.

The Zoom tool

Sometimes you need to zoom in on your diagram to make fine adjustments. Select the Zoom tool and click anywhere on the canvas to center on that point and double the zoom percentage. Use multiple clicks to zoom in quickly and

Option+click on the canvas to zoom out. To select a specific portion of your canvas, click and drag a box while the Zoom tool is active. If you click and drag while holding the Option key, the selection centers itself on your starting point. Shift+click the Zoom tool to return your canvas to its actual size.

In addition to the Zoom tool, you can adjust the zoom level of your OmniGraffle document with the Zoom iconic button in the lower-right corner of the main canvas window, shown in Figure 13-2.

The Hand tool

This tool lets you grab and move the canvas. It is most helpful when you are zoomed in for detail work.

The Browse tool

You can build interactive OmniGraffle presentations that transition between diagrams. Use the Browse tool to set specific actions to objects on your canvas for the presentation. In practice, my OmniGraffle diagrams are always a part of a bigger presentation in Keynote. As a result, I find little use for this feature.

To get a separate floating tool palette with all the available drawing tools, choose Window ▶ Tool Palette.

The remaining tools in the toolbar include the Front and Back iconic buttons to set the order of objects in your OmniGraffle diagram, and Group and Ungroup iconic buttons to combine (or separate) multiple objects.

Using stencils

The Stencils tool is one of OmniGraffle's best features. When you activate the Stencils inspector using the Stencils iconic button in the toolbar, you get the window shown in Figure 13-4. The Stencil library includes several prebuilt objects that you can drag and drop on your OmniGraffle document.

Using stencils takes the drudgery out of creating diagrams. You just drag in a series of prebuilt elements and arrange them on the OmniGraffle canvas. OmniGraffle ships with several stencil sets, including shapes, connections, textures, and flowcharts. Additional stencils are available at www. graffletopia.com, including network diagramming, shapes and figures for presentations, wireframe models for programming, and mind-mapping. As of this writing, the Web site has 80 pages of downloadable OmniGraffle stencils. Whether you are designing a new kitchen or creating the next great iPhone app, there are stencils for you.

The most recent version of OmniGraffle has built-in support for Graffletopia. (Choose Help ▶ Visit Graffletopia.) You can also search www.graffletopia. com from the Stencil inspector and import new stencil sets without leaving

OmniGraffle. To search Graffletopia from within OmniGraffle, click the selection triangle iconic button in the Stencil inspector's search bar and choose Graffletopia.

Inspectors

OmniGraffle's inspector, activated by clicking the Inspector iconic button in the toolbar (shown in Figure 13-2), includes many fine controls for your shapes. If, for example, you want to change the shape of the arrows at the end of your lines, go to the inspector.

OmniGraffle also has the Mini Inspector, a context-sensitive bar just below the toolbar that displays attributes and tools for the selected object. The Mini Inspector is similar to the context-sensitive toolbar in the iWork applications. If, for example, you select a rectangle, the Mini Inspector indicates the size, location, line size, and other elements of the rectangle. The Mini Inspector also allows you to make adjustments, including adding fills, shadows, line weight, and other rectangle attributes.

Organizational charts

Making organizational charts is easy with OmniGraffle. To do so, start with one of the organizational chart templates. You can create an organizational chart on the OmniFocus canvas with the graphic objects (using the Diagramming tool covered earlier is helpful here) or create it as an outline in the View mode. As you

FIGURE 13-4

The OmniGraffle Stencil inspector

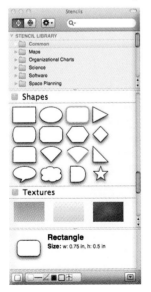

type in parent and children outline levels, OmniGraffle automatically creates a graphic representation on the canvas, as shown in Figure 13-5.

After you are done, you can change the look and orientation of the organizational chart using the Diagram Layout inspector, shown in Figure 13-6.

The magic of OmniGraffle is the ability to quickly create diagram elements and arrange them on the screen in relation to one another. You can label, connect, and color elements to create impressive-looking diagrams. There is an iPad version that lets you create, view, and edit OmniGraffle diagrams on the iPad. You can also add downloaded stencil sets to the OmniGraffle iPad application through iTunes (see Chapter 7).

Once your diagram is complete, OmniGraffle offers several export options, including Photoshop (.psd), PDF, JPEG, and vector images. Normally, I export completed OmniGraffle images as PNG files and deselect the Include Non-Printing Layers check box. The image has a transparent background and can be imported into Keynote or Pages without a background.

OmniGraffle also has a professional version that costs $200. It includes several additional features, including subgraphs (which can be contained inside larger graphs), shared layers, support for multiple windows, and greater export options, such as to Microsoft Visio.

FIGURE 13-5

Creating an organizational chart with OmniGraffle

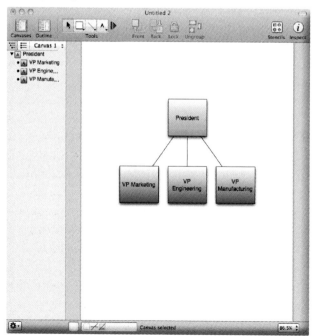

FIGURE 13-6

OmniGraffle Diagram Layout inspector

OmniGraffle is one of my secret weapons. Often, in advance of an important meeting or presentation, I will spend just a few minutes putting together a diagram of important points. It doesn't take long once you get the mechanics of OmniGraffle down. Then inevitably someone who attended the meeting will ask what company I used to produce my graphics. My answer is always the same. "You can't afford my graphics department."

Apple Preview

Apple Preview comes free on every new Mac. Chapter 12 covers Preview's PDF features, but it has more capabilities than just working with PDF files or looking at other images. Although you cannot create graphics with Preview like you can with OmniGraffle, it is handy for working with existing images.

Quite often you have an image that needs resizing, cropping, or other tweaking before you can use it in a graphic or a presentation. Previously, Mac users used expensive image applications for this purpose. But for most needs, you can now get away with using Preview.

Preview image tools

To change an image's size, open the image in Preview and choose Tools ▶ Adjust Size. You then get the dialog box shown in Figure 13-7, which lets you resize an image. You can change the size using pixels, inches, centimeters, and several other units of measure. To keep the image proportional, select the Scale Proportionally check box. Selecting the Resample image check box helps keep the image quality as you make it smaller. It is usually a bad idea to make an image bigger in Preview: The enlargement process makes the image look pixelated (blocky).

Cropping is also easy with Preview. Click the Select button in the Preview toolbar, then (using the mouse) select the portion of the image you want to keep. If the Select button's icon is not a square, click and hold it and choose the

FIGURE 13-7

Resizing an image in Preview

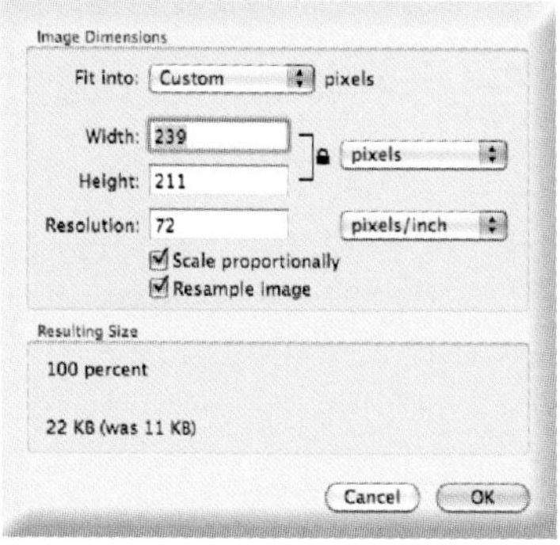

Rectangle Selection tool. Once you've selected the portion of the image to crop, choose Tools ▶ Crop or press ⌘+K.

The annotation tools covered in Chapter 12 are also available for images. You can add lines, ovals, and rectangles to your pictures. You can also type in labels and annotations. Preview lets you adjust colors, brightness, exposure, and other image settings. Using Preview, you can avoid loading a separate image editor for most small adjustments.

Removing backgrounds

Preview also lets you remove backgrounds from images. Let's say you have an image of a baseball and you want to include it in a presentation. You only want the round ball in the Keynote slide, though. You don't want a rectangular image and the background.

First, you need to extract the image, so choose the Smart Lasso tool from the Select pop-up menu in the Preview toolbar. Then use the mouse to trace the edge of the image you want to extract (in this case, the ball). Make sure the thick lasso line does not touch the edge of the ball.

Once you complete the circle with the Lasso tool, you can delete the background, as shown in Figure 13-8. First, reverse the selection (choose Edit ▶ Invert Selection), then press Delete.

If the Smart Lasso tool doesn't completely remove the background, Preview has another tool, Instant Alpha, that will finish the job. The Instant Alpha tool, found in the Select pop-up menu in the Preview toolbar, looks at an image and tries to remove the background. To use the Instant Alpha tool, place the cursor in the background and then hold down the mouse button as you slowly drag the mouse away from the point of origin; Preview removes the background. The further away you drag the mouse, the more aggressive Preview is about removing the background. If you go too far, move the mouse back toward the point of

FIGURE 13-8

Removing a background in Preview

FIGURE 13-9

An image in Keynote after removing the background with Preview

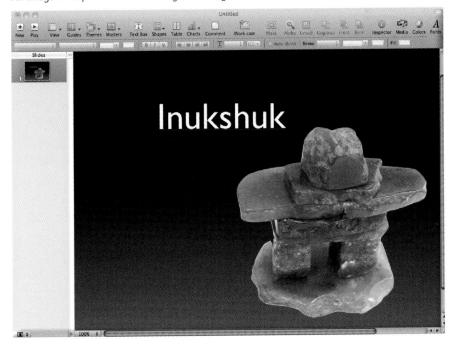

origin. Once you have it just right, press Return. Although not perfect, Instant Alpha does a good job removing the background.

The Instant Alpha tool is also available in Keynote (covered in Chapter 14), Pages (covered in Chapter 11), and Numbers (covered in Chapter 15); in Keynote, Instant Alpha is really helpful for pulling the background off images. Figure 13-9 shows the finalized image in a Keynote slide.

Removing backgrounds from images used to be a painstaking process accomplished only with expensive graphics software. Using Preview's Smart Lasso and Instant Alpha tools, you now have this ability on every Mac.

Other Graphics Software

Adobe Photoshop ($700; www.adobe.com/products/photoshop) and Adobe Illustrator ($700; www.adobe.com/products/illustrator) are the leading photo and drawing applications for Mac OS X. They are also very expensive and, for the types of graphics contemplated by this book, something like killing a gnat with a hand grenade. These applications are powerful and complicated. Some users spend years perfecting their skills with these tools but they are not necessary for making simple graphs, charts, and illustrations.

Pixelmator ($60; www.pixelmator.com) and Acorn ($50; www.flyingmeat.com/acorn) are both less-expensive alternatives to Photoshop and Illustrator with smaller feature sets. Both applications are good options for drawing and working on images. Pixelmator uses more of the look and feel of Adobe Photoshop, while Acorn has its own unique interface.

Using OmniGraphSketcher for graphs ($30; www.omnigroup.com/products/omnigraphsketcher) and Timeline 3D for timelines ($65; www.beedocs.com) are also useful niche graphics applications. OmniGraphSketcher is covered in more detail in Chapter 15, and Timeline 3D is covered in Chapter 14.

Presentations

ecause I'm a trial lawyer in my day job, I've spent a lot of time thinking about and giving presentations over the years. There was a time when going to trial meant heading to the local copier to get blow-ups the size of coffee tables and loading up on felt-tip pens. Presentation software started as a new and liberating tool to avoid the super-sized copies and let people create interactive presentations. Sadly, presentation software has been abused to such an extent that audiences now groan when they walk in a room and see a projector.

In many ways, presentation software is the poster-child example of why the Mac is such a great fit for work. Macintosh hardware and software combine to let you make fantastic presentations that will turn your audience from a "death by PowerPoint" mentality to attentive listeners while you make your case.

Keynote versus PowerPoint

Keynote is the presentation component of Apple's iWork office suite ($79; www.apple.com/iwork). In comparing iWork's other components (Pages and Numbers) to Microsoft Office (Word and Excel), I've found an argument for all contenders. But this is not the case with Keynote. Keynote is so superior to PowerPoint that even if you have no intention of ever using Pages or Numbers, Keynote alone is worth iWork's $79 price tag.

Although PowerPoint has made progress with recent releases, it still does not hold a candle to Keynote on the Mac. This is partly because of how well Keynote integrates with Mac OS X, as covered later, and also partly because of the complete saturation PowerPoint has obtained in corporate America. PowerPoint is everywhere, and people are sick of it. They are tired of the same themes, transitions, and fonts. Often jurors who work in sales will ask me for copies of my "PowerPoint" after a trial. They know it is better (and different) from their own, but they can't put their finger on why. I wish I had a cut of all the Macs I've sold after explaining it was a Keynote presentation that I gave.

FIGURE 14-1

Selecting a Keynote template

Apple iWork Keynote

Keynote is, in my opinion, the best presentation software available on any computing platform.

Creating a presentation

When creating a presentation in Keynote, you first choose a theme and screen resolution, as shown in Figure 14-1. The resolution should match your projector but can be changed later in the Keynote inspector's Document pane (press Option+⌘+I).

As an alternative, Keynote can import PowerPoint presentations, doing a credible job of importing PowerPoint files. However, because the Keynote transitions, graphics, and fonts are different, you will need to check your slides.

Like the other applications in the iWork suite, there is no automatic save function in Keynote. Remember to save your file (press ⌘+S) often.

Keynote includes 44 built-in themes, which are professionally designed and look great. You can also create your own custom themes or purchase third-party themes. A good source of Keynote themes is www.keynoteuser.com.

Setting a theme does more than give you a color scheme and font selection. The Keynote themes also include stylized graphics and a series of professionally designed slides for different elements of a presentation, including bullet points, pictures, and graphics. You can access these master slides by clicking the Masters iconic button in the toolbar, as shown in Figure 14-2.

FIGURE 14-2

Keynote's master slides

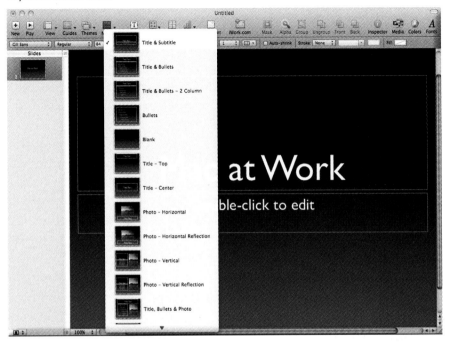

There are several advantages to using slide masters. Master slides provide an easy way to apply consistent formatting throughout your presentation. When an audience sees a presentation that has different indentation on every slide, it notices. Indeed, they may start thinking more about where the next text block will appear than the actual content of your presentation. The slide masters also provide unified animations, frames, and media presentation.

A lot of users don't realize you can use more than one theme in a single presentation. If you want the presentation to use the Gradient theme but prefer how the Showroom theme displays pictures, you can mix and match the two themes. To do this, first build your presentation in Gradient theme, then select the photo slide only and change the theme to Showroom (using the Theme iconic button in the toolbar).

Outlines and Keynote

It is a good idea to start your presentation with an outline. There are several ways you can do this with Keynote. In Keynote, you can create an outline by using the Keynote Outline view by choosing View ▶ Outline; the application presents an outline view of your presentation in the slide navigator on the left side of the screen. You will see the title and bullet points for every slide; if the slide does not contain any text, it appears empty. You can edit the text directly in the slide navigator, which is useful for proofreading slides. In Outline view, you can further delete, duplicate, move, and add slides. If you select a slide in outline view and press Tab (or drag the slide's icon to the right), you demote that slide into a bullet point on the prior slide. Conversely, you can Shift+Tab a bullet (or drag it to the left) to make it an independent slide.

You can create an outline in OmniOutliner (covered in Chapter 10) and export it directly to Keynote; you get a new presentation with bullets for each of your subpoints. If you choose to outline your Keynote presentation in OmniOutliner, each new slide must be a Level 1 outline item. If your OmniOutliner outline only has three Level 1 points with many subpoints, your imported Keynote presentation will have only three slides with many, many bullet points.

When starting a presentation from an outline, be careful. Just because you can create outlines with bullet point slides, don't create a text-heavy, boring Keynote presentation that puts your audience to sleep. Instead, use the outlining procedure to create a structure for your presentations. For example, I might make a Level 1 outline entry in OmniOutliner called Hammer Photo. When imported into Keynote, that Level 1 entry becomes a slide named Hammer Photo that serves as a reminder to find an interesting image to hammer home whatever point I am making. Many of the Level 1 outline entries I use are simply labels (like Timeline, Graph, or Image) for slides that never get any text.

Using objects

Objects are the bits of text and graphics you put on a blank slide. Keynote objects include text, graphics, tables, charts, pictures, movies, and links. You can select, move, copy, resize, rotate, and flip objects. Keynote's copy and paste functionality not only remembers the object size and look but also its location. If, for example, you want your company logo to appear in the lower corner of a series of slides, you can put it in the same position on each slide by copying it from one slide and manually pasting it into every subsequent slide.

The trick to using Keynote objects is to keep the inspector open (open it by pressing Option+⌘+I). A little known Keynote fact is that you can open multiple inspectors by choosing View ▶ New Inspector. When building a presentation, I open three inspectors: one with text tools, another with graphics tools, and a third with animations. As long as you have the available screen real estate, it speeds things up for you.

Once you've created a slide, you can resize the text box or click inside it and start typing. By default, if your text exceeds the size of the box, Keynote displays an icon of a small box with a + (plus) inside it at the bottom of the text box, to indicate there is additional text. You can resize the box to display all your entered

FIGURE 14-3

Keynote's Text inspector

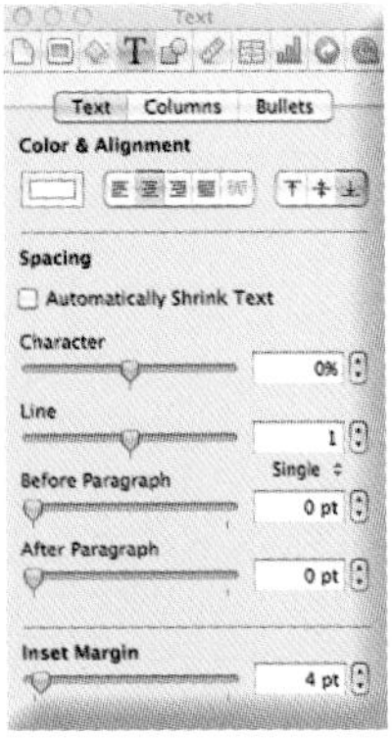

text, or you can click the + iconic button to shrink the text to fit in the box. Keynote also spell-checks your text, and puts a dotted line under suspect words.

You can adjust the text formatting using the Text inspector, as Figure 14-3 shows. Using the Text inspector, you can adjust the justification, spacing, margins, and other text attributes.

Use text sparingly in your presentations. A good rule of thumb is to make certain no text in your presentation is set to a point size smaller than one-half the age of the oldest listener in your audience. Lots of small type on the screen simply doesn't get read. Also, don't go crazy with fonts and colors.

Keynote gives you the option of adding hyperlinks to your text, using the Hyperlink inspector. When you click hyperlinked text, Keynote jumps to the designated slide, to a separate Keynote presentation, or to an external Web page. Hyperlinks can be very powerful: If you're giving an interactive presentation where the order of the slides may vary, you can create an index slide with a list of the available subjects and hyperlink each entry to the starting slide number for that subject.

Keynote provides a full suite of graphics tools, including lines and shapes. Graphics can be added using the Shapes iconic button in the toolbar or choosing Insert ▶ Shapes. Once you create a shape in your Keynote slide, you can resize it, move it, and change its formatting using the graphics inspector. The Graphics inspector is contextually sensitive to the selected shape: If you select a line, you get line tools (including end points and thickness). If you select a rectangle, you get fill and gradient tools. When working with shapes, I recommend keeping the Graphics inspector open.

One of the biggest advantages of creating your graphics in Keynote is the Keynote smart guides feature. Keynote includes an ingenious system for constantly measuring the relative position of all objects on the screen in

FIGURE 14-4

Keynote's smart guides in action

comparison to other objects. This capability lets you snap a line of text to the center or offset two boxes with very little work, as shown in Figure 14-4.

Using Keynote's tools, you will quickly be able to put together formidable graphics. But you can also create your own graphics for Keynote in other applications, like OmniGraffle (covered in Chapter 13) or OmniGraphSketcher (covered in Chapter 15). When exporting graphics for Keynote, save the image as a PNG file with a transparent background. This way, when you drag the image into Keynote, the background is already removed. If you need to remove the background from an imported graphic, you can use the Instant Alpha tool (covered in Chapter 13) in the Keynote toolbar.

You can also add hyperlinks to graphics. If, for example, you create a Keynote presentation with an index slide that has a list of subjects, you can create a small icon (I make one that looks like a home button) and put it in the bottom-right corner of each slide. At any point during the presentation, I can return to the index slide by clicking on the icon.

Keynote includes impressive table and chart tools. (The 3D charts are particularly attractive.) You can create your own tables and charts in Keynote or import them from Numbers (covered in Chapter 15). If you're using a consistent theme, Keynote automatically applies theme-based formatting to charts and

FIGURE 14-5

A 3D chart in Keynote

tables. You can adjust individual charts and tables using the Chart inspector, which is context-sensitive. For example, the tools for a bar chart are different from the tools for a pie cart. Figure 14-5 shows a sample Keynote chart.

You can add images to Keynote slides by simply dragging them onto the slide. You can then format them using the Graphics inspector. Keynote also lets you add masks, frames, lines, and shadows to the image, as well as adding a text box to annotate an image.

If you want to show multiple images on a single Keynote slide, you can use the Keynote smart build feature (choose Insert ♦ Smart Build). When creating a smart build, you can choose the transition method and drag in multiple images. When you arrive at that slide in your presentation, Keynote transitions through each image. If you use images repeatedly, add them to your iPhoto library so you can access them directly in Keynote using the Inspector iconic button in the toolbar.

You can import an iMovie or a QuickTime movie onto a slide. Using the Keynote QuickTime inspector, you can set the start and end playback points, as well choose the poster frame, which is the image shown on the screen when the movie is not playing.

When working with multiple objects, you need to pay attention to the display order (also called the *stacking order*) of each object. If, for example, you want text to appear on top of a solid box, make certain the object holding the box is behind the object holding the text. Otherwise the text is hidden.

You can adjust the order of your objects by selecting an object and then choosing Arrange ❥ Bring Forward or Arrange ❥ Send Backward to change its place in the display order. You can also adjust the order of objects by Control+clicking or right-clicking on the object and then, via the contextual menu, move the object forward or backward.

Animations and transitions

You can animate objects (making them appear, disappear, and move) in Keynote using the Build inspector. Depending on the type of object you are animating, Keynote provides a variety of effects.

With animations, less is more. Despite the fact that Keynote gives you the ability to make words in the text box appear to burn up in flames, it is not a reason to use it on every slide. Indeed, I'm still waiting for a presentation where that particular animation would be appropriate. Audiences quickly grow tired of excessive animations in your slides: It is like ending every sentence with an exclamation point!

You can instruct Keynote to perform animations when you click the mouse or after a set amount of time. You can also set up animations to run in relation to one another. For example, you can animate the drawing of an arrow and then have Keynote create a text box at the end of the arrow. To do this, you use the Build inspector. First, click the More Options button at the bottom of the Build inspector to open a drawer that lists each object and its build order, as shown in Figure 14-6. You can click and drag objects in the build order list to change their appearance relative to other objects. When working on complicated animations, I keep this inspector open on the side of the Keynote window.

You use the slide inspector to access slide transitions, those interesting animations between slides. The same advice I gave in using animations applies to using slide transitions: Don't overdo it.

Keynote offers several 2D and 3D transitions. For most purposes, the Dissolve transition is all you need. However, when moving between major points in your presentation, you may want to find a more distinctive transition to cue the audience that you are moving to a new subject.

One of the best additions to the most recent release of Keynote is Magic Move. Magic Move is a slide transition that lets you select a series of objects on one slide and move them to pre-ordained positions on the next slide. To do this, first create a slide with objects. Then duplicate the slide (press ⌘+D or choose Edit ❥ Duplicate). In the duplicated slide, move and resize your objects to their

FIGURE 14-6

Keynote animations

new locations. Finally go back to the first slide and set the slide transition to Magic Move. That's it!

When you give the presentation, the objects will automatically move and resize themselves. Before this feature was added to Keynote, moving multiple objects in one transition required you to painstakingly set the motion track and destination for each object. For complicated slides, this took hours.

Timelines

Quite often, you want to insert a timeline in your Keynote presentation. There is no timeline object in Keynote so creating timelines is often a matter of building the individual graphic objects. If the timeline is simple, you can use a series of lines and text boxes. Using animation, you can build a timeline in front of your audience one piece at a time. If you have more complicated timelines, you can use a separate timeline application.

One of my favorites is Timeline 3D ($65; www.beedocs.com), shown in Figure 14-7. Timeline 3D does all the hard work of putting the text and timeline on the screen and finding a way to make everything fit. You can then display the timeline as a static image or open it in 3D mode and move between each point on the screen. You can display your animation directly from Timeline 3D, using the arrow keys to move through the timeline. If you do so, be sure to hide your Keynote presentation by pressing the H key before switching to Timeline 3D.

Alternatively, you could export the timeline from Timeline 3D as a QuickTime movie file and place it in one of your Keynote slides. This is safer in front of an audience than exiting your presentation and displaying the timeline

FIGURE 14-7

Timeline 3D

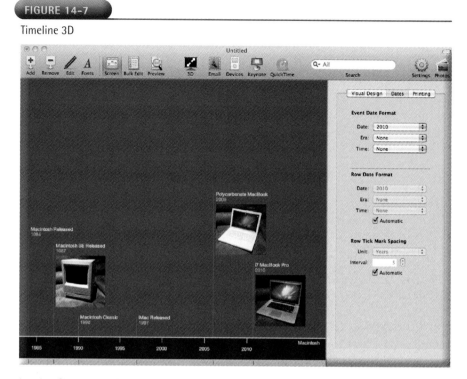

in Timeline 3D. It lets you avoid that awkward moment of finding your way back into Keynote and restarting the presentation. However, displaying the timeline as a pre-rendered movie does not let you fluidly move forward and backward in it as you can when working directly in Timeline 3D.

Organization and sharing

As your slideshow begins to take shape, you will inevitably want to reorganize. Keynote's Light Table view (choose View ▶ Light Table) is made for this purpose. Keynote presents thumbnail images of your slides, which you can select and move at will. The Light Table view is a good place to choose which slides you will want in your presentation. You can hide an individual slide by Control+clicking or right-clicking it and choosing Skip Slide from the contextual menu. The slide is then skipped when you give your presentation. You can add the slide back into the presentation by Control+clicking or right-clicking the slide and choosing Don't Skip Slide from the contextual menu.

As you finish building your presentation, always remember to put a blank slide at the end. This way, if you accidently click Forward at the end of your presentation, the presentation doesn't exit to Keynote but instead just leaves an attractive blank screen.

FIGURE 14-8

Exporting a Keynote presentation for QuickTime playback

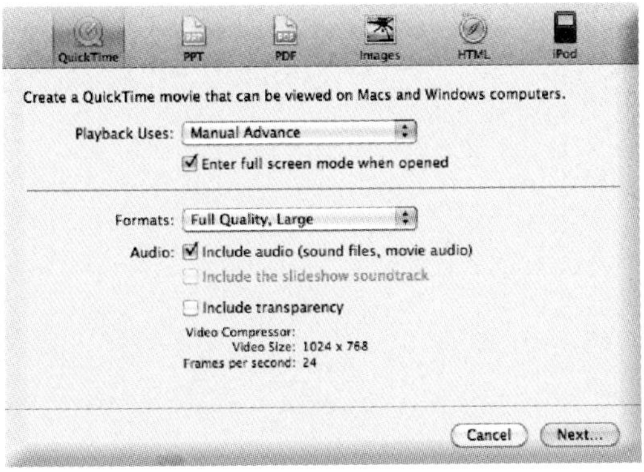

Once your presentation is finished, you have several methods for sharing it. You can export it as a QuickTime movie and then play it on any computer (including Windows PCs) that has QuickTime installed. As part of the export settings, you can set the Keynote presentation-turned-QuickTime-movie for manual advance, as shown in Figure 14-8. The finished movie will wait for a mouse click before each build — just as if it were being presented in Keynote. When giving important presentations, I always export and save a QuickTime version of the presentation on a USB thumb drive. That way, when I arrive for the presentation and all my computers choose that moment to implode, I can load the movie file on any computer with QuickTime and give the presentation.

You can also save your completed Keynote presentation as a PDF file or as a set of Web pages. You can even export it to PowerPoint. However, because PowerPoint does not support the same transitions and effects as Keynote does,

OTHER USES FOR KEYNOTE

Keynote is surprisingly useful. The Keynote graphic tools combined with the easy ability to animate objects makes it perfect for simple video effects processing. You can create animated words or objects and then export the Keynote presentation as a QuickTime movie for later import into your movie editing software as a graphical effect.

Another interesting use for Keynote is as a sales kiosk. You can create a hyperlinked presentation with an index screen. Potential customers can then use the mouse to click any icon or words of interest and have the presentation jump to those slides. You can set up automatic transitions that, ultimately, return to the menu. I recently attended a conference where there was a 27-inch iMac with a mouse set up for just this purpose, and people were lined up in front of it all day.

FIGURE 14-9

Keynote's Presenter Display view mode

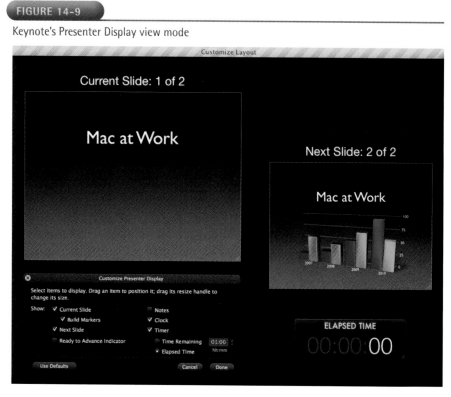

you will most likely not be satisfied with the results. Sending a well-designed Keynote presentation to PowerPoint feels something like putting Cheez Whiz on artisan bread.

Do note that Keynote's collaboration tools are limited. Using iWork.com, you can share your Keynote file (for download as images or in Keynote or PowerPoint formats) or allow co-workers to annotate images of the Keynote presentation directly on iWork.com. I find this useful when working with clients, as it allows them to make suggested changes and annotations without accessing the source file.

Presentation day

As presentation day approaches, make sure to test your Keynote presentation with whatever projecting hardware you will be using. Make a list of whatever cables and extension cords you need — and check it twice.

Keynote has the Presenter Display view mode that provides critical data on your Mac's screen while projecting your presentation on the projector screen. Access this mode by choosing Play ▶ Customize Presenter Display, as shown in Figure 14-9.

TABLE 14-1

Keynote's Presentation Keyboard Shortcuts

Shortcut	Effect
Option+⌘+P	Play slideshow.
Option-click the Play button in the toolbar	Play the slideshow from the beginning.
Click the mouse or press any of the following: N, spacebar, Return, Page Down, →, or ↓	Go to the next build.
Press any of the following: P, Delete, Page Up, ←, or ↑	Go to the previous build.
Home	Go to the first slide.
End	Go to the last slide.
Z	Go back through the previously viewed slides.
H	Hide the presentation and show the last application used.
F	Freeze (pause) the presentation and show the current slide. (To resume, press any key.)
B	Pause the presentation and show a black screen. (To resume, press any key.)
W	Pause the presentation and show a white screen. (To resume, press any key.)
C	Show or hide the mouse pointer.
Type the slide number and press Return	Go to a particular slide.
X	Switch to the primary presenter display. If you stand up to give your presentation and, by some cruel twist of fate, your presenter display shows up on the big screen and your presentation appears on your laptop, dive for the X key.
R	Reset the timer in the presenter display.
Press any of the following: Esc, Q, or . (period)	Quit the presentation.

You can customize the Presenter Display view mode to your liking. It includes options to show the current slide, the next slide, notes, a clock, a timer (showing time elapsed or time remaining), and an indicator that Keynote has completed all animations and is ready to advance to the next slide. I usually run it with a preview of the next slide and a clock.

Get to the location of your presentation early. Make certain you have enough time to set up and get through any last-minute problems before anyone arrives. I always make sure to run through the entire presentation once before anyone in the audience shows up, so my movies are already in Keynote's memory cache (which speeds up display and avoids awkward load times).

While you are giving your presentation with Keynote, there are several handy keyboard shortcuts to remember, shown in Table 14-1.

You can advance your slides remotely using the $19 Apple Remote. I'm not a fan of Apple's remote because it uses infrared wireless technology. Thus, if the remote loses the line of sight with your Mac's infrared sensor, the Mac can't see any of your remote control actions, so slides and builds will stop advancing. There are also a variety of iPhone applications and non-Apple remotes that work over Wi-Fi and Bluetooth. I recommend those instead. If you give lots of presentations, get a remote with a built-in laser pointer.

Microsoft PowerPoint

PowerPoint is the presentation component of Microsoft Office 2011 ($200; www.microsoft.com/mac). PowerPoint started life as a Mac application in 1987 called Presenter. It was eventually acquired by Microsoft and incorporated into Microsoft Office. Shown in Figure 14-10, PowerPoint for Mac has traditionally lagged behind PowerPoint for Windows. For example, PowerPoint 2008 for Mac was unable to track changes if you were working on presentations with co-workers despite this feature being available on the Windows version. The ability to track changes was added in PowerPoint 2011. Microsoft also restored Visual Basic support to PowerPoint 2011.

Like the rest of the Microsoft Office suite, PowerPoint now uses the improved ribbon interface, making it easier to find desired features. It also includes improved SmartArt graphics that makes it easier to generate common graphics such as organizational charts and Venn diagrams.

In my years of using a Mac for presentations, I have never encountered another speaker that uses PowerPoint on the Mac. In fact, the truth is quite the opposite: I've met some speakers who want nothing to do with Mac OS X but nevertheless own a MacBook that is only used with one application, Keynote. Keynote has always had the edge with respect to clean font rendering, animations, and ease of use. Microsoft has made lots of progress in streamlining PowerPoint 2011's interface. It will be interesting to see if the changes cause more users to use PowerPoint.

So where does PowerPoint fit on the Mac? I still think it sits a distant second behind Keynote. However, if your co-workers don't have Keynote and if you are required to use PowerPoint, it is at least available on the Mac. PowerPoint 2011 is much closer to the Windows version than PowerPoint 2008 was, so there'll be fewer hassles. Nevertheless, the graphics-intensive nature of presentation software

FIGURE 14-10

PowerPoint 2011

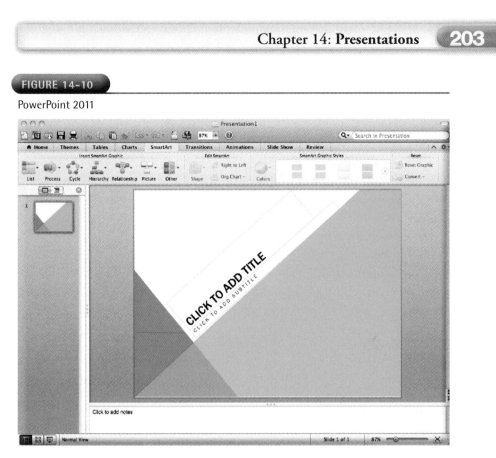

means that compatibility issues will continue to arise between the Mac and Windows versions of PowerPoint. If using PowerPoint for Windows is absolutely critical, you are better off running it using virtualization software (covered in Chapter 22).

Presentation Mojo

So now that I've covered the how of presentation software, I'd like to cover the why. Specifically, why do so many presentations stink and put the audience to sleep? Many users fundamentally misunderstand the purpose of presentation software. Presentation software does not exist to *replace* the speaker, it is there to *enhance* the speaker. But most presentations are all icing and no cake.

Many people are afraid of public speaking, so they look at presentation software as the ultimate crutch. They type their entire speech into the presentation and then proceed to project it on the screen, turn their back to their audience, and read it.

Every time I watch one of these presentations, my head gets fuzzy with the long sentences in small typeface and multiple bullets. Despite my best intentions, within minutes I am completely checked out and thinking about going to the beach. I'm not alone. The audience needs cake.

Presentation software gives the speaker a tremendous opportunity. Studies have shown that most people don't learn (and rarely remember) information presented to them in a verbal-only fashion. But when information is presented both verbally and visually, people are much more likely to understand and retain it.

Presentation software lets you combine verbal and visual learning to make a maximum impact on your audience. But to do so, you need to stop using slides as giant shared cue cards and instead use them as tools to hammer your key points visually. This is not easy. It starts with you breaking down each presentation into its key components. A presentation is much like a story. It needs a beginning, middle, and an end. It needs to be emotional and involve your audience.

I plan presentations using mind-mapping software (like MindNode, covered in Chapter 10). In addition to outlining the general chronology of my presentation, I also give thought to the ebb and flow of the points and how they fit together. Any presentation has high and low points. Spend time thinking about how best to fit them together. It is important that you arrange your presentation in a way that makes it relevant to your audience. Do not let them mentally go to the beach on your watch.

This initial planning takes time. In my case, it usually takes hours (sometimes days). I was told once as a young lawyer that if I couldn't summarize any case in two sentences, I didn't know the case well enough. This advice applies equally to planning presentations. You need to spend lots of time looking at each component and distilling it down to its simplest form for your presentation. Your audience is not interested in doing the hard work of figuring out your product, plan, or case. You have to do it for them, in advance.

Once you have those simple pieces laid out, begin making slides. Pick the most important points and reinforce them with slides. The slides shouldn't be filled with bullets and words but instead with visual representations of your most important points.

As an example, I once had a very complicated business case that involved a once-successful but now failed business, and there was a lot of talk about how and why that happened. I struggled with how to represent that business to the jury until I noticed a neighbor's lawn was dying. I took a close picture of all this dead grass and then took another close picture of a different lawn that was healthy and green. I then used two slides (one with a green lawn and one with a dead lawn) to explain the business and the relative causes for why the grass died. It worked brilliantly, and the other lawyer's random scribbling and ranting on a chalkboard never sunk home with the jury. Because the audience understood my analogy, they understood my argument. Pictures, analogies, and simplified data and graph slides are a great way to reinforce your points without losing your audience.

Once you've prepared a polished slide deck that includes fantastic icing, you still need to work on another part of the cake: your own presentation style. The sad truth is there is no magic formula to giving a good presentation. Instead, it comes down to spending an obscene amount of time practicing. When I give a big presentation, I practice it endlessly. I script it in my mind as I prepare the slides. I say the presentation out loud as I revise the slides. I give it in the mirror. I give the presentation to patient family members. I even talk through the presentation as I sit in traffic. There is no substitute for the process of getting the words from your mind to your lips many times. Until you are comfortable verbalizing your presentation, you are not ready. After you spend the time and effort perfecting your presentation, you will be full of confidence and fantastic.

PART

IV

Advanced Business

Spreadsheets

S preadsheets, and their ability to quickly run many calculations, were the first "killer apps" for business computers. Thirty years later we still use spreadsheets on our computers, and there are several options for crunching numbers on your Mac. This chapter focuses on three — Microsoft Excel, Apple iWork Numbers, and Google Spreadsheets — that take different approaches to spreadsheets. You'll also learn about OmniGraphSketcher, an application to help make better graphs and charts from your spreadsheet data.

Microsoft Excel

Microsoft Excel, shown in Figure 15-1, is part of the Microsoft Office suite. The Office suite (www.microsoft.com/mac/products/office2011), includes Microsoft's Outlook, Word, PowerPoint, and Excel. The price for Office varies from $120 (for the Home and Student Edition) to $200 (for the Home and Business Edition).

Excel is the 800-pound gorilla of spreadsheet applications. Microsoft has been building on the Excel code for two decades — in fact, it was first created for the Mac back in 1985, then went on to Windows two years later — and has no equal in terms of calculating capability and features.

Microsoft's primary focus with Mac Excel is making it compatible with its Windows sibling. The Mac team at Microsoft strives to have the spreadsheet you create on your Mac in the airport open and run on the PC in the boardroom. If cross-platform compatibility with Windows Excel is essential, Mac Excel is your best bet.

However, if you are switching from Windows, don't expect Excel to look like Windows Excel. Two separate teams at Microsoft develop them. The user interfaces are different and so switching between them can take some getting used to.

Also, even with the emphasis on cross-platform compatibility, it doesn't always work. Opening Mac-created spreadsheets in Windows sometimes brings unexpected surprises. Missing fonts or differences in how Windows handles files may distort or even break a Mac Excel spreadsheet. Mac Excel 2008 removed the Visual Basic macro language, making it impossible to use many Windows-based

FIGURE 15-1

Microsoft Excel

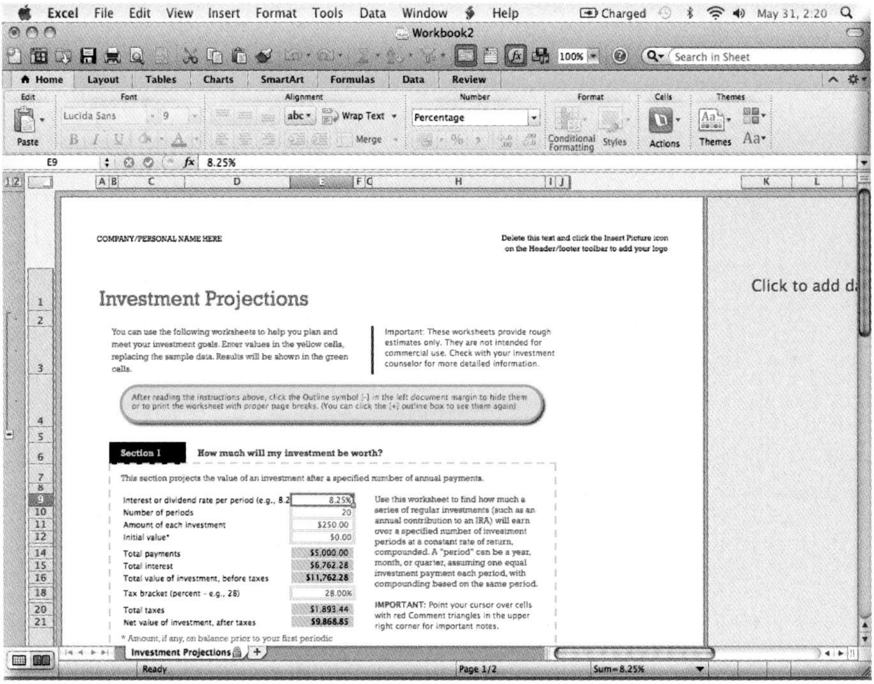

Excel spreadsheets. This was, fortunately, remedied with the release of Mac Excel 2011, which returns Visual Basic to the Mac.

In addition to cross-platform compatibility, Excel is a powerful spreadsheet. It has more built-in calculations, formulas, and computing tools than any spreadsheet application. No matter how esoteric your formula, Microsoft has probably built a formula for it; and if Microsoft hasn't, there's likely a third-party add-on available. This is no small accomplishment, and it's the reason most large companies rely so heavily on Excel. If, for example, you need to use the Weibull Statistical Probability Distribution, you need Excel.

Despite its power, Mac users do not universally love the Microsoft Office suite. Traditionally, using Office felt something like piloting a battleship. It was slow to start, slow to maneuver, and involved way too many buttons, switches, and levers. Microsoft has addressed some of these complaints with the release of Microsoft Office for Mac 2011. Its user interface borrows the ribbon look from the Windows version of Office, as shown in Figure 15-2. This is a notable improvement over prior versions that had mushroomed into a jumbled mess of options, buttons, and toolbars.

In the past, Microsoft Office did not follow conventions used in most Mac OS X applications; it tended to use Windows conventions and some unique

FIGURE 15-2

Microsoft Excel's ribbon toolbar

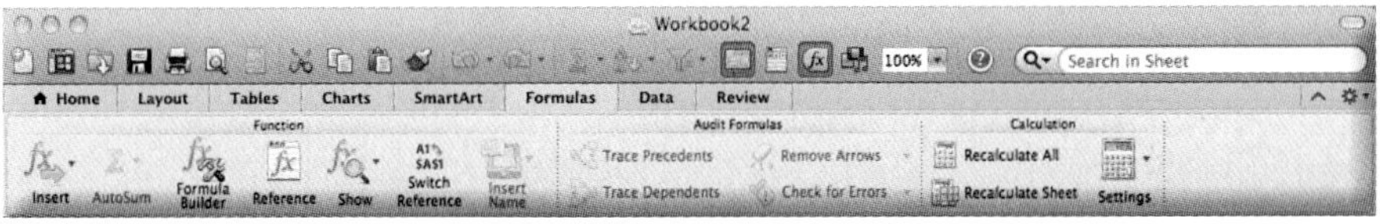

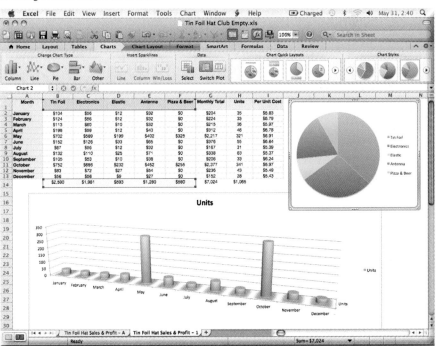

approaches Microsoft's Mac Business Unit added that were neither Windows- nor Mac-standard.

The newest version is more Mac-like. For example, the toolbar is displayed using Mac OS X's Core Animation framework, which provides smooth animations between the different ribbons. The Mac ribbon is not identical to that in the Windows version but is close enough for users transitioning between operating systems.

Although Microsoft is moving it in the right direction, Mac Excel remains very much a Microsoft product and still does not follow many standard Mac OS X guidelines. For example, although virtually all Mac applications tie into the Mac OS X Recent Documents framework, Microsoft uses its own recent documents system, thus excluding the Office applications from quick-launching documents in LaunchBar (covered in Chapter 3).

FIGURE 15-3

Creating a chart in Microsoft Excel

FIGURE 15-4

Microsoft Excel's new sparkline charts display at the very bottom of this spreadsheet.

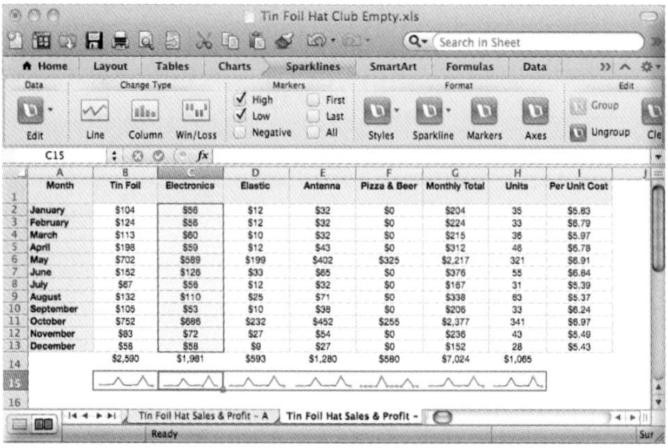
Tin Foil Hat Club Empty.xls
Search in Sheet
Home Layout Tables Charts Sparklines SmartArt Formulas Data
Data Change Type Markers Format Edit
High First Low Last Negative All
Edit Line Column Win/Loss Styles Sparkline Markers Axes Group Ungroup
C15
Month Tin Foil Electronics Elastic Antenna Pizza & Beer Monthly Total Units Per Unit Cost
January $104 $56 $12 $32 $0 $204 35 $5.83
February $124 $56 $12 $32 $0 $224 33 $6.79
March $113 $60 $10 $32 $0 $215 36 $5.97
April $198 $59 $12 $43 $0 $312 46 $6.78
May $702 $589 $199 $402 $325 $2,217 321 $6.91
June $152 $126 $33 $65 $0 $376 55 $6.84
July $67 $56 $12 $32 $0 $167 31 $5.39
August $132 $110 $25 $71 $0 $338 63 $5.37
September $105 $53 $10 $38 $0 $206 33 $6.24
October $752 $686 $232 $452 $255 $2,377 341 $6.97
November $83 $72 $27 $54 $0 $236 43 $5.49
December $58 $58 $9 $27 $0 $152 28 $5.43
$2,590 $1,981 $593 $1,280 $580 $7,024 $1,065
Tin Foil Hat Sales & Profit - A Tin Foil Hat Sales & Profit -
Ready

Microsoft Excel offers multiple chart styles, as shown in Figure 15-3. As a result of the application's maturity, there are a variety of three-dimensional and two-dimensional charts available. Whether you require stacked pyramids, exploding pie charts, or a mixture of both, Excel has you covered.

Mac Excel 2011 adds a new type of chart called *sparklines*. Sparklines are charts and graphs the size of words that fit directly in the spreadsheet. Rather than just looking at numbers in your table, sparklines can, at a glance, give meaning and context to your data. Sparklines show trends, highs, and lows. Because they fit right in your table, you don't need to go looking for the information. Figure 15-4 contains a sparklines-enabled table showing manufacturing costs over time. Excel's implementation of sparklines allows pie charts, lines, bar charts, and other graphs styles.

Another key Excel capability is its long-time support for pivot tables, which allow you to summarize categories of data. Pivot tables sort, count, and total the data stored in a table, giving you additional information not otherwise available. (Apple's competing iWork Numbers can categorize a table, but that capability is not as mature as the pivot table support in Microsoft Excel.)

Excel for Mac 2011 provides access to the Microsoft cloud-based data service, which provides online access and collaboration, as well as the cloud-based file storage. Although cloud-based Excel is still in its infancy, its mere existence is a step in the right direction.

Power users can take advantage of the Visual Basic macro language, which allows them to customize the Office applications. Talented Visual Basic programmers can dramatically improve Excel's functionality by automating complex calculations and spreadsheet formatting. I've seen some Visual Basic-driven Excel files reduce hours of work into a few minutes of automated computing.

THE OPENOFFICE ALTERNATIVE

If you want the Excel experience without the cost of Microsoft Office, try OpenOffice (free; www.openoffice.org). OpenOffice reads and writes the Microsoft Office formats. Although OpenOffice does not have all the bells and whistles of Microsoft Office, it has enough to get the job done for many users — and it's free.

Ironically, Microsoft Excel embraces Mac OS X automation tools better than Apple's iWork does. Some editions of Microsoft Office ship with built-in Automator actions, and Excel has an extensive AppleScript library (Automator and AppleScript are covered in Chapter 24). I once witnessed a nerdy CPA use a combination of AppleScript and Visual Basic macros to make Mac Excel do nothing less than integer ballet.

Microsoft Excel 2011 is a very powerful spreadsheet application with many features simply not available in other Mac OS X spreadsheet programs. Although it still suffers from the feature glut found in all Microsoft Office applications, the Microsoft Mac team has made notable strides with Mac Excel 2011 toward making it a more Mac-like application.

Apple iWork Numbers

Although one of Excel's strong points is the years of development and weight of features behind it, that is also one of its weaknesses. Excel is anchored to decades of feature bloat. For many users, Excel is overkill. Fortunately, Apple developed its own spreadsheet application as part of the iWork suite ($79; www.apple.com/iwork) called Numbers, shown in Figure 15-5.

Where the focus of Excel is to provide maximum compatibility and nearly all the features and formulas from Windows Excel, the focus of iWork Numbers is to provide a simple to use alternative for everyone else. This design mandate appears in little ways throughout the application. For example, the menu bar is context-sensitive: If you select a data table, you get data table tools. If you select an image, you get image tools.

The first thing you notice when opening a new Numbers spreadsheet is that it does not include the familiar Excel cell table grid to infinity. A Microsoft employee once told me, proudly, that every new Excel sheet provides the user more than 1 billion cells. The default table size in Numbers provides just 585 cells. The tables resize to fit the data set, and no more.

The tables are also smart. If, for example you make a table and use column headings such as Name, Address, and Phone Number and then drag a contact list onto the table from Apple's Address Book application, Numbers automatically imports those contacts and fills in the appropriate data.

Although Numbers does not support Excel pivot tables, it has a similar feature, called *categories*. Numbers tables can look for recurring entries in a designated column and then sort the entire table around those items. For example, if you have a column listing manufacturing costs, with recurring entries of research, materials, and labor, Control+clicking or right-clicking the column title and then choosing the Categorize by This Column contextual menu option, Numbers sorts and counts each entry. You can even categorize by multiple columns.

Because the tables scale to the size of your data, you can put multiple tables in a single sheet. If your spreadsheet includes monthly sales figures, you can place a separate table in the same sheet with fixed costs, such as mark-up and commission rates.

The tables can share data, and you can then model different options without flipping through different sheets. Because each table is independent, resizing and changing one does not affect the others. If you use multiple sheets in one spreadsheet, you can move the tables to different sheets, and Numbers keeps track of your formulas.

In addition to placing multiple tables in a sheet, you can place other objects outside the table such as text, graphics, objects, and charts. With very little work, you can create a sheet with a corporate logo next to a data table and above an attractive chart. The application has automatic layout guides that help you align objects on the sheet. The final product is much cleaner on the screen and printed page than what Excel produces, as shown in Figure 15-5.

Entering data is also intuitive. Numbers allows you to change cell formatting from the toolbar. To prevent errors in data entry, you can set up sliders (where you click and drag a slider to adjust entries), steppers (where you increase or decrease a value by a set amount), and pop-up menus (which allow you to choose from a group of preset values) to adjust cell contents with mouse clicks. Once you format a cell for sliders, steppers, or pop-up menus, the appropriate interface appears any time you select that cell. This is especially helpful for reference cells. For example, if you want to create a percentage discount calculation, you can set up the discount reference as a slider as shown in Figure 15-6 and then easily adjust the amount.

Check box cells are also helpful; they provide a Boolean value of 1 (for yes) and 0 (for no) for your calculations. If, for example, you have a row that has the product price and then a check box for whether a commission is earned, you could set up a formula that multiplies the product price times the commission rate times the commission check box (which is 1 for checked and 0 for unchecked). It would look like:

FIGURE 15-5

Apple's iWork Numbers

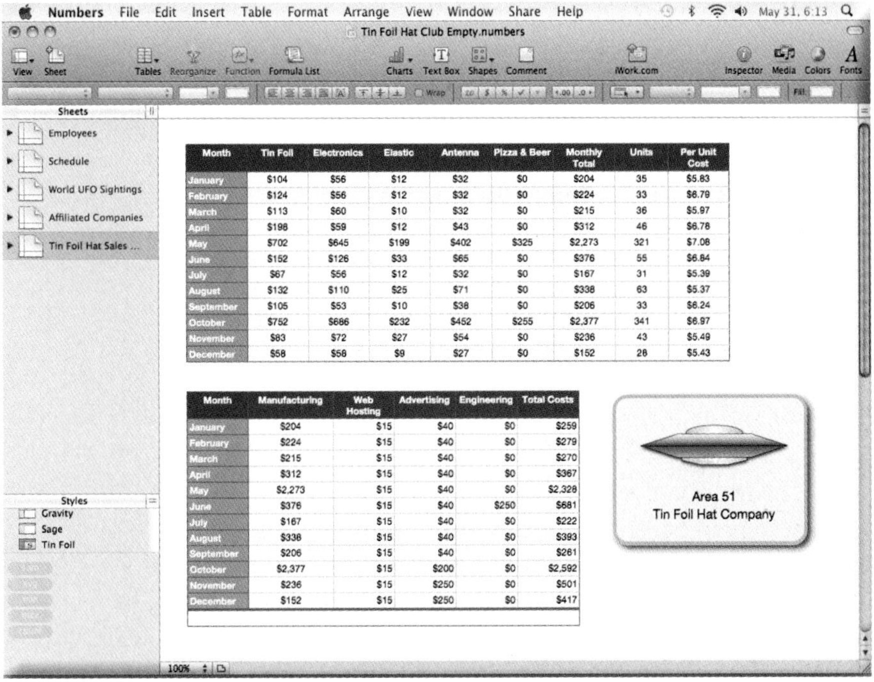

(Product value * (Commission Rate * Commission Check Box))

This equation allows you to turn certain portions of your spreadsheet on or off with one mouse click.

Apple also made Numbers more accessible by using the standard Mac OS X application interface. If your spreadsheet has multiple sheets, the Sheet Navigator, shown in Figure 15-7, located on the left side of the screen — just like in iTunes,

FIGURE 15-6

Numbers' cell slider setup

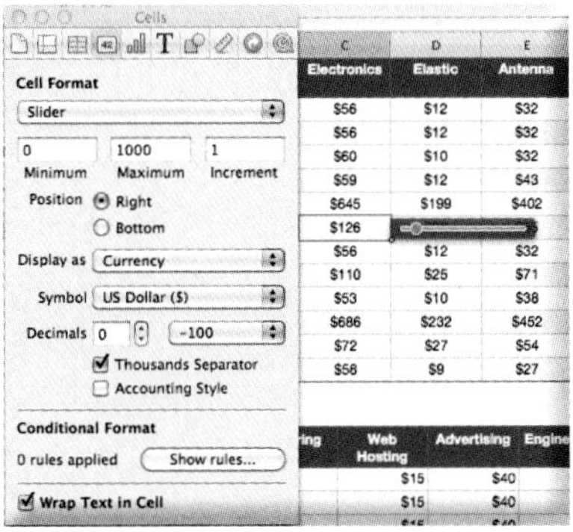

FIGURE 15-7

The Numbers Sheet Navigator

Mail, and several other Apple applications — lists every table, chart, and sheet in your spreadsheet for quick access.

Formulas allow spreadsheets to do calculations without a lot of work on your part. By applying formulas, you can add and subtract dates or perform complex financial and statistical calculations. Numbers does not support as many formulas as Excel; Apple ships Numbers with about 250 formulas. If you need to run formulas that are unsupported by Numbers, you simply can't, and you'll have to work instead in Excel. For the formulas it does support, Numbers makes them easy to use by explaining each formula, as shown in Figure 15-8, and giving usage examples.

Once you insert a formula into your Numbers spreadsheet, the application puts color-coded placeholders in your tables over each variable. You can change

FIGURE 15-8

Numbers' Functions dialog box shows the available formulas and explains their use.

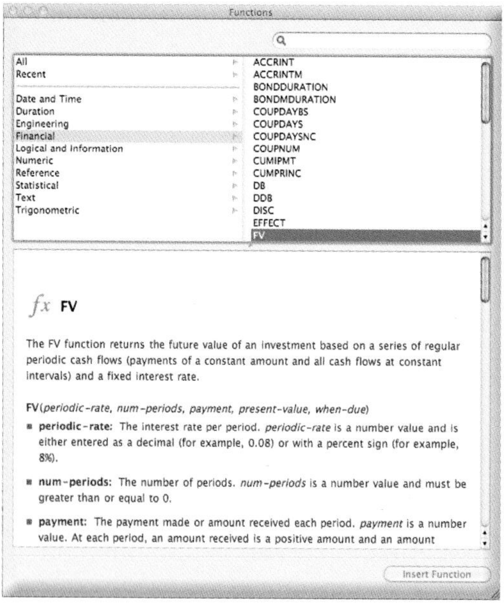

variables by dragging the placeholder to a different cell. The Formula List view displays all your calculations.

A show-stopper for some Excel users is Numbers' inability to work with linked spreadsheets. Using Excel, you can link to a separate spreadsheet file and use its data. This feature is useful in business where, for example, different departments prepare their own spreadsheets that are later tied together in one master spreadsheet.

Numbers sheets look better than Excel sheets. The combination of limited sized tables and easy customization of fonts, sizes, colors, styles, and borders allow you to quickly make visually attractive spreadsheets. The Mac OS X Media Browser is available from Numbers, so you can add pictures from your iPhoto library. Numbers also includes alignment guides and rulers for laying out your worksheets. You can even use iWork tools, such as Instant Alpha (covered in Chapter 13), to remove backgrounds from images. This feature, which was only available in expensive graphics applications, is now (remarkably) available in Apple's spreadsheet application.

The Numbers built-in templates are a mix of business and personal spreadsheets, all professionally designed. The templates provide a starting point that can save you hours of work in making your own custom spreadsheet.

Charts in Numbers are easy to create and customize: You select the data set and click on the desired chart format. If you want to add a data set to a chart, just highlight the data set and drag it onto the existing chart; Numbers does the rest. Although it doesn't support as many chart types as Excel, Numbers supports all the standard chart types — bar, pie, line, and scatter point — in 2D and 3D models, as shown in Figure 15-9. You can also combine chart types such as lines

PIE CHARTS OR BAR CHARTS?

There is a raging battle between nerdy spreadsheet types as to which is better: pie charts or bar charts. The answer is usually bar charts. Although it can be easy to show small differences in data with a bar or line chart, it is nearly impossible to do so with a pie chart. Pie charts with multiple data sets in the same ballpark make each pie slice appear as if they were the same size, so the differences are easily missed. That's much less likely in a bar chart. Also, when using 3D pie charts, the angle of the chart can misleadingly skew the look of the data; that distortion is less in a 3D bar chart.

So, whenever you're making charts, stick with lines and bars and avoid pie charts. The big exception is when there is a significant difference in data sets. For example, if you want to call out a data set that is only 10 percent of the total, using a big pie chart with the tiny 10 percent slice exploded out is an effective presentation technique.

FIGURE 15-9

The Numbers charting tools

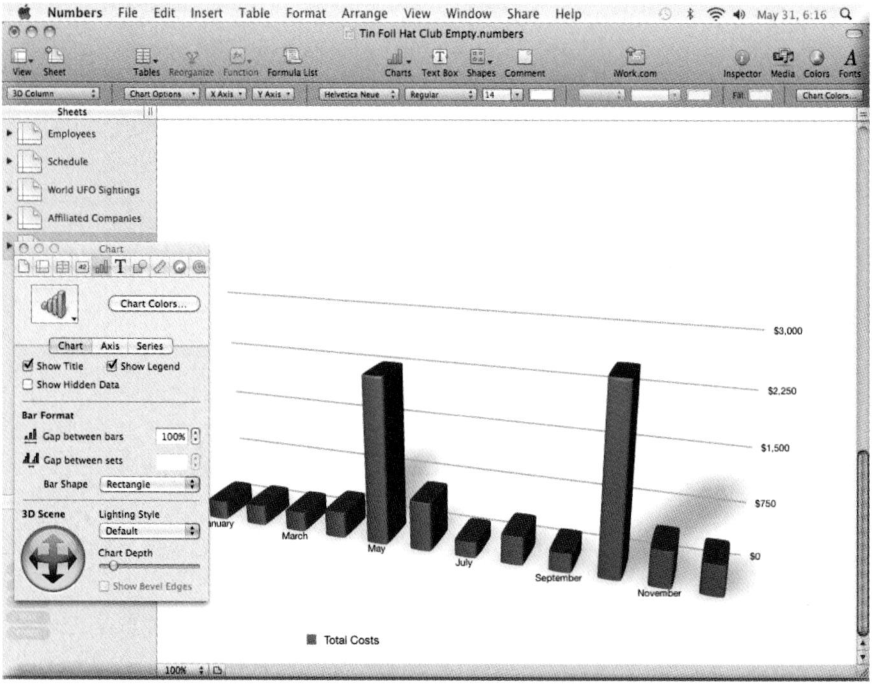

and columns. If you use iWork Pages and Keynote, you can link the charts across the two programs and have them auto-update.

Although Numbers opens Microsoft Excel files and exports to Microsoft Excel format, Apple does not put the same priority on Office compatibility that Microsoft does. The fancy layouts, graphics, and titles in a Numbers spreadsheet often get mangled in the export to Excel.

Likewise, some elements of a Numbers spreadsheet get modified during export to Excel. For example, Numbers allows you to put multiple tables on a single sheet whereas Excel does not. When you export to Excel, each table is broken into a separate sheet. Another Numbers feature is footer rows. You can create footer rows in Numbers that exist independently of the table data. Because Excel does not support footer rows, the export process converts the footer rows into a bottom row on your Excel sheet.

Apple has its own cloud-based collaboration service, iWork.com, that allows you to publish your Numbers sheet to the Web. Other people in your group can review and comment on the data or even download their own Numbers or Excel versions of the data. Although iWork.com is a good first step for Apple, it is not as capable as Google Spreadsheets or Microsoft's Office Web Apps cloud service. The main reason: iWork.com does not host the source file but instead merely provides a copy of it. iWork.com also does not allow multiple users to modify a spreadsheet at the same time. If your co-worker modifies a spreadsheet from iWork.com while you are making changes at the same time on your local copy, there is no easy way to reconcile the different versions.

Still, Apple has succeeded in its goal with iWork Numbers to create a spreadsheet application that is simple to use and visually appealing. Because I so often use spreadsheets in presentations and I want them to be easy to build and look great, I find that Apple's Numbers is the right fit for me.

Google Spreadsheets

Google has its own spreadsheet application as part of the free Google Docs online applications package (http://docs.google.com). Shown in Figure 15-10, Google Spreadsheets is all about collaboration. Multiple users can access and edit the data, with the changes immediately available to everyone. There is no need to e-mail the most recent file or synchronize changes, just log in and open the file. If you are working on a spreadsheet with multiple users in multiple locations, it is hard to beat Google Spreadsheets.

Because it is a cloud-based application, you need an Internet connection for Google Spreadsheets to work. There are some workarounds for offline use, but they all require extra steps and, by their nature, destroy the biggest reason to use the Google Applications: immediate online collaboration.

FIGURE 15-10

Google Spreadsheets

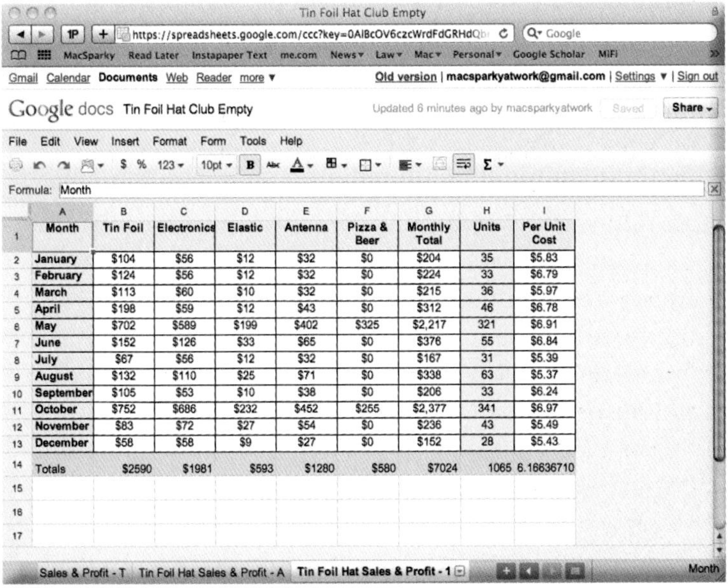

	A	B	C	D	E	F	G	H	I
1	Month	Tin Foil	Electronics	Elastic	Antenna	Pizza & Beer	Monthly Total	Units	Per Unit Cost
2	January	$104	$56	$12	$32	$0	$204	35	$5.83
3	February	$124	$56	$12	$32	$0	$224	33	$6.79
4	March	$113	$60	$10	$32	$0	$215	36	$5.97
5	April	$198	$59	$12	$43	$0	$312	46	$6.78
6	May	$702	$589	$199	$402	$325	$2,217	321	$6.91
7	June	$152	$126	$33	$65	$0	$376	55	$6.84
8	July	$67	$56	$12	$32	$0	$167	31	$5.39
9	August	$132	$110	$25	$71	$0	$338	63	$5.37
10	September	$105	$53	$10	$38	$0	$206	33	$6.24
11	October	$752	$686	$232	$452	$255	$2,377	341	$6.97
12	November	$83	$72	$27	$54	$0	$236	43	$5.49
13	December	$58	$58	$9	$27	$0	$152	28	$5.43
14	Totals	$2590	$1981	$593	$1280	$580	$7024	1065	6.16636710
15									
16									
17									

The user interface is Web-based and thus rudimentary. However, Google is always making improvements and I have no doubt that in the future we'll look back at any productivity application that does not have cloud-based collaboration as quaint.

Except for its superior collaboration tools, Google Spreadsheets does not stack up well against Excel and Numbers; there are simply too many compromises required to make a browser-based spreadsheet application. For example, Google Spreadsheets does not include a deep formula set like Excel or Numbers and does not include Numbers' layout and printing tools. The best use for Google Spreadsheets is a starting point with team members ultimately importing the file into Numbers or Excel for the final push.

OmniGraphSketcher

If you make charts as part of your work, another useful Mac application is OmniGraphSketcher ($30; www.omnigroup.com/products/ omnigraphsketcher). Despite the recent improvements to Numbers' and Excel's charting tools, creating charts and graphs is still often much harder than it should be. For example, if you want to call out one data point on your chart or selectively fill in space in a line chart, it is often not possible to do so without additional editing in a graphics application.

OmniGraphSketcher, shown in Figure 15-11, fills this void by taking graphing out of the spreadsheet. It essentially combines a charting tool with a drawing application. You can quickly create accurate graphs with colorful data sets and highlights, curves, and shading without requiring an advanced degree in mathematics and statistics.

FIGURE 15-11

OmniGraphSketcher

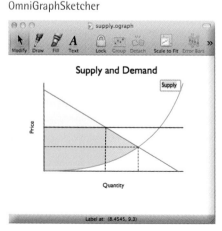

Using OmniGraphSketcher, you can input your own data set or copy data from Numbers or Excel. You can then make your graphs with annotations, shapes, arrows, and check marks. OmniGraphSketcher also makes it easy to export graphics for text-editing, presentation, and other applications.

Databases

D atabase management is the meat and potatoes of workplace computing. Using a database, you can track customers, employees, students, projects, products, inventory, and anything that fits in a list. Databases also occupy a unique position among computer technologies: They were some of the first applications developed for workplace computers so they've been around for a long time. And, because nobody wants to lose their data, databases are probably the single most upgrade-resistant applications in any workplace. Once a company has a working database in place that holds precious company data, it is easier to convince management and IT staff to dynamite the building than to change the database software.

As a result, the database applications and computers that run them are usually the most antiquated in the office. They are difficult to upgrade and modify, and they require copious amounts of consultant time and duct tape to keep going. Fortunately, there are several modern database applications on the Mac. Two of the best are FileMaker Pro and Bento.

FileMaker Pro

FileMaker Pro (starting at $299; www.filemaker.com) is the premier database application on the Mac. Shown in Figure 16-1, FileMaker Pro has long roots on the Mac; in fact, its first Mac OS release was on the original Macintosh. Although initially developed by another company, Apple has long owned and published FileMaker Pro through its old Claris subsidiary or its current FileMaker subsidiary.

FileMaker Pro is a relational database with both Windows and Mac OS X versions. Most commercial database applications are built with two pieces: the database engine (which does all the sorting and storage) and the user interface (which displays the data on computers). FileMaker Pro, as one of the first database applications to embrace the graphical user interface, doesn't split the database engine from the user interface. Instead, it keeps them together, making it possible for users to drag elements of the interface into new forms and layouts. Because of FileMaker Pro's graphical approach, users can adjust and customize

FIGURE 16-1

FileMaker Pro on Mac OS X

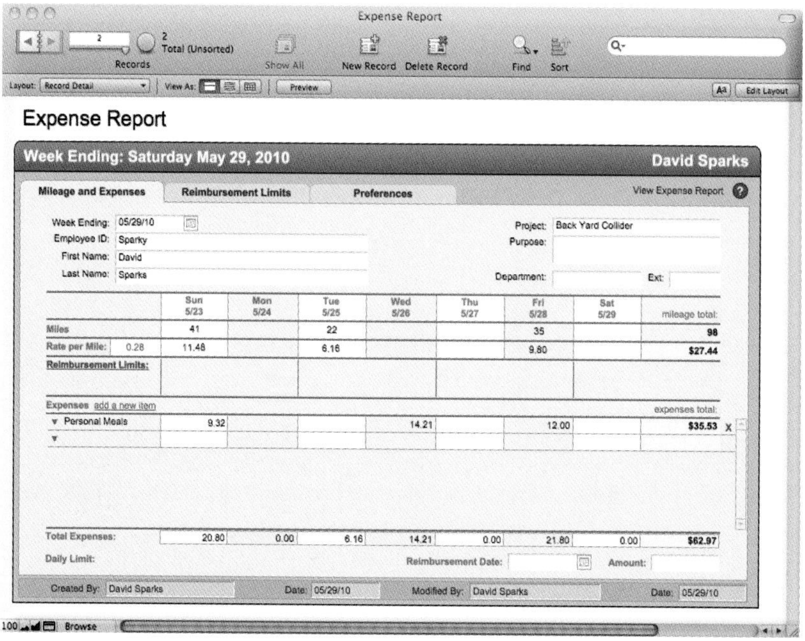

their own database. If you want to change your database, you don't need to call in a database guru to perform special incantations. You can change it yourself.

Using FileMaker Pro

FileMaker Pro ships with more than 30 built-in Starter Solutions that offer a jumping-off point to customize your database. There are several business-friendly Starter Solutions, including expense reporting, customer lists, and inventory tracking. Each template is attractive and professionally designed. The Starter Solution databases are ready for business without any additional work. For example, the invoicing Starter Solution database, shown in Figure 16-2, includes customer and inventory databases and combines them with a tax schedule to create invoices. You can customize the template, but if you just want to get started, everything works out of the box.

If you have an Excel-based spreadsheet "database," you can drag the Excel file onto the FileMaker Pro icon; FileMaker autogenerates a database using the Excel data. You can then add fields and further customize it as needed. This takes much of the pain out of transitioning your databases from spreadsheet to FileMaker Pro.

Whether you start with a template or roll your own database, once you have it set up, FileMaker Pro provides several viewing options. The Table view provides spreadsheet-like columns for each database field, with records listed as rows

FIGURE 16-2

FileMaker Pro's Inventory Starter Solution

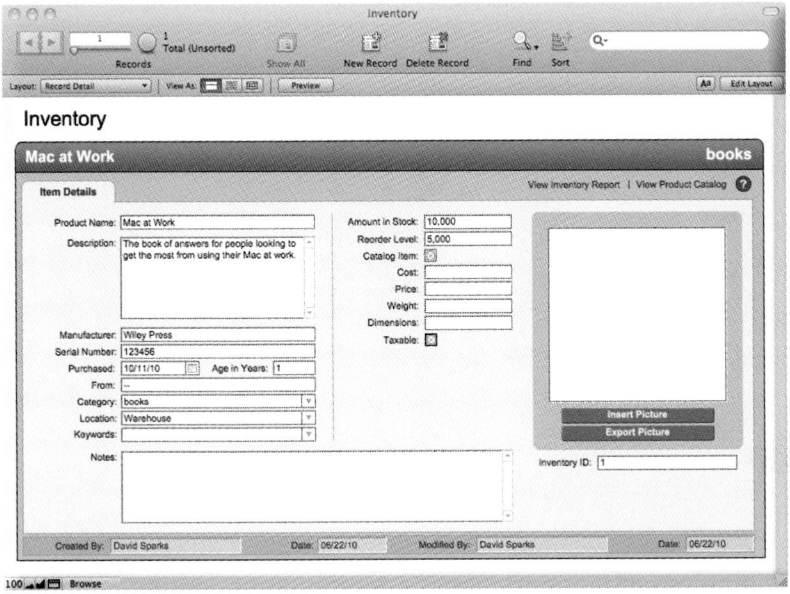

below the field. This view combines the look of a spreadsheet with the sorting capabilities of a database. You can define fields and enter data in Table view. You can even hide or show fields in this view.

The Table view is the default view when you create a new database, which helps with initial organization and record entry. But there are other views: The Form view taps into the FileMaker Pro database but uses a custom screen form to enter and review data. The Layout Mode view allows you to customize the look and feel of your database.

Although FileMaker Pro does not have the computing power of a dedicated spreadsheet application, it does include the functions often needed for a database. For example, you can total sorted groups of records by record state, average, sums, and several other mathematical functions.

You can search all the fields in your FileMaker Pro database using the Quick Find feature, which provides a search bar that quickly searches all the fields in the current layout. Quick Find is helpful when you are not sure which field contains the data you are looking for, and it's faster than using an advanced search.

FileMaker Pro helps you visualize your database with easy chart creation. To create a chart, set your database to Layout Mode view and click Charting Tools to get the dialog box shown in Figure 16-3. You can then choose a chart format and select the data sets you want to chart. It takes just a few minutes;

FIGURE 16-3

Creating charts in FileMaker Pro

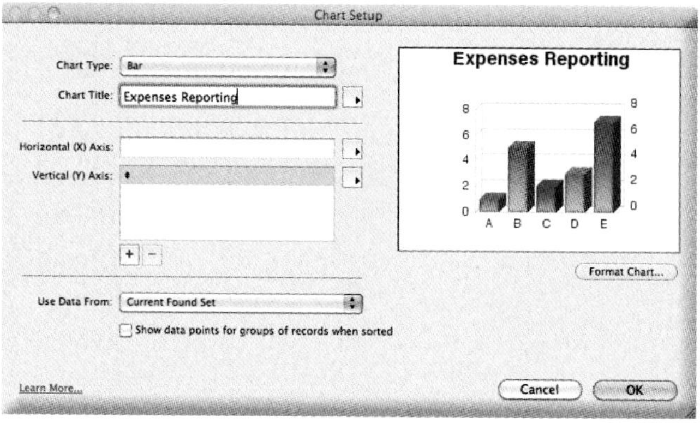

when completed, you have an attractive chart that visually displays your data and updates as you enter new data.

In addition to the ability to make your own database adjustments, graphs, and reports, FileMaker Pro has a plug-in architecture that enables you to add features and custom databases. Although you can manage your FileMaker Pro database yourself, there is an active community of FileMaker Pro developers releasing industry-specific and networking plug-ins. Whether you are manufacturing buggy whips or running a dental office, there is probably a customized FileMaker plug-in for you. FileMaker developers also contract with companies to construct their databases to specific requirements.

Sharing data with FileMaker Pro

Once you've built your database, you will want to share the data. FileMaker Pro has extensive reporting functions that are user-adjustable. You can export it to PDF, Excel, or the Web's HTML format. The Quick Reports feature allows you to make detailed reports without entering the sometimes-intimidating Layout Mode view. If you want more granular control over reporting, the Layout Report Assistant allows you to make custom reports with the data and layout you specify.

FileMaker Pro also includes powerful networking tools. Using its Server editions, you can deploy FileMaker Pro in large companies and share data throughout the network. You can use FileMaker Pro Server to host your database on the Web, allowing remote users to access and modify data from their browsers. It can even be set up for customers to fill in Web forms and automatically update your local FileMaker Pro database. Internally, users can share snapshots of data. A snapshot can contain a specific view of the data, such as a list of customers with orders more than two days old. This allows employees on a network to easily share managed lists.

You can also take your data with you using the FileMakerGo iPad application.

There are four versions of FileMaker Pro. The $299 FileMaker Pro 11 is the standard FileMaker Pro database software covered in this chapter. The $499 FileMaker Pro 11 Advanced version includes more advanced design and layout tools, such as a custom menu user interface and the ability to cut and paste custom functions in your database. Using FileMaker Pro 11 Advanced, you can build a kiosk-style database where users just see the entry form and all menus are hidden.

The $999 FileMaker Pro 11 Server lets you connect as many as 250 users and gives you server management tools such as the ability to manage the database remotely, schedule automatic backups, and automate tasks. You can also share your data with the Web. You can create customer feedback forms or surveys for customers to fill in from the Web. The $2,999 FileMaker Pro 11 Server Advanced allows an unlimited number of users and as many as 100 concurrent Web users. It also provides more administrative tools appropriate for large installations.

In the years since it first appeared on the original Macintosh, FileMaker has matured into a feature-rich database that combines a user-controllable architecture with strong plug-in support. Most remarkable, despite its powerful database engine (FileMaker Pro can manage data files as large as 8TB), the interface has maintained its original vision of making it easy to use and modify.

DATABASES AND SPREADSHEETS

If you have Numbers or Excel on your Mac, you can create a database using spreadsheet tables. But the trouble with using a spreadsheet to manage data is the lack of tools for data management.

Although you can keep a customer list in a Numbers spreadsheet, you cannot filter the data with the same flexibility as with a database application. For example, what if you want all customers who have moved to Wyoming in the last year and have made a purchase in the last nine months? Data sorting and filtering is where a database earns its keep. Spreadsheets just don't have the ability to keep up.

Spreadsheets also do not provide the same network sharing and filtering options that you get with a dedicated database like FileMaker Pro or Bento. Spreadsheets also limit your ability to view the data: Spreadsheets only provide a table view, whereas a database application allows you to create lists and custom forms for displaying your data.

It is possible to manage databases on a spreadsheet, but data management is easier with a dedicated database application. The point is that you should use the right tools for the job. Nothing beats a spreadsheet for computing data, and nothing beats a database for organizing, sorting, and viewing data.

Bento

Small businesses and consultants have database needs, but they often don't need the 8TB capacity and Web-active features that come with FileMaker Pro. For them, FileMaker Pro is overkill. Instead they just want a simple database they can install and start using. For these users, FileMaker publishes Bento.

Bento ($49; www.filemaker.com/bento), shown in Figure 16-4, is a user-friendly database that trades some of FileMaker Pro's power and flexibility for simplicity and ease of use. Despite its limited scope, Bento is useful for getting work done.

Creating a database with Bento

Opening Bento for the first time, you will find 35 professionally designed database templates. The New Library window, shown in Figure 16-5, includes many useful work templates, including inventory, time billing, customers, and issue tracking. Each template can be further customized.

If Bento doesn't include the template you are looking for, you can visit the Bento Template Exchange (shown in Figure 16-6) at http://solutions. filemaker.com/database-templates; it lists user and professionally designed templates for download. The template exchange includes templates such

---

FIGURE 16-4

Bento in Form View mode

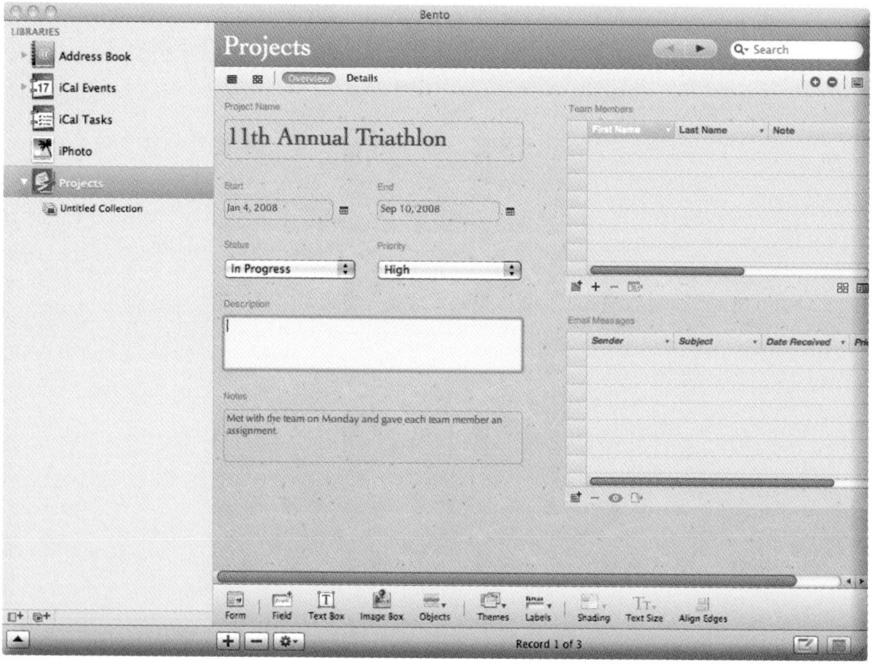

FIGURE 16-5

Bento's New Library window

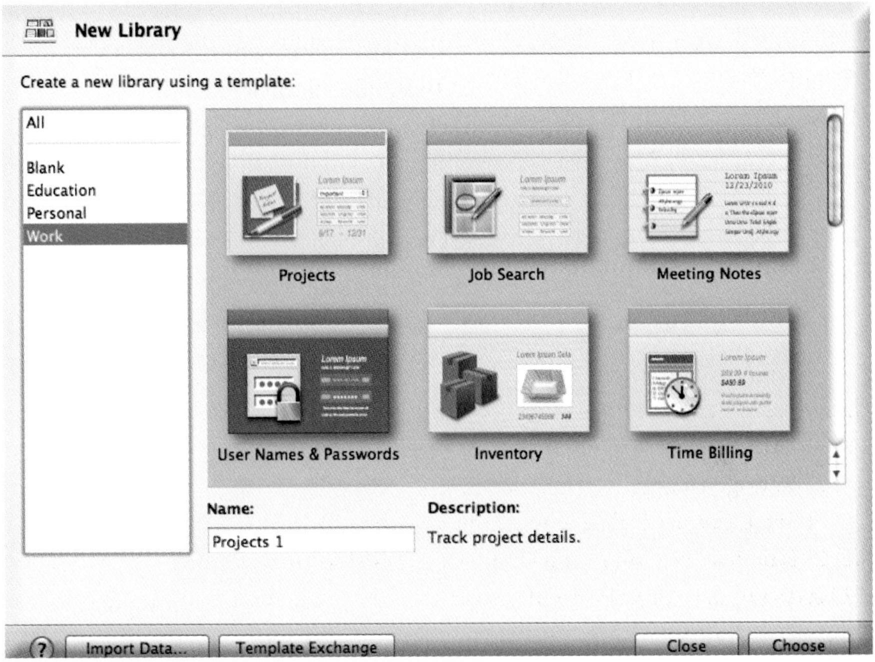

FIGURE 16-6

The Bento Template Exchange

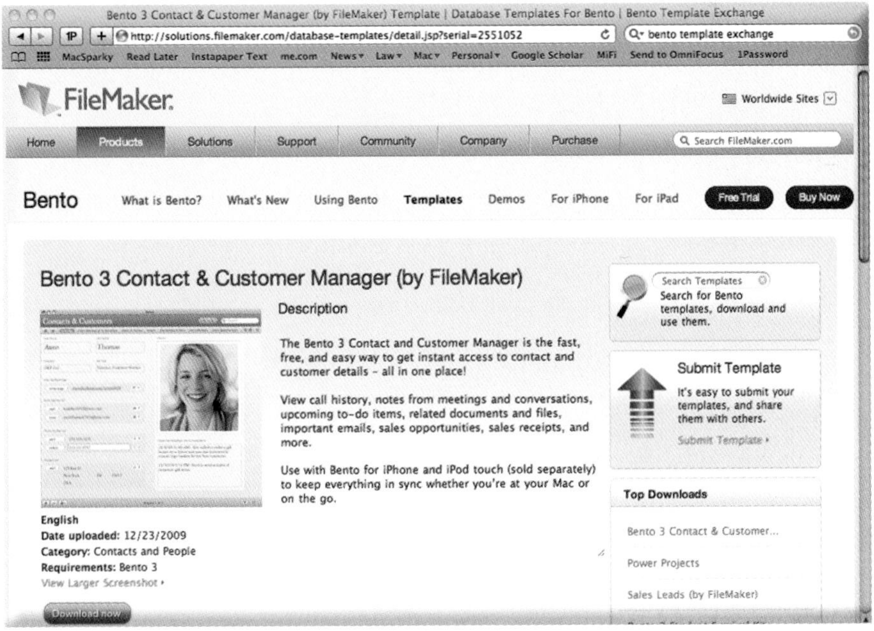

as mail management, sales leads, contact and customer manager, and product research libraries. If you create your own specialized template, you can upload it to the exchange to share with other users.

If you'd rather start from scratch, open the blank template. Customizing or creating a new template is easy in Bento: Click the Form tool in the lower-right corner and begin adding fields to your form. You can also delete, modify, and move fields that are already on your form.

Databases in Bento are called *libraries*. Rather than reloading a different database every time you need access, Bento keeps a list of all your libraries in its left pane. For example, you can have your customer list library right above your supplier and inventory libraries. You can then jump among the libraries with one click; you do not need to separately load and close your Bento libraries. As long as the application is running, all your libraries are available.

When working with libraries, Bento uses a two-pane window similar to that in iTunes. In addition to displaying your libraries, the left pane also displays *collections*, which (following the iTunes metaphor) are record clusters within libraries. Building collections inside your Bento libraries allows you to further refine your database and make it more manageable. You can add a collection to a library by Control+clicking or right-clicking on the library to display the

FIGURE 16-7

Bento showing a library in Table View

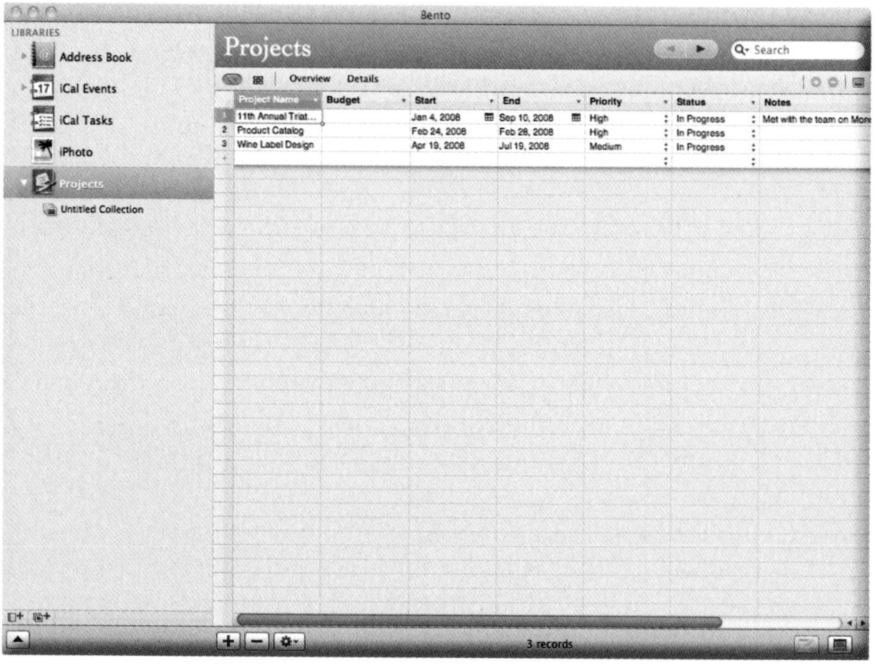

contextual menu, from which you choose the New Collection option to create the collection. For example, if you have an address book library, you can have a collection that just includes customers.

You can add records to the collection by dragging them from the library. You can also create "smart" collections that populate with records based on the conditions you set (just like Mac OS X, iTunes, and Apple Mail let you create smart folders, smart playlists, and smart mailboxes, respectively).

The right pane in the Bento library window is the Records pane where you access and modify the data in your libraries. The records can be displayed in Table View, as Figure 16-7 shows, or in Form View, as Figure 16-4 shows. There is also the Grid View that displays a thumbnail for each record and the Split View that mixes two views (for example, Table View and Grid View) in one window. Bento simplifies database management by tying together your libraries, records, and fields in one interface.

Data fields

Fields are the basic building blocks of a database. A field is a lot like Tupperware: You have different kinds of Tupperware containers for different kinds of food. The Tupperware is not the food but simply where you hold the food. Fields serve the same function with data: They are not the data you put in the database but instead the containers for it. You have different types of data — such as dates, numbers, and names — so Bento has a lot of different field types, as shown in the Create a Field dialog box in Figure 16-8.

In addition to the usual text, dates, and numbers, Bento includes fields for time, currency, and rating. The Rating field allows you to grade a record with up to five stars. On first glance, the Rating field doesn't seem useful for work, but it can be: You can use it to rate sales leads or new product ideas and later sort in order of rating.

You can also create a Media field in Bento to hold images, video, and sounds. If you have customers in your iPhoto database, for example, you can display them in your Bento database on the customer contact form. There are also several Internet fields, including URL, Email Address, and IM Account.

You can use the Checkbox field to create filters for items such as a company holiday card list. The Simple List field creates a list in your database. The File List field allows you to make a list of files. You can, for example, keep a list of artwork for a customer account in a File List. Double-clicking the file name in the File List opens the file in its associated application.

Bento also simplifies data entry with the Choice field that creates a pop-up menu limiting data entry to a group of predefined options. The Calculation field manipulates existing fields similar to how a spreadsheet's formulas work on cells.

FIGURE 16-8

Adding a field to a Bento database

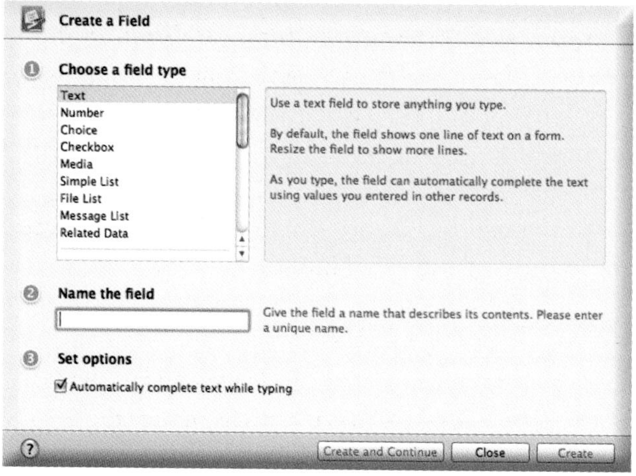

Create a Field

① **Choose a field type**

Text
Number
Choice
Checkbox
Media
Simple List
File List
Message List
Related Data

Use a text field to store anything you type.

By default, the field shows one line of text on a form. Resize the field to show more lines.

As you type, the field can automatically complete the text using values you entered in other records.

② **Name the field**

Give the field a name that describes its contents. Please enter a unique name.

③ **Set options**

☑ Automatically complete text while typing

(?)　　　Create and Continue　　Close　　Create

For example, you can use the Calculation field to combine a first and last name into a single field or to perform basic math operations.

Once you have created your database and set up the fields, you can customize the look of the database by dragging the individual fields from the field list in the lower left pane onto your database layout. It is as simple as that: Click and drag. You can add and remove fields and add bits of text or graphical elements to make your form easier to follow and more attractive. You can also change texture and colors of your library using the Theme button in the Form Tools bar at the bottom of the screen.

Making a database in Bento can be a pleasant distraction. Just make sure to remember to start filling in your data at some point.

FIGURE 16-9

The Bento Sharing preferences pane

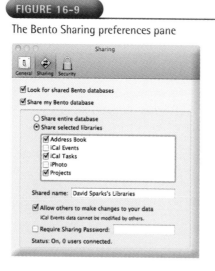

Sharing

General　Sharing　Security

☑ Look for shared Bento databases
☑ Share my Bento database

　○ Share entire database
　⊙ Share selected libraries

　　☑ Address Book
　　☐ iCal Events
　　☑ iCal Tasks
　　☐ iPhoto
　　☑ Projects

Shared name:　David Sparks's Libraries

☑ Allow others to make changes to your data
　iCal Events data cannot be modified by others.

☐ Require Sharing Password:

Status: On, 0 users connected.

Sharing Bento libraries

You can share your Bento libraries with as many as five users on your network. Users can then view and modify the data in your library based on the permissions you set in the Bento Sharing preferences pane, shown in Figure 16-9. (For user sharing to work, each user must have his or her own Bento license.)

Bento also has versions available for the iPhone, iPod Touch, and iPad that allow you to use your database on the go. Using the mobile editions, you can view, edit, and add new records to your Bento data remotely. When you sync your device back to Bento, it adds any changes to your library.

Enhancing Mac OS X applications

Bento also adds some much needed functionality to Apple's Address Book and iCal. If you use these applications, Bento may be worth its cost for these features alone.

The Bento Address Book template ties into the Mac OS X's built-in Address Book database. This means the Apple Address Book and Bento share the same contact data. If you make a change to a phone number in Address Book (or on your iPhone tied to your MobileMe account or synced via iTunes), the next time you launch Bento, that changed number is reflected in your Bento library. It works in both directions: If you update an e-mail address in your Bento library, it is reflected in Address Book.

You can customize the data layout in Bento in ways not possible with Address Book. Rather than being forced to display your contact entries one record at a time, you can display them in a tabular format. You can also add new data fields. For example, you can place a check box labeled Vendors or Customers in Bento and then sort your list using those values.

Bento is one of those tools that either works spectacularly or fails entirely. Bento's simple interface and low cost makes it perfect for a small business or consultant practice. Bento falls down, however, when you need database features such as networking with large groups, Web hosting, and the customization tools found in FileMaker Pro.

Whether you want to organize a customer list for your home crafting business or manage 8TB of data for a global product release, there is a database on the Mac for you.

Project Management

C hapter 9 is full of great tools to help you manage tasks and projects. Managing teams, however, is different: You must manage deadlines, collaborative resources, and, most important, time. Scheduling large groups of people can be daunting: Certain tasks are always contingent on the completion of other tasks. A setback in one small part of the project can send shock waves down the entire project plan, resulting in delays and more expenses.

Because of the contingent nature of each piece in a project plan, there can be a lot of calculation and rejiggering of schedules involved. This is exactly the kind of tedium that computers manage. And you'll find many project management tools available for the Mac, in both desktop application and online varieties.

Desktop Project Management

As you dip your toes in the world of Web-based software, there are good reasons to keep your project management software on your desktop. Desktop applications are usually more secure, because the data is normally located on local drives and not available on the Internet. Furthermore, desktop applications are built using Apple's Mac development software, so they usually have more features and always look better. Two of my favorite Mac OS X project management applications are OmniPlan and FastTrack Schedule.

OmniPlan

OmniPlan ($150; www.omnigroup.com/products/omniplan) comes from Omni Group, which is regarded as one of the best Macintosh productivity software companies. Indeed, the Omni Group software appears several times in this book, including OmniOutliner (see Chapter 10), OmniFocus (see Chapter 9), and OmniGraphSketcher (see Chapter 15). Its software is known for its stability and clean interfaces.

OmniPlan, shown in Figure 17-1, lives up to the Omni Group's reputation. Project management software is legendary for a steep learning curve, and many applications are so complicated that you have no hope of operating them without several days of training. This is not the case with OmniPlan.

FIGURE 17-1

OmniPlan's main window

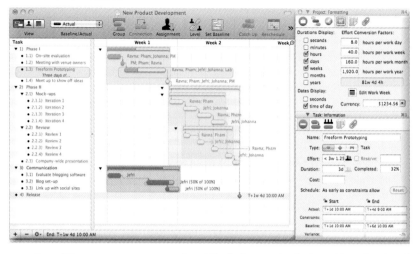

OmniPlan uses a two-pane view. The left pane includes a list of tasks while the right pane lays out a Gantt chart (see the sidebar "How Henry Gantt Became Famous") showing the start and end dates for each task. The first time you open OmniPlan, a new project is already created with the first task entry.

Adding new tasks in OmniPlan is simply a matter of clicking in the Task pane, pressing Enter, and typing in your new tasks. When starting from scratch on any large project, it's a good idea to brainstorm in the Task pane and create a long list of all the relevant tasks. Once you have your list of tasks, you can sort and reorganize them by clicking and dragging on any task entry. You can also group tasks by selecting multiple tasks and clicking the Group iconic button in the toolbar or pressing Option+⌘+L. The objective is to have your tasks in chronological order and grouped appropriately. Like OmniFocus and

HOW HENRY GANTT BECAME FAMOUS

Virtually all self-respecting project management applications include a Gantt chart function. So what is a Gantt chart anyway? Around 1910, Henry Gantt designed a new type of chart that included a list of tasks to be completed with a line representing the start and end date for each task. Productivity nerds loved the idea and immediately adopted it. They were so thankful that they named the chart after Henry.

Gantt charts really came into their own with the arrival of computers with graphical user interfaces (like the Mac). Computers automate the labor-intensive process of laying out Gantt charts and making adjustments when the inevitable delay occurs.

FIGURE 17-2

Sorting tasks and assigning time estimates in OmniPlan

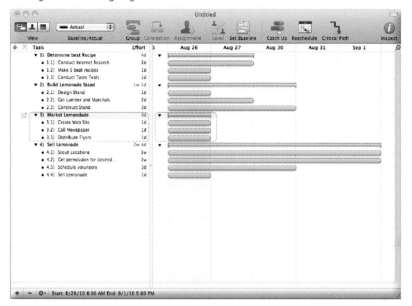

OmniOutliner, OmniPlan has a note field for each entry where you can enter detailed notes concerning any particular task.

Once you have an outline of all the steps in your project, you add a time estimate for each task. At this point, you are not worried about *when* any particular task will be completed but instead *how long* each task will take. You do the estimation in the Task pane, under the Effort column or in the Task inspector, shown in Figure 17-2. It is easiest to enter the time estimates directly in the Task pane. Using the inspector requires several extra clicks for each entry. When inserting time estimates, you can use a type of shorthand: 3d for three days, 2w for two weeks, and 1w3d for one week and three days, for example. At this stage, your project plan should look something like Figure 17-2.

You can also input costs for each task in the Task inspector. Depending on your type of business, this could be material costs, labor, or both. Although OmniPlan includes support for costs, it is primarily a scheduling tool. The calculation of costs is better done in a spreadsheet like Microsoft Excel or iWork Numbers (covered in Chapter 15). Nevertheless, those amounts can be referenced in your OmniPlan.

Once you have your list of tasks and an estimate as to how long each task will take, OmniPlan needs to know which tasks must wait for the completion of other tasks, called *dependencies*. For example, in Figure 17-3, the group of tasks called Sell Lemonade, is dependent on the group of tasks called Build Lemonade Stand. In OmniPlan you create dependencies by selecting two tasks and clicking

FIGURE 17-3

Creating task dependencies in OmniPlan

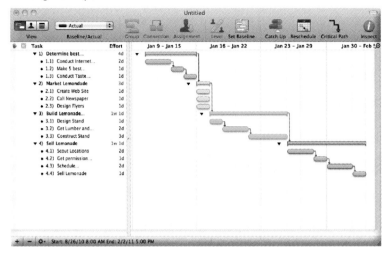

the Connection iconic button in the toolbar, by pressing Control+⌘+=, or by dragging an arrow from one task to another. Once you do this, OmniPlan moves the second task to begin at the conclusion of the first task and draws a line between the two. You can have dependencies between two individual tasks, two groups of tasks, or any combination of the two.

OmniPlan provides several ways to customize the dependencies. You can create prioritizations in the dependencies in relation to material supplies. For example, you could relate the Make Lemonade group with the acquisition of lemons. As you create dependencies, OmniPlan builds a Gantt chart that graphically shows each task. OmniPlan will schedule the entire project using your estimates and dependencies. Alternatively, you can set the finish date and have OmniPlan schedule backward, based on your estimates and dependencies. The OmniPlan Gantt chart in Figure 17-3 shows an example: If you plan to become a captain of industry in the lemonade business and you want to open your stand on February 5, you need to start on January 9.

In addition to scheduling tasks, OmniPlan lets you schedule people. You can assign individual team members to tasks. OmniPlan tracks each person and their assignments in the background and makes certain you don't have any of your team members working on two tasks at the same time. (To assign team members, switch to Resource view by choosing View ▶ Resource View or pressing Option+⌘+2.)

Once in Resource view, the task list in the left pane is replaced with a resource list. You can enter your resources the same way you add tasks. Type the team member or resource name and press Return. Resource view lets you see a convenient list of all your team members and their contributions as shown in Figure 17-4.

FIGURE 17-4

OmniPlan's Resource view

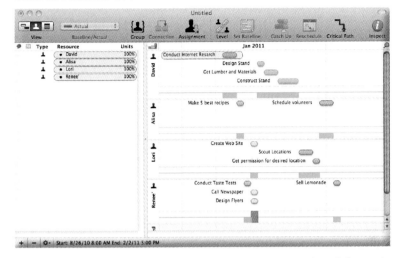

In addition to project planning, OmniPlan is a good tool for project management. Using OmniPlan, you can track the progress of all the tasks in your project as it progresses. Project management with OmniPlan enables you to anticipate problems ahead of time and schedule time and resources accordingly as you move forward.

You can also share your OmniPlan, so multiple team members can access the OmniPlan data at once and make changes and adjustments to it. OmniPlan tracks the changes and lets the project administrator review and approve (or reject) the changes later. OmniPlan also has an iPad application that can access the OmniPlan data. (There is no Windows PC version of OmniPlan, so to modify the OmniPlan data, users must have a Mac or an iPad.) OmniPlan can save your data file to the Internet using a MobileMe account or WebDAV server. (WebDAV is a protocol that allows you to share files using Internet servers.)

OmniPlan also offers several export options to share data. It exports to Microsoft Project, iCal, HTML, OmniOutliner, OmniGraffle, and PDF. Most of my staff uses Windows computers, so I regularly export OmniPlan data to PDF to share it with them.

FastTrack Schedule

FastTrack Schedule ($350; www.aecsoftware.com/project-management-software/fasttrack-schedule-mac) is another desktop project management tool on the Mac. (The networked five-user version costs $3,000.) Shown in Figure 17-5, FastTrack Schedule has both Mac and Windows versions.

FIGURE 17-5

FastTrack Schedule's main window

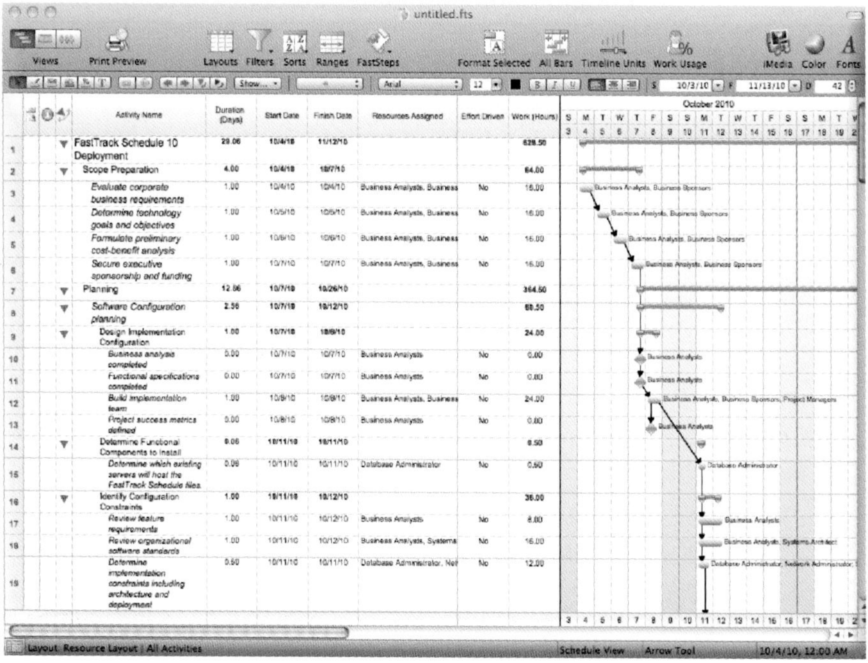

The workflow in FastTrack Schedule is similar to that of OmniPlan, covered earlier in this chapter: You create a list of tasks, set dependencies, and assign resources. FastTrack Schedule includes additional features worth noting.

One additional feature is FastTrack Schedule's inclusion of project templates. These are a great way to get a head start on planning a new project. The templates include varied projects that range from construction management to wedding planning. FastTrack Schedule also has an online depository with more project templates at www.aecsoftware.com/resources/project-management-templates.

While in the midst of a project, you sometimes need to change team members' assignments. FastTrack Schedule's Effort-Driven Scheduling automatically adjusts task durations as resources are added (or removed). If, for example, you realize a project is behind schedule, you can throw more resources at a lagging task in FastTrack Schedule and see how that would impact the schedule before committing to it.

The Assignment Contouring feature, shown in Figure 17-6, analyzes the most labor-intensive portions of a task and helps you assign staff when they are needed most, based on the contour of the resource requirements. For example, a bell-contoured task requires more labor in the middle of execution whereas a front-

FIGURE 17-6

Assignment contouring in FastTrack Schedule

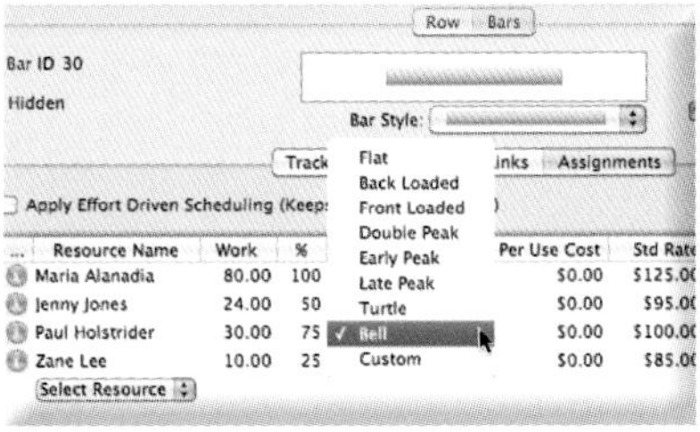

loaded task requires more staff at the beginning. Using Assignment Contouring and FastTrack Schedule, you can predict the particular labor needs of any task.

Despite the fact that it is multiplatform, FastTrack Schedule takes advantage of several Mac OS X conventions: It integrates with the built-in Address Book and also uses FastTrack Schedule's own iMedia browser (which keeps images in a pop-up window) to apply images to your project plan. Overall, it very much *feels* like a Mac application.

If you are working in a multiplatform office, FastTrack Schedule is the best tool. If you're a Mac-only office, take a careful look at both OmniPlan and FastTrack Schedule. In my experience, OmniPlan is easier to get up and running but lacks some of the features offered by FastTrack Schedule. Both applications are well-designed, are stable, and have a free trial period.

WORKING WITH MICROSOFT PROJECT

The most used project management application in Windows is Microsoft Project. Many large companies have employees whose sole job is managing Microsoft Project data files. If your office lives and breathes by Microsoft Project, you have several options on the Mac.

Both OmniPlan and FastTrack Schedule can import and export their data files to Microsoft Project with varying degrees of success — the conversion process can cause loss of data, and specific features in Microsoft Project do not always translate.

For general project management, exporting to Microsoft Project should do the trick. However, if you find the exported files do not have all the required information, the best solution is to run Microsoft Project on your Mac. Although there is no Mac OS X version of Microsoft Project, you can run the Windows version using desktop virtualization software (covered in Chapter 22). Microsoft Project is not resource-intensive and thus can run just fine in a virtual environment on a modern Macintosh.

Web Tools

In addition to desktop tools, there is a growing crop of Web-based project management software. Web-based project management applications share their data in a centralized database available to all team members given access. Because they are browser-based, these tools eliminate all compatibility problems across different computing platforms.

Web-based project management software is still in its infancy and generally does not have the exhaustive feature sets available in applications such as OmniPlan and FastTrack Schedule. However, what they lack in features, they make up in collaboration. Two of my favorite Web-based project management applications are 37signals' Basecamp and Tom's Planner.

Basecamp

Basecamp (starting at $24 per month; `www.basecamphq.com`), shown in Figure 17-7, seeks to provide one centralized location for all elements of project management.

The Web service includes modules to share communications between teams. Instead of tracking multiple e-mail chains, Basecamp has a centralized message board where all team members can share information. Basecamp also can prepare and mail a daily digest of all communications to team members.

Basecamp provides a depository for documents. Team members can upload to it Microsoft Office documents (including Word, Excel, and PowerPoint), Photoshop documents, movies, Zip files, and PDFs. Everyone with access to the Basecamp project can download and review the shared documents. It also includes version tracking so if a team member modifies a document and uploads it back to the Basecamp project, both versions are available to team members.

Basecamp has scheduling modules to track project deadlines and milestones. Like more traditional project management applications, you can track each task related to a project and who is responsible for getting it done.

Basecamp also includes several features not found in traditional Gantt chart-style project managers, such as tracking team members' time. This feature, which is normally associated with financial management software (covered in Chapter 18), is an interesting addition to project management software. It is, however, only available in the higher-tier Basecamp pricing plans (those starting at $50 per month).

Basecamp also includes other innovative features such as writeboards, which allows members to collaboratively write text documents, and Campfire, which is a useful group chat tool that works within Basecamp projects.

FIGURE 17-7

Basecamp project management

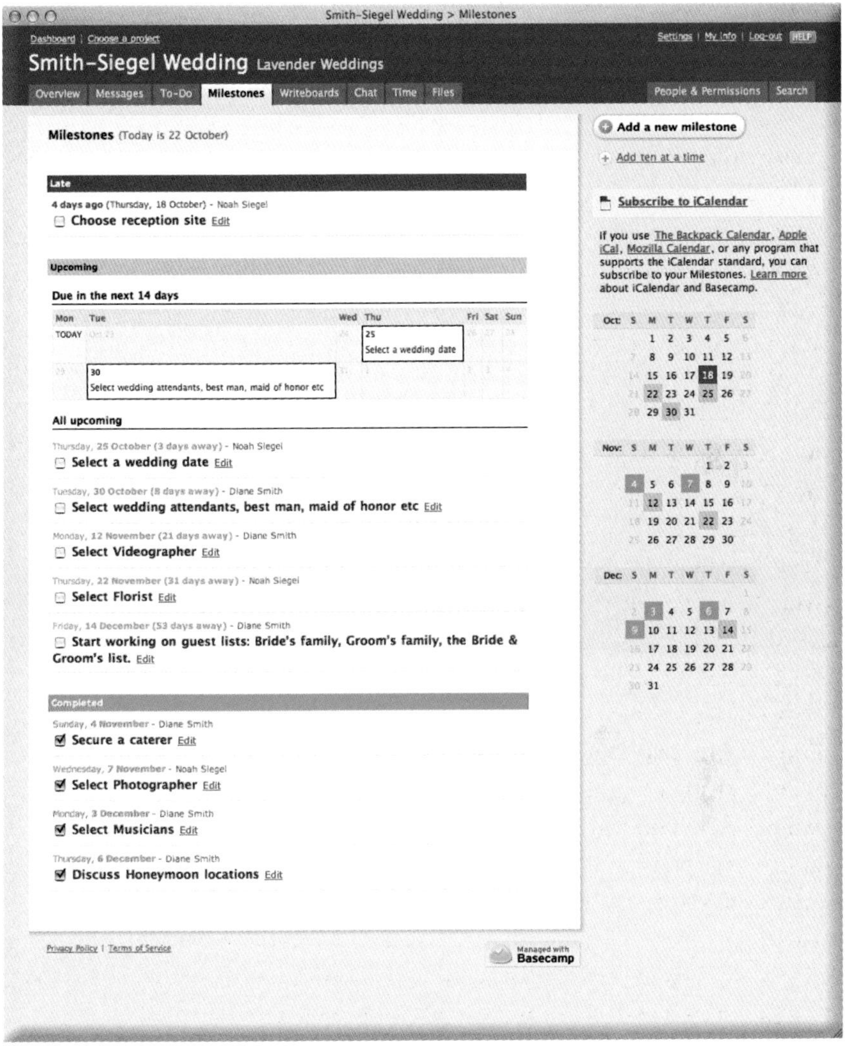

What makes Basecamp so interesting are its innovative features and fresh take on project management. There is nothing else like it. When combined with 37signals' Highrise Web-based contact management service (www.highrisehq.com), it provides a powerful management tool for small to medium companies.

Tom's Planner

Tom's Planner (www.tomsplanner.com) is a no-nonsense Web-based Gantt chart project management tool. It is free if you just have one project. You

FIGURE 17-8

Tom's Planner project management

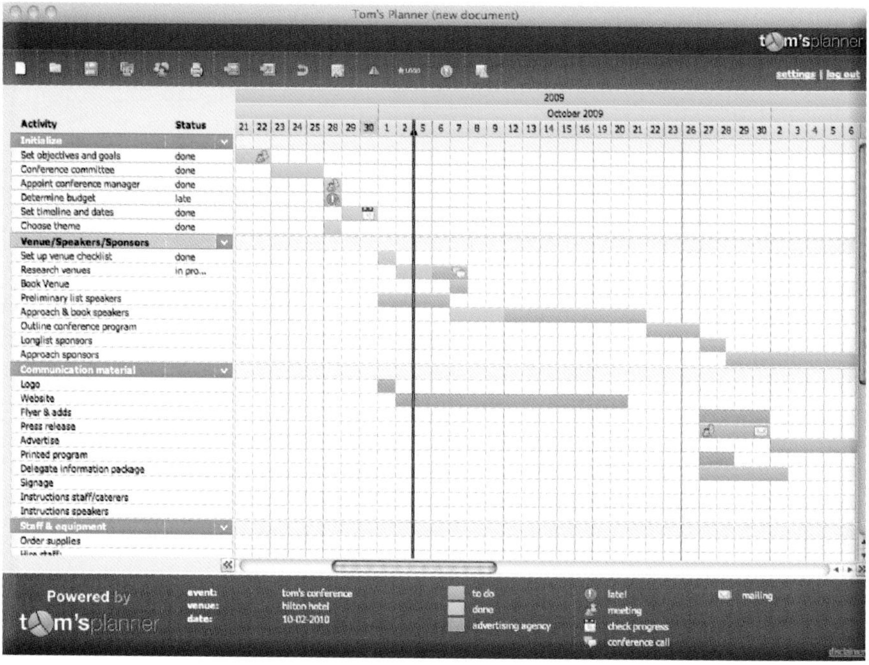

can have up to 20 projects for $9 a month, and an unlimited number of projects for $19 a month.

Shown in Figure 17-8, Tom's Planner lacks much of the sophistication and polish of OmniPlan and FastTrack Schedule. Nonetheless, it is absurdly easy to use. Furthermore, as a Web-based application, you can access it from any computer.

As Figure 17-8 shows, Tom's Planner tracks project task, resources, and status all in one view. You simply Control+click or right-click on a task item to make adjustments to the task list. You can change or add new tasks, and adjust the timing and dependencies of specific tasks by dragging and dropping the task on the Gantt chart. Tom's Planner is very intuitive: If you have no interest in learning the more sophisticated tools available in OmniPlan or FastTrack Schedule, spend five minutes with Tom's Planner and you may find that it has all the project planning tools you need.

Whether you are planning a new Web site or managing a multimillion-dollar construction project, the project management tools on the Mac are up to the task.

18

Billing and Invoicing

U sing the applications in this book, you are doing some great work on your Mac. So how about getting paid? That's where billing and invoicing software comes in, to track your product (whatever that may be) and who pays for it. There are several Mac products to do so, including accounting packages, which manage all the financial aspects of your business, to more focused packages that track just your time. This chapter looks at some of the best billing and invoicing options and answers the question of what to do if you are working in an office that requires QuickBooks for Windows.

QuickBooks

QuickBooks, published by Intuit Software, is the default billing and invoicing software package for most small and medium companies. Just like most graphics designers learn their trade on a Mac, most bookkeepers and CPAs learn the ropes using QuickBooks on a Windows PC.

QuickBooks for Mac ($200; `http://quickbooks.intuit.com/ product/accounting-software/mac-accounting-software`) is Intuit's Mac-friendly version of QuickBooks. QuickBooks has an erratic history on the Mac. For the longest time, QuickBooks on the Mac felt like a poor quality port of prior releases of QuickBooks for Windows. Most Mac offices that relied on QuickBooks kept around one Windows PC for no other reason but to run QuickBooks. Indeed, some Mac offices *still* do this.

More recently, Intuit tried to close the gap between the Mac and Windows versions with QuickBooks 2009 for Mac. With this release, Intuit scrapped the prior code and started over. QuickBooks was rewritten for the Mac — and the results bear that out: The application was suddenly more Mac-like. However, although Intuit definitely gave the application a new coat of paint in QuickBooks 2009, the software remained a clunker under the hood: Several features that are staples on the Windows version (multiple users, credit card processing, and cross-platform data files, and online bill pay) were left out.

The current iteration, QuickBooks 2011 (shown in Figure 18-1), improves on these deficiencies, but not enough. The new version does provide for

FIGURE 18-1

QuickBooks for Mac

in-application credit card processing and multiple users but several features, as covered later in this chapter, are still missing.

QuickBooks 2011 for Mac eases new account setup with a streamlined process that lets you start a new file in minutes. Intuit also added improved support for new users with Guide Me, a virtual helper that walks you through how to set up and maintain your books. Guide Me will be a big help with the initial learning curve for new users.

QuickBooks lets you track inventory, expenses, and income. Using its tools, you can issue payroll checks and client invoices. It is intended to be a complete business accounting tool, and so has more than 100 customizable reports to analyze your data. The application speeds up monthly reporting by remembering your favorite report formats. Intuit also added a time-tracking module to QuickBooks, called My Time, where you can bill time directly to projects and clients. For MobileMe subscribers, QuickBooks can automatically back up your data file to the MobileMe cloud storage service.

Although QuickBooks for Mac is better than it used to be, it falls down with its continuing inability to match features in the Windows version. QuickBooks for Mac 2011 still does not allow online bill-pay, or have a file format compatible with the Windows version.

QuickBooks Online Edition

Because nearly all bookkeepers and CPAs speak QuickBooks and nearly all are using Windows computers, it is important that the QuickBooks for Mac data file is readable by QuickBooks on Windows. You need to be able to share your files and send a copy of your data to your CPA for review. Unfortunately, QuickBooks for Mac doesn't use the same data file type as QuickBooks for Windows, but instead offers a very convoluted file-sharing process: You have to click the Windows Backup toolbar icon in QuickBooks for Mac and export your .mac.qbb Mac file as a .qbb Windows file. You can then import the .qbb file on a Windows PC to work with QuickBooks for Windows. When finished working on Windows, you have to then save the file for QuickBooks for Mac (.mac.qbb) and then, back on your Mac, restore the file. There are multiple steps (and opportunities for data corruption) involved.

The best reason to use QuickBooks is its near-universal adoption in the Windows world but Intuit still hasn't released a Mac version that easily works with its Windows cousin. It's baffling.

An interesting development is Intuit's recent release of QuickBooks Online Edition (www.quickbooksonline.intuit.com). This is a hosted version of QuickBooks accessed through your browser for a monthly fee, starting at $10 per month. Although the online edition does not have as many features as a locally installed version of QuickBooks, it does solve the disparity between Windows and Mac versions. Plus, your offsite accountant can access the data. QuickBooks Online Edition is shown in Figure 18-2.

QuickBooks Online works with both Mozilla Firefox and Apple Safari (both are covered in Chapter 4). QuickBooks Online data can also be accessed with iOS (iPhone, iPad, and iPod Touch), BlackBerry, and Android smartphone operating systems. Although the idea of keeping a company's financial records with an online service may leave some managers running for the hills, most people's banking information is already online in one form or another, so putting financial management online is not as much of a stretch as it may first seem.

Still, most businesses will insist on using locally installed software. For them, until Intuit improves QuickBooks for Mac, the software is not worth the trouble. Go elsewhere: If you do not need QuickBooks for Windows compatibility, there are better tools available on Mac OS X (as covered in this chapter). If you are working with QuickBooks to share data with Windows users, you are better off installing a Windows virtual machine on your Mac (covered in Chapter 22) and just running QuickBooks for Windows on your Mac or using the QuickBooks Online service.

AccountEdge

Acclivity (formerly called MYOB) is an accounting software company with several products for Mac OS X. Acclivity AccountEdge ($299; www. accountedge.com/mac) is Acclivity's flagship product, business accounting software built from the ground up for the Mac. Where QuickBooks has suffered from years of Intuit's changing priorities on the Mac, AccountEdge has steadily improved to provide solid business accounting for the Mac.

AccountEdge, shown in Figure 18-3, manages the financial aspects of a small to medium business with tools to manage employee wages, pay bills, create invoices, and track inventory.

Like QuickBooks, AccountEdge tries to help with the initial learning curve. The New Company File Assistant lets you choose from 100 editable business

GETTING HELP WITH ACCOUNTING

Whether you use AccountEdge or QuickBooks, simply buying a license and installing the software usually is not enough. Although QuickBooks and AccountEdge do a valiant job of explaining accounting principles with their tutorials, there is no accounting software package that can automatically bestow on you the underlying principles required to properly use it. That's why, no matter which accounting package you use on your Mac, it is important you have an understanding of how accounting works.

Just as important, you need to work with your accounting professional to do the initial software setup. Getting off on the right foot makes all the difference. If you enter the data wrong, your accounting fees to sort it all out will eclipse any license fees for the software.

FIGURE 18-3

Acclivity AccountEdge for Mac

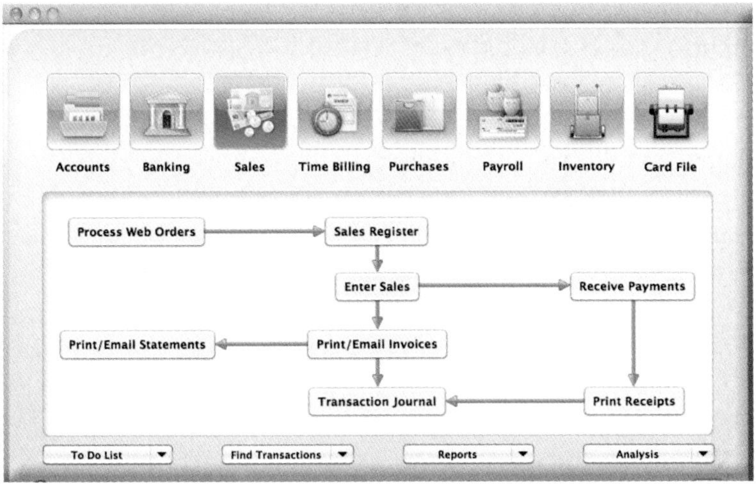

templates. Alternatively, you can start your accounting file from scratch. AccountEdge also has an Accounting 101 Guide to help with setup.

AccountEdge handles all financial aspects of your business. You can create sales quotes and invoices using its built-in forms or customize your own. The application supports print and e-mail forms, so you can electronically communicate with your customers. In addition to taking orders, AccountEdge tracks your accounts payable. It can track taxes, discounts, and returns. AccountEdge lets you make electronic vendor payments and even create the necessary federal tax forms. The inventory tools are also impressive: You can track inventory in multiple locations, check shipments against purchases, and keep digital reference photos.

The time-billing component is customizable with multiple billing rates and can track chargeable and non-chargeable time. There are also several time-billing reports that let you track productivity. You can enter time manually or use the built-in timer. The employee payroll tools include withholdings, allowances, and bonuses. Employee wages can be calculated by set hours or time sheets. AccountEdge also interfaces with outside payroll services.

AccountEdge includes more than 200 reports that show key financial indicators for your business, including profit margins, inventory, and receivables. The reports' formatting looks better than the comparable reports in QuickBooks.

The security features go beyond a simple login password. The trouble with having login-based security in business accounting software is that employees who get *any* access get *all* the access to the data. To prevent that, AccountEdge lets you set security within the application. For example, an employee can have access to

PERSONAL FINANCE

You can also manage your personal finances on the Mac. Quicken, published by Intuit, has a Mac version, Quicken Essentials for Mac ($50; quicken.intuit.com/personal-finance-software/mac-personal-financial-software.jsp), but again the Mac version's features trail behind the Windows version.

One of the better personal finance applications is iBank ($60; www.iggsoftware.com/ibank), which connects directly with your bank and does its best to automatically categorize your transactions. iBank also includes the best reporting and investment tracking tools of all the Mac personal financing software applications.

One of the most interesting developments in personal financial management is the rise of the Web-based money manager Mint (www.mint.com). Mint interfaces with your financial institutions, so you can manage your expenses and income from any computer with Web access. Mint was so successful that Intuit bought it. The security concerns of online financial management aside, Mint's success indicates people are ready to move their financial management to the Web. In the end, Web-based financial management may put an end once and for all to the disparity between Intuit's Mac and Windows-based software.

inventory data but no access to personal data about employees. AccountEdge also tracks all changes so you can see who made what changes and when.

AccountEdge has a network version ($300; www.accountedge.com/mac/networkedition) that supports as many as 15 simultaneous users (its client licenses cost $150 each or five for $500). Acclivity also has a Windows edition ($300; www.accountedge.com/windows). If your accountant doesn't use AccountEdge, Acclivity will send him or her a free copy.

AccountEdge also embraces AppleScript automation. (AppleScript is covered in Chapter 24.) Even if you are not an AppleScript guru, AppleScript automation support can still benefit you because third-party software developers use AppleScript code to link applications. For example, Marketcircle (makers of Daylite, covered in Chapter 6) publish AccountEdge Connect ($99; www.marketcircle.com/daylite/addons/accountedgeconnector.html) that connects AccountEdge data to Daylite.

Acclivity also publishes FirstEdge ($100; www.firstedgeapp.com/firstedge), which includes AccountEdge's quotes, invoices, and expenses modules. It does not, however, handle payroll, inventory, and time-billing.

Acclivity gets the Mac in a way that Intuit has yet to demonstrate. It has steadily developed an accounting package for the Mac that, for most small to medium companies, just works.

Billings

QuickBooks and AccountEdge are the kitchen-sink class of financial software. They track everything you need for your business including costs, time, customers, and invoices. Marketcircle's Billings ($40; www.marketcircle.com/billings) does not boast the full accounting features of QuickBooks and AccountEdge but instead is limited to time billings often used by accountants, attorneys, artists, and other professionals. If time is your stock in trade, Billings may be all you need.

Billings, shown in Figure 18-4, is a well-designed Mac OS X application that borrows the iTunes interface paradigm, with projects and accounts in the left pane and data in the right pane.

Billings interfaces with the Apple Address Book (covered in Chapter 6) to manage your clients; Billings creates an Address Book group containing all your clients. Using Address Book for client contacts lets you use MobileMe syncing with an iPhone, iPad, or iPod Touch or with another Mac; you can also use Address Book's Google and Yahoo sync tools to automatically synchronize your contacts with other devices (see Chapter 6).

There are several ways to track your time in Billings. You can track time from inside the application or use a menu bar timer, which makes it easy to run a clock while you are working in other applications. The timer continues to run even when Billings is closed. Additionally, you can manually enter time in the editor,

FIGURE 18-4

The Billings main window

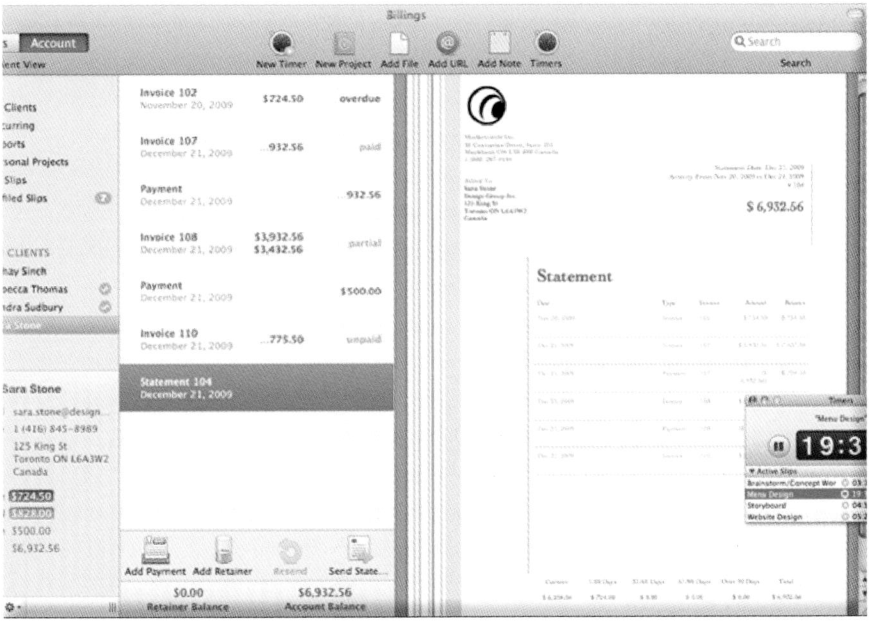

as shown in Figure 18-5. There is also an iOS application that lets you enter time on your iPhone, iPad, or iPod Touch.

FIGURE 18-5

Entering time in Billings

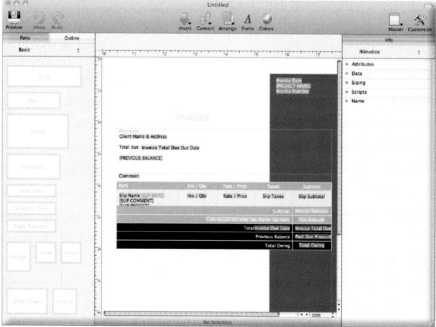

FIGURE 18-6

Billings' invoice template

FIGURE 18-7

The Billings Pro main window

Billings includes several professionally designed invoice templates and includes an editor so you can modify the included template, shown in Figure 18-6, or create your own. Once your invoice format is done, you can generate client invoices by choosing Client ▶ Send Invoice. Billings supports multiple currencies, which can be set on a per-client basis, so American clients receive their bills in dollars while European clients will receive invoices in euros, for example.

Billings, which has more than 30 built-in reports to analyze your accounts, also lets you track payments. The entire experience is user-friendly and intuitive. For example, if you want to quickly find all clients with past-due accounts, their names appear in red in the left sidebar.

Daylite (covered in Chapter 6) is published by the same developer. As a result, Billings and Daylite feature tight integration. Working together, you can send existing Daylite events, such as calendar appointments, to Billings as billing events.

Billings Pro ($200; www.marketcircle.com/billingspro) is an enhanced version of Billings. Shown in Figure 18-7, Billings Pro allows multiple users to access the data at the same time. Billings Pro also includes a Web interface from which timekeepers can enter time and expenses from their Web browsers (including Windows and mobile browsers).

The Paperless Mac

P eople have been talking about "going paperless" and transferring all their records to digital form for years, but this ideal has been largely unavailable to anyone except large corporations until recently. Fortunately, paperless technology is finally here for small and medium businesses. This chapter covers how to get your records into digital form and to use available Mac tools to sort and organize them.

Getting Paper Records on Your Mac

Transferring existing records to a digital format requires that they be scanned into the computer. For large corporations, there are commercial scanners and copiers that can process thousands of documents at a time. These devices are too costly for small and medium businesses. Likewise, digital conversion is not a job for a your traditional flatbed scanner: The scanners on your multifunction printer or flatbed scanner are slow and usually require that you manually feed each page (or limit you to maybe a dozen or so pages at a time). If the page is double-sided, you have to scan it twice. Although flatbed scanners are great for getting high-resolution scans of photographs, when scanning multipage documents, they are unworkable.

Instead, you need a dedicated document scanner. Just not the expensive types that large companies use. Some of the best paper digitizers on the Mac platform for small and medium businesses are the Fujitsu ScanSnap scanners.

The Fujitsu ScanSnap S1500M ($500; `http://scansnap.fujitsu.com`), shown in Figure 19-1, is Fujitsu's premier desktop scanner. The S1500M document scanner holds up to 50 pages and scans at a rate of 20 pages per minute. The unit has two scanners, so it can simultaneously scan both the front and back pages of a document as its pages are fed through the scanner. The result: The ScanSnap flies through scanning projects. (There is also a networked version, the ScanSnap fi-6010N, which costs $2,500.)

The S1300 ($280) mobile scanner is the portable ScanSnap model. At 3.1 pounds and 11 × 3 × 4 inches, it can fit in a medium-size briefcase. It can run off AC power or a powered USB port. Like the S1500M, the S1300 also includes front and back scanners. The S1300 can scan up to 10 pages per minute.

FIGURE 19-1

The Fujitsu ScanSnap S1500M

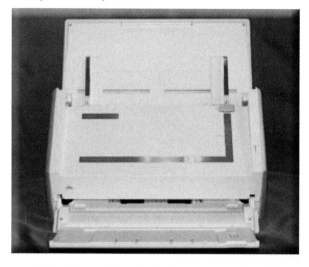

Fujitsu has embraced the Mac community with custom software for Mac OS X. Just as important as the ScanSnap hardware, is the software, included with both the S1500M and the S1300. The ScanSnap software is fully customizable but defaults to save scans to the near-universal PDF format (see Chapter 12). The scanner software has built-in logic to align the paper correctly. Thus, if you scan a page sideways, the ScanSnap software recognizes the text direction is wrong and rotates the page image automatically. The software also includes automatic size detection, which allows it to distinguish between a business card and a letter easily.

With years of experience, Fujitsu has made a lot of progress with common problems associated with scanning lots of documents. For example, sometimes the sheet feeder grabs more than one page at a time, but the ScanSnap has a sensor that checks for this problem. And often, extra-long documents cause scanners to seize; again, the ScanSnap handles long pages (including grocery receipts).

One challenge of going paperless is making the text of the scanned documents searchable using optical character recognition (OCR; covered later in this chapter and in Chapter 12). The ScanSnap software checks your scanned documents for highlighted text (green highlighters work best) and then selectively performs OCR on just the highlighted portions. For example, you can highlight the words "Smith Sales Report" on a document. After you scan the report with your ScanSnap, the software sees those highlighted words, performs optical character recognition on them, and adds the words "Smith Sales Report" to the file's Spotlight index. You can then find the document by searching for those words using Mac OS X's Spotlight utility (covered in Chapter 1).

The Fujitsu scanning software lets you save multiple scanning profiles, so you can have one setup for getting fast low-resolution scans of black-and-white records to PDF and slower high-resolution scans of color pictures to JPEG format. You can also set a custom destination for your scanned documents. I save mine to a folder on my Dropbox account (covered in Chapter 21) so I can sort and organize them from any computer with Dropbox access.

Both the S1300 and S1500M include additional software, including Abbyy FineReader (`www.abbyy.com`), which performs optical character recognition on your scans and converts them into Microsoft Word and Excel documents. The scanners also ship with Cardiris, which scans business cards and saves them directly into the Mac OS X Address Book. The S1500M also ships with Adobe Acrobat Professional for Mac, version 8. Although this is one version behind the current Acrobat Pro, it originally sold for $500.

If your office has more unscanned documents than you can handle, there are services that will do bulk scanning. This can be helpful for getting your paperless systems started. However, when choosing a vendor to scan documents, make certain it is trustworthy. Depending on your industry, there may be privacy concerns that prohibit this option.

Once your physical documents are scanned, what do you do with them? Some industries require that original documents be retained. In that event, look for an offsite storage service. There are many companies that will pick up boxes of documents and store them for a fee. If there isn't a good reason to retain documents, shred or discard them. After all, the point of this exercise is to get that paper out of your life.

Saving Electronic Records

Once you commit to a paperless system, you are also going to *generate* electronic documents you want to file. You can't simply save your Pages, Excel, and Keynote documents in their native formats to your paperless archive. A paperless archive needs to be viewable on any system, regardless of what software is installed on those systems; thus you need to store your documents in a universal format. Also, saving your archived documents as application files lets later users open and modify the files (if they have compatible editing software), which is bad for version control and records management.

The answer is to save the files in an uneditable but widely readable format, of which there are several options.

▶ **TIFF**, the Tagged Image File Format, uses different compression types to minimize the file size of scanned documents. Not all TIFF decoders work the same way: Some do a better job at compression than others. Because there are different decoding algorithms, occasionally you will come across TIFF files that will not open in Mac OS X Preview, Adobe Reader, or other viewer. Although TIFF was often used for scanned documents several years ago, its popularity has ebbed.

▶ **JPEG**, the Joint Photographic Expert Group format, is a compressed image type most often used for Web and digital photographs. Most cameras automatically compress photos to JPEG. JPEG does a great job of reducing file sizes but it can throw away detail and quality in the process, making it generally inappropriate for archiving diagrams and documents.

▶ **PNG**, the Portable Network Graphics, format is a newer Web graphics standard. PNG is useful for graphics but not suitable for scanned documents. It has several features not available to JPEG, including the use of an alpha channel (transparency) background. Thus, graphics created in the PNG format can have their backgrounds removed (as Chapter 13 explains), which is useful when using graphics in documents and presentations.

▶ **PDF**, the Portable Document Format, is the clear winner for a paperless system file format. PDF is ubiquitous. Free software exists on all the major computing platforms to view and annotate PDF files. Mac OS X's Preview application has PDF tools built in, and you can easily create PDFs from any file that can be printed (see Chapter 12).

Organizing Scanned Documents

Once you commit to saving and scanning documents, you need to decide where they go. An electronic document depository has a few specific needs:

1. **Accessibility.** The documents need to be in a centralized location where everyone that needs access has access. For a small consultancy, this could be on a single iMac with file sharing turned on (see Chapter 20). In a larger office, it makes more sense to store paperless documents on a central server (also covered in Chapter 20). If you are part of a virtual office with team members all over the country, you are better off using an online service such as Dropbox or Box.net (covered in Chapter 21).

2. **Privacy and security.** The document organization needs to reflect any security requirements. Health records, for example, have very specific legal requirements for keeping their information private. But a scanned copy of the menu for that rib joint everyone is considering for the next office party has no such security concerns. The amount of privacy and security depends on your specific industry but must be considered when deciding where to keep your paperless files.

3. **Automated backup.** A paperless system needs multiple backups, with at least one automated system for daily backups. To do this, you could use any of the backup plans covered in Chapter 2. One advantage of going paperless is the relative ease of creating copies of the files; it is much easier to make copies of electronic documents than physical ones. In 1994, I had a work project that included 32 banker's boxes full of documents. It cost nearly $4,000 to make copies for everyone involved. Today, I could make those same copies for the $30 price of a spindle of blank recordable DVDs.

Having decided where to store documents, you need to devote time deciding how you will organize the documents. Investing time upfront figuring out the document organization will save you multiples of that time later.

Specifically, you need to settle on a naming convention and hierarchical file structure. There are a couple ways to go about this. One popular approach is the use of nested folders, technically called a *hierarchical file structure*. This is how I do it. I have a master folder called Client Folder on my Mac that contains separate folders for each client. Each client folder has separate folders for each of that client's business dealings. Figure 19-2 illustrates this organization.

Because the folder names indicate the type of documents stored (letters are, for example, located in the Correspondence folder), I use the filenames to provide the date and detail. The format I use is the date, in the format *yyyy-mm-dd*

FIGURE 19-2

A hierarchical file structure

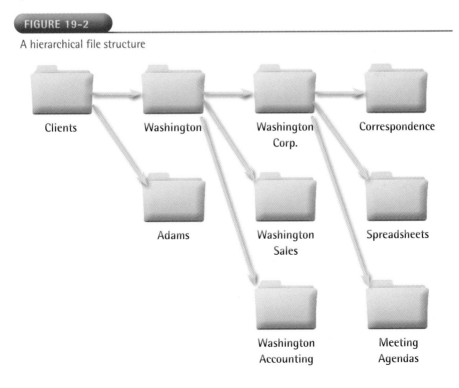

OCR AND STORED DOCUMENTS

Optical character recognition, the technology that enables your Mac to read and index the words on your scanned documents (covered in Chapter 12), lets you search all your documents. PDF documents with embedded text (which is added as part of the OCR process) are indexed by the Mac OS X Spotlight service (covered in Chapter 1). Thus, if you set up a scanning process that OCRs documents as they are scanned, you can later search them.

One advantage of the Fujitsu ScanSnap software is that it can automatically OCR every document it scans. There are other ways to perform OCR, however. PDFpen and Adobe Acrobat Pro (covered in Chapter 12) both perform automatic OCR on PDF documents. The paid Evernote service (covered in Chapter 10) also recognizes text in scanned and saved PDF (and JPEG) files. There are also independent software tools; one of the best is Abbyy FineReader ($100; www.abbyy.com).

Despite the increasing ease of performing OCR on a file, I still do not OCR every document in my paperless system. The OCR process takes time, and many of my scanned documents are meant only as a historical archive, so the time investment to OCR them isn't worthwhile. Think about your paperless system and what documents are worth the trouble of OCR before devoting time to the process.

followed by a brief description. For example, I might call a file 2010-12-18 Letter to Lynn re Meeting.pdf. (I automate the date entry with my TextExpander date-stamp macro, covered in Chapter 3.)

Although the file is date-stamped by Mac OS X, the date for a scanned file is the date the scan occurred, not when the original file was created, so putting the date in the filename assures an accurate date for scanned files. It also helps if I need to copy documents to another disk, which can change the copies' date stamp to the date of the copying. Also, naming files in this way makes it very easy to find documents and gives you the ability to quickly sort documents in chronological order. This system makes it easy for others to use and understand your file system.

You can further automate this process using Hazel, covered in Chapter 3. For example, you could create a rule in Hazel that any scanned file named Smith-Ltr gets a date stamp added by Hazel to the front of the filename and saved to the Clients/Smith Co/Correspondence folder.

Another way to save paperless documents is to just assign it an index stamp (usually a series of letters and numbers) and then use a separate application like Bento or FileMaker (both covered in Chapter 16) to create a detailed index for each document. Using a database application gives you more flexibility to organize your documents. For example, you could create a search that includes just letters to Smith and Jones between January and March. Provided you set

FIGURE 19-3

Yep document management

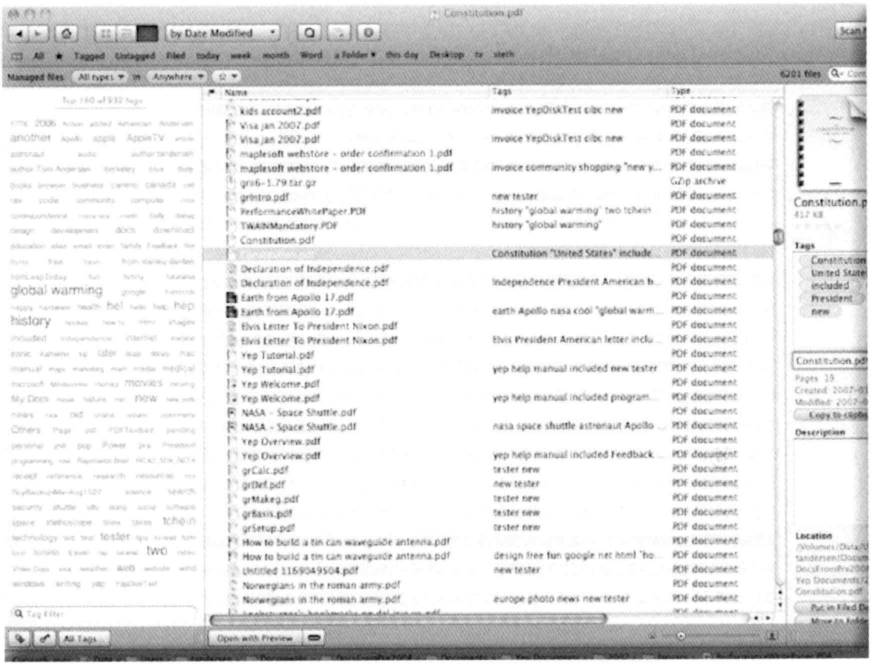

up clickable links from the database to your file storage system, you can then immediately get access to the documents.

Although not as prevalent on the Mac, there are several document management systems available in Windows. In my experience, these systems are expensive and cumbersome. Moreover, I am always leery of these closed systems because of the inability to get the documents back out later. What if, in two years, you want to get access to your documents but your license to the $800 management software has expired? If you must have a document management system, roll your own in FileMaker Pro.

Still, there are consumer-focused document organization applications for Mac OS X that can be used for business.

Yep ($39; www.ironicsoftware.com/yep), shown in Figure 19-3, presents an interface that is, essentially, iTunes for documents. The Sidebar is a list of your keywords letting you selectively filter your documents, which appear in the right pane. The documents can be kept in their original location and format, so you have a clean set of hierarchal folders in addition to the Yep tools. If you are willing to commit the additional time to tag your files, Yep is a good tool for viewing and indexing your documents.

EagleFiler ($40; http://c-command.com/eaglefiler) is another tool to consider. You can import PDF (and several other formats, including e-mail) into EagleFiler and set up smart folders and smart folder actions. One advantage of EagleFiler is that it lets you save a separate library for every project so you can easily separate your data.

DevonThink Professional Office ($150; `www.devon-technologies.com`), shown in Figure 19-4, is a popular document manager for the Mac. The software interfaces directly with the Fujitsu ScanSnap to import PDF documents as you scan them. DevonThink uses artificial intelligence to assist you in filing documents, reading the document and suggesting where to file it. In addition to reading PDF files, DevonThink can also store and organize e-mails, Word documents, multimedia files, and other file types. DevonThink includes sharing tools so you can post documents to the Web or share them with co-workers on a local network.

A final possibility for paperless document management is to use one of the "everything bucket" applications for Mac OS X such as Evernote (covered in Chapter 10) or Yojimbo ($40; `www.barebones.com/products/yojimbo`). Yojimbo is designed to capture all those bits and pieces of data on your Mac that you don't know where to keep. It can include snippets of text, e-mails, images, and PDF files. For a modest PDF paperless system (a few thousand documents), Yojimbo provides impressive indexing and organizational tools. You can tag your documents and selectively encrypt secure documents in it.

FIGURE 19-4

DevonThink Professional Office

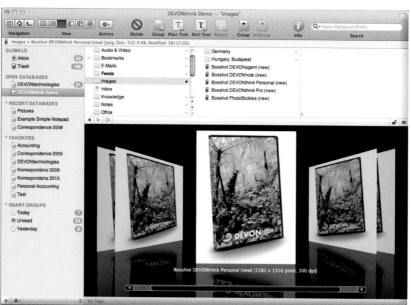

FIGURE 19-5

The PageSender faxing software

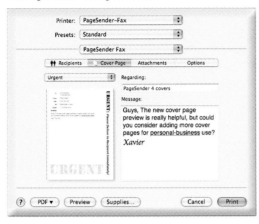

There is no one right tool for managing your paperless documents. I've tried most of them but keep gravitating back toward a simple hierarchical file structure. It is easy to maintain using automation tools and the data is extremely portable.

Faxing on a Mac

Once you have your paperless system in place, what about faxes? Fax machines are so 1990s. Still, Mac OS X includes built-in fax support, accessed in the Print & Fax system preference. In it, you can configure a modem attached to your Mac and use it to send and receive faxes. Although this is fine for the occasional fax, the built-in tools are not suitable for daily business use.

My favorite Mac faxing application is PageSender ($40; www.smilesoftware.com/pagesender). PageSender, shown in Figure 19-5, provides drag-and-drop simplicity to faxing from your Mac. PageSender works with just about any modem you can use with your Mac, including internal, Bluetooth, USB, serial, and PC Card modems. It includes spam filtering and multiple styles of cover pages (you can also design your cover page in the application).

The faxing tools (such as retry counts, redial interval, and electronic delivery of fax confirmation) are easy to configure. PageSender also supports AppleScript (covered in Chapter 24) and can be scripted to send faxes using FileMaker Pro lists. PageSender, developed by the same company that publishes PDFpen (covered in Chapter 12), works well with PDFpen. For example, you can sign a document in PDFpen and send it (via PageSender) directly from PDFpen.

Using modern document scanners and Mac OS X software, small companies (and individuals) can easily take the plunge and go paperless.

PART

V

Advanced Topics

Networking

A computer network includes at least two computers communicating with each other. Although modern computers are fast and powerful, they are even more useful when they can work with other computers. In addition to allowing communication between computers, a computer network allows Macs to share files, hardware, and software.

There are two basic types of networks: server networks and peer networks. Server-based networks have a central computer serving the files and data to the attached client computers. On peer-based networks, each computer holds its own files and shares them directly with the other computers on the network. The server and peer-based networks are illustrated in Figure 20-1.

With the emergence of standard protocols used in both Windows and Mac OS X, networking is easier than ever. The largest computer network is the Internet, which is covered in Chapter 4. This chapter focuses on local networks of computers attached to your Mac, on your wireless network, and on remote networking that allows you to access your work network from a distance.

The Mac Server Network

The best tool for creating a Mac server network is using Apple's Mac OS X Server software ($499, `www.apple.com/server/macosx`). The most recent edition, Snow Leopard Server, is a 64-bit operating system with advanced file-sharing tools such as the ability to read from and write to multiple clients simultaneously and virtual local area networks (VLANs) that allow different departments in different locations to appear to be on the same network. Mac OS X Server also includes security controls that allow network administrators to set specific access for each user as well as global security settings on the network. Mac OS X Server makes it possible to efficiently share, control, and manage files.

Mac OS X 10.6 Snow Leopard Server provides useful services for network users. iCal Server manages calendars for network users and allows users to see co-workers' schedules and set up meetings when everyone is available. It supports push notification that immediately notify team members when a meeting is set.

FIGURE 20-1

Server-based (top) and peer-based (bottom) networks compared

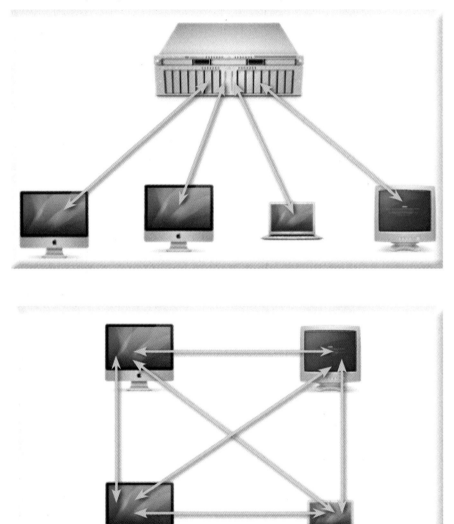

The Address Book Server keeps a master list of names and addresses that can be shared with each computer. Users can add, modify, and delete contacts for the entire network.

For group projects, Mac OS X Snow Leopard Server includes Wiki Server; a wiki is a Web site that provides the ability for the group to easily review, modify, and collaborate on data. Users can create links between different data sets and collaborate on large projects. A wiki is best used with groups of people adding bits and pieces of data to a larger whole. (The most popular wiki is Wikipedia.)

Mac OS X Server's Wiki Server brings this power to your local network: You can create a locally hosted internal wiki shared by everyone on the network where they can collaborate on information and ideas for a specific project. Participants can upload files and images, add comments, and access the wiki pages from their iPhones and iPads. Tapping into other Mac OS X Server tools, the wiki can include mailing lists and its own calendar.

Mac OS X Server also includes Mail Services. Using this tool, small offices can create their own e-mail server on the local network server. Mail Services include tools for junk mail filtering, virus detection and quarantine, and setting up vacation messages. Administrators can also create server-based rules to scan and filter e-mail messages before they are delivered to users.

For companies where in-person collaboration is not always possible, Mac OS X Server includes iChat Server to permit secure confidential iChat sessions and persistent chat rooms. Using iChat Server, you can keep track of ongoing projects even when you are away from your Mac. Every time you log in, all communications from the chat that occurred while you were logged off is loaded for review.

Finally, Mac OS X Server simplifies file management. Keeping all your key files on a central server makes a lot of sense, even in small offices. Mac OS X Server's file sharing works with Macs and Windows computers. File access and security can be set for each user. Network administrators can control access to data and make certain everything is backed up (Mac OS X Server includes support for Time Machine backup). Mac OS X Server also includes tools for file-level locking that keep Mac or PC clients from overwriting changes when more than one user has a file open at the same time.

The best hardware options for running Mac OS X Server are Apple's dedicated server products (see Chapter 1): the Mac Pro, the Mac Mini, and the recently discontinued Xserve. The Mac Pro, starting at $2,499, provides the most power. A Mac Mini bundled with Mac OS X Server ($999) provides a simple server solution for offices that don't require the additional computing power offered by the Mac Pro. Before buying a server, talk to a networking consultant.

File Sharing

Mac OS X makes it easy to share files, even if you don't use Mac OS X Server. If you just need to host and serve files, you could set up a dedicated Mac using the standard Mac OS X; such a server could benefit from using a RAID 1 or Drobo external drive (see Chapter 2) to handle the volume of files. You can also have each Mac act as a file server to the other computers on your network. Or you can have both: a dedicated file server (Mac OS X Server or just Mac OS X) for common files, plus individual Macs set up for file sharing so individuals can share their own files.

Sharing files from a Mac

For basic file sharing, you do not need a dedicated server. Every Mac has the ability to share files directly with other computers, including PCs, on a network.

To permit sharing on your Mac, open the Sharing system preference, shown in Figure 20-2. If the Lock iconic button (located in the lower-left corner) displays as a closed padlock icon, you can't make changes to the preferences until you unlock the Sharing system preference by clicking the Lock iconic button and entering your system password; the button then displays as an open padlock icon.

The first step is to select the File Sharing option from the list on the left side of the Sharing system preference. Then designate folders to share by clicking the + iconic button below the Shared Folders list. This presents a dialog box where you can navigate to the folder you want to share. Repeat this step for each folder you want to share. If you want to share folders with Windows computers, click the Options button and select the Share Files and Folders Using SMB check box; then click Done.

Once you've chosen which folders to share, you need to identify which users get access, then specify what access they get. To add users, click the + iconic button below the Users list. You can add individuals or groups from your network. Conversely, you could limit access by removing users; select them one at

The Sharing system preference

a time and click the – (minus) iconic button. Once you have added and removed specific users and groups, you set the access privileges for each using the following options, which are available in a pop-up menu adjacent to each user or group name (select Everyone to apply privileges to all users on the network):

- **Read Only:** This is the default setting. Other users can read or copy files from the shared folder but cannot write to the folder or modify files inside it.

- **Read & Write:** This allows other users to read, copy, edit, and delete the contents of the folder.

- **Write Only (Drop Box):** This option allows users to drop files in the folder. Users cannot view the contents of the folder or pull files back out. The Drop box is useful if you want to collect different files from team members in a central location. (The Drop box feature should not be confused with the Dropbox synchronization service covered in Chapter 21.)

- **No Access:** This option, available only for groups and Everyone, allows you to prohibit access to certain folders. Note that if the permissions separately set for an individual user in this group allows access to the selected folder, that user will still have access even though the group he or she is in is set to prohibit access.

Once you're done, other users on the network (including Windows users) can access your shared folders consistent with the permissions you set.

Sharing Files from a Windows PC

Your Mac can also access files stored on a Windows PC. Just like on your Mac, the Windows PC needs to enable sharing. The steps involved to enable sharing on a Windows PC depend on which version of Windows you are running.

In Windows XP, choose Start ▶ My Network Places. Then click Set Up a Home or Small Office Network in the left column. Windows XP presents the Network Setup Wizard, which allows you to set up file sharing and printing. Once enabled, the Shared Documents folder is available for sharing. You can add additional folders by right-clicking the folders and adjusting their sharing properties.

In Windows 7, you set file sharing in the Network and Sharing Center in the Control Panel. Select Choose Homegroup and Sharing. Then select the Change Advanced Sharing Settings option and enable File and Printer Sharing. You can then designate a folder for sharing by right-clicking the folder in the Windows Explorer and choosing Share.

The Mac OS X Finder is always on the lookout for shared folders, including shared Windows folders. So, once you share a Windows folder, it should appear in your Finder's sidebar.

Online file sharing

Another way to share your files is through the use of Internet-based file storage. Services such as MobileMe, Dropbox, and Box.net allow you to keep files on Internet-based servers. These cloud services seek to take the place of a traditional server: You can designate shared folders on your cloud-based storage, so co-workers can upload and download shared files (see Chapter 21 for the details).

Sharing external media

Before computer communication protocols existed, computer networking was accomplished with a box of floppy disks and your feet. We called it "sneakernet." Although technology has moved on, using portable media still serves in a pinch. USB flash drives fit on your key ring and can hold gigabytes of data. Likewise, portable hard drives with large capacities are sometimes the best way to move gigabytes of data between Macs. In short, the sneakernet still lives.

Using portable media is easy when you are moving data between two Macs or two Windows PCs. When you move data between Macs and Windows PCs, however, things can go a bit sideways if you're using hard drives. The trouble is that Mac OS X and Windows use different file systems. Mac OS X uses HFS Extended formatting, referred to in Mac OS X as *Mac OS Extended (Journaled)*. Every version of Windows since Windows NT uses the New Technology File System (NTFS) format. Unfortunately, these formats don't get along as well as we'd like them to. Mac OS X can read NTFS but not write to it. You are out of luck getting Mac data on a Windows computer because Windows can't read from or write to the HFS Extended format. Table 20-1 summarizes the disk formats and their platforms support.

(If you're using flash drives, don't worry: Mac OS X and Windows use the same format for these devices — FAT32 — so there's no problem sharing data across the two platforms.)

There are applications to help out. If you want to read an HFS drive on a Windows PC, you need MacDrive 8 ($50; www.mediafour.com/products/macdrive), which gives Windows the ability to read and write to HFS Extended

TABLE 20-1	Mac OS X and Windows Disk Format Compatibility		
Platform	HFS Extended	NTFS	FAT32
Mac OS X	Read and write	Read only, can't write	Read and write
Windows	Can't read or write	Read and write	Read and write

drives. On the Mac side, NTFS for Mac OS X ($40; `www.paragon-software.com/home/ntfs-mac`) allows Macs to read from and write to NTFS.

Another solution is to skip NTFS and HFS Extended altogether and format your portable drives with the older FAT32 format. Both Mac OS X and Windows can read and write FAT32. But there are some limitations: It is slower than both HFS Extended and NTFS, and you can't store files larger than 4GB. Nevertheless, FAT32 is an excellent choice for transferring files between operating systems. To format a disk in FAT32 in Mac OS X, erase and reformat the drive (using the Mac OS X Disk Utility) in the MS-DOS (FAT) format.

Sharing Printers

Sharing a printer in Mac OS X is painless. To make your printer available to other computers, go to the Print & Fax system preference shown in Figure 20-3. Select the printer you want to share from the list of available printers and click Share This Printer on the Network. Next go to the Sharing system preference and click Printer Sharing in the list on the left to display its options. You can adjust user access just as you set user access for file sharing (covered earlier in this chapter). Computers on your network can then use the printer connected to your Mac. If you use a Mac as your central file server, you can also make it a print server by attaching printers and turning on sharing. This is illustrated in Figure 20-3.

Remote Access

Another way to network computers is through remote access, which allows you to log in to a local computer network, such as at your office, through an

FIGURE 20-3

Printer sharing is enabled in the Print & Fax system preference

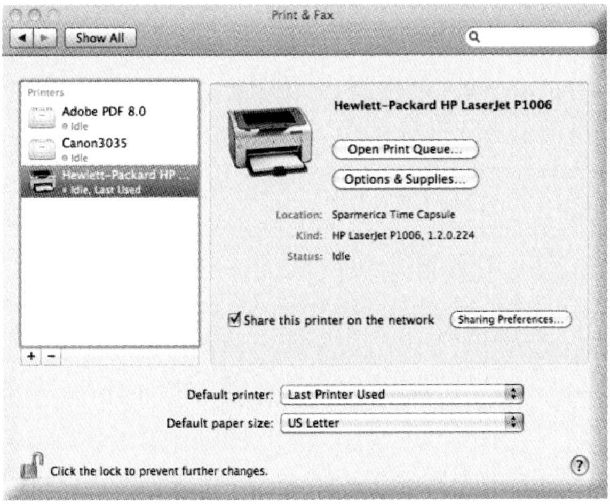

Internet connection. Depending on the network type, you can then download files from the remote network or take control of a remote computer and make its screen appear on your Mac.

Remote access is one of the best tools for a Mac worker connecting to a Windows PC network. It allows you to put a Windows PC, and all its accompanying software, on your Mac without loading Windows on your Mac. There are several ways to pull this off in Mac OS X.

Microsoft Remote Desktop Connection

 Microsoft's Remote Desktop Connection (free; `www.microsoft.com/ mac/products/remote-desktop`) is one of the best tools for remote access into a Windows network. Remote Desktop Connection uses standard Windows authentication and allows you to log into Windows computers. You provide Remote Desktop Connection with the Internet Protocol (IP) address of the computer you are connecting to, and Remote Desktop Connection does the rest of the work for you.

To use Remote Desktop Connection, you need to enable your office Windows PC to receive and authorize the connection. This may require some network settings (such as assigning an IP address and adjusting the firewall settings) but is not difficult with the assistance of your network administrator. Also, when you log in, the remote computer must be turned on.

Once Microsoft Remote Desktop connects, you are asked to enter your user name and password as if you were sitting in front of your Windows PC. After you log in, your office computer appears in a window on your Mac. You can use the Start menu and run your software as if you were in your office. As long as you have a broadband Internet connection, your remotely connected computer will respond at an acceptable speed. You can write documents, create spreadsheets, and even e-mail yourself missing files. If you don't want to tangle with Windows virtualization on your Mac (covered in Chapter 22) but are saddled with a Windows PC at work that you sometimes must run, Remote Desktop Connection may be all you need.

CoRD

 The open source (free but donation requested) CoRD (`http://cord. sourceforge.net`) is another Remote Desktop client that works similarly to Microsoft Remote Desktop Client. It supports multiple logins for different PCs (Microsoft Remote Desktop supports only one) and makes it easier to change settings than Microsoft Remote Desktop. CoRD has a slide-out drawer on the left side of its window that keeps a list of all your logins and allows you to log in using hot keys, which is convenient.

I prefer CoRD over Microsoft Remote Desktop, but they both get the job done. If your network administrator is already nervous about you using a Mac, use the Microsoft Remote Desktop Connection (IT people are more comfortable with Microsoft tools); otherwise, give CoRD a try.

VNC applications

Where Microsoft Remote Desktop Connection and CoRD allow you to remotely log into a Windows PC, an alternative technology, called *virtual network computing (VNC)*, lets you share the screen of another computer. This is not the same as a remote login covered earlier but often can obtain the same result. There are two pieces to VNC, the server and the client. The VNC server allows other computers to log into it and the client allows a remote computer to access and control a computer with a VNC server enabled. VNC server software is built into Mac OS X and can be turned on with the Computer Settings button in the Remote Management pane in the Sharing system preference, shown in Figure 20-4.

There are two VNC client applications on the Mac worth noting:

▶ **Chicken of the VNC** (free; http://sourceforge.net/projects/cotvnc) is an open source tool that has been popular for years. Chicken of the VNC can automatically discover available servers on your network and work in full-screen mode. This application is a simple VNC client without many bells and whistles but with an uncanny ability to establish a VNC connection where other VNC clients cannot.

▶ **RealVNC** ($50; www.realvnc.com) is a commercial VNC tool. If you use VNC in a large corporate network, you are more likely to be successful

FIGURE 20-4

Enabling VNC in the Sharing system preference

	Sharing

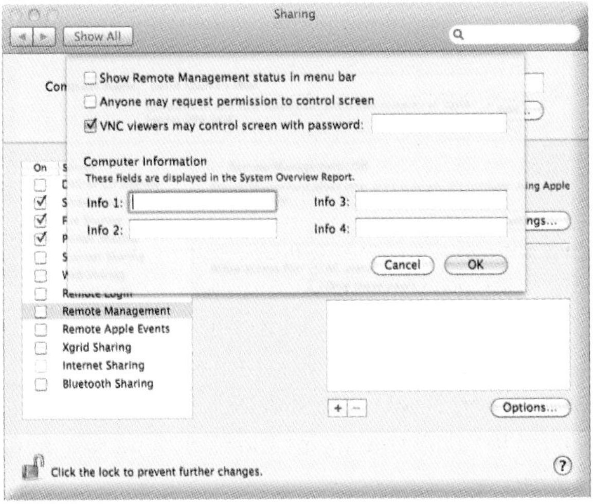

convincing the IT staff to let you use RealVNC rather than Chicken of the VNC. RealVNC includes several security features including 2,048-bit server authentication and 128-bit encryption. RealVNC is multiplatform, supporting Windows, Linux, and Mac OS X. To operate it on Mac OS X, however, you need to purchase the $50 Enterprise edition.

Apple Remote Desktop

For controlling multiple Macs on a single network, use Apple Remote Desktop (`www.apple.com/remotedesktop`), which allows you to access and control multiple Macs. You can manage 10 systems for $299 or an unlimited number of systems for $499.

Apple Remote Desktop goes beyond mere remote access to provide administrator tools for software distribution, automation, and remote search. It is ideal for a network of managed Macs. You can install applications and even restart machines remotely. Apple Remote Desktop can be automated, allowing the administrator to quickly apply settings to all computers on the network.

Moreover, Apple Remote Desktop has a "curtained" mode where system maintenance and updates can be applied in the background without local users seeing the administrator do so. If you need to report on computer activity, Remote Desktop compiles application usage and hardware reports with more than 200 attributes about networked Mac OS X systems.

FIGURE 20-5

Enabling Back to My Mac in the MobileMe system preference

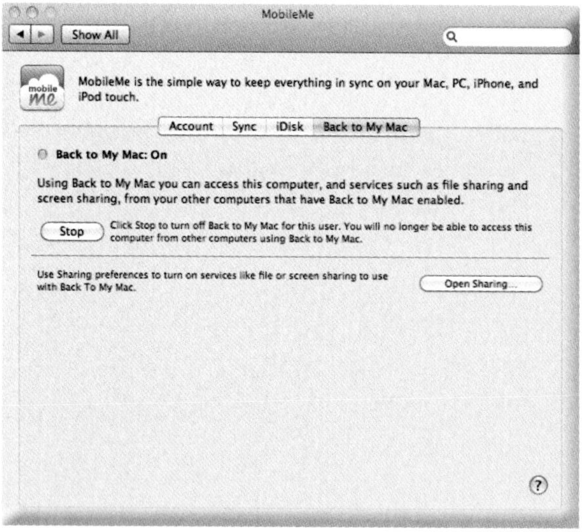

Back to My Mac

Back to My Mac is a part of the MobileMe service, covered in detail in Chapter 21. It allows you to easily create a virtual connection between Macs registered to your MobileMe account. Although Apple markets it as a consumer service, it is also useful for work. If you have an iMac at the office and a MacBook for home, you can remotely control your office iMac and access files over the Internet using Back to My Mac. You enable Back to My Mac in the MobileMe system preference shown in Figure 20-5. Additionally, you need to enable Screen Sharing and File Sharing on your remote Mac in its Sharing system preference.

Once enabled, your other Mac should appear in your Finder's sidebar. Clicking on the remote Mac's name in the Finder sidebar connects you to the remote Mac, allowing you to access files and, if Screen Sharing is enabled in the remote Mac's Sharing system preference, share screens with the remote Mac.

We've come a long way since sneakernet. Using the products covered in this chapter, you should have no trouble networking your Mac to get work done.

Synchronization

Having more than one computer is great. It gives you the flexibility of having a nice big screen on your desk and the ability to escape to the coffee shop with a laptop. The trouble occurs when you get seated with your venti triple-shot mocha latte and realize that the spreadsheet you need is on your office computer and not on your laptop. Your computers are out of sync, and you are unable to work.

Syncing used to be a real pain in the neck involving color-coded floppy disks and lots of praying. But it's much easier now with local and Internet-based tools.

Local Syncing

ChronoSync ($40; `www.econtechnologies.com`) was covered in Chapter 2 as a backup tool. However, ChronoSync really shines as a synchronization tool. Using ChronoSync, shown in Figure 21-1, you can synchronize files among multiple computers.

ChronoSync can share any files your Mac sees. If you have PC files or servers networked to your Mac (see Chapter 20), you can synchronize the files to your Mac. For example, if your office's Windows server holds your project documents, you can mount that server on your Mac and ChronoSync will synchronize those files to your Mac's internal hard disk. That loads your Mac with all the files you need for your next trip to the coffee shop. When you return, you can run ChronoSync again, syncing your changed files back to the network drive.

Even if you use more complicated syncing and file-management tools, ChronoSync is great for helping things along. For example, if you have a mission-critical project that requires lots of work and you cannot lose any data, you can create a ChronoSync template that saves that project folder to a thumb drive or even to the cloud-based synchronization tools covered later in this chapter.

Internet Synchronization Tools

With the advantage of high-speed Internet connections and cheap storage, several companies now offer file synchronization among multiple computers

FIGURE 21-1

ChronoSync's settings

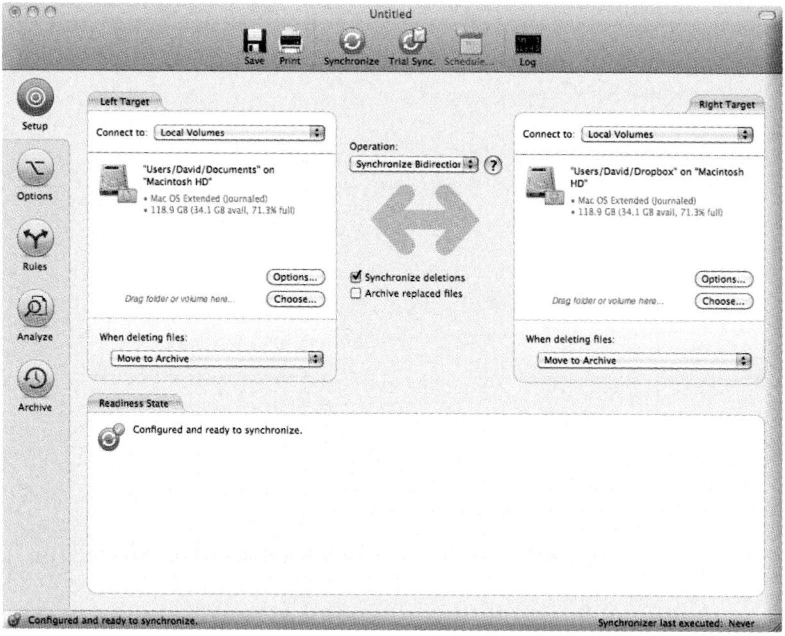

using Internet-based (or *cloud storage*) synchronization services. This industry is in its infancy but is already proving useful to Mac workers. Three of the best tools are MobileMe, Dropbox, and Box.net.

MobileMe

MobileMe ($100 per year; www.apple.com/mobileme) is Apple's tool for online synchronization. MobileMe synchronizes many of the user settings on your Mac and is configured in the Sync pane of the MobileMe system preference, shown in Figure 21-2.

MobileMe synchronizes calendars and contacts, as explained in Chapter 6. It also synchronizes e-mail account settings and rules. Synchronizing e-mail settings is handy when working with multiple Macs. For example, if you have to change your e-mail server settings on one computer, most likely you need that change on all your computers. Using MobileMe, you only need to make the adjustment once. The MobileMe server keeps copies of your e-mail account settings and automatically updates the other devices. If you create custom rules and mailboxes, covered in Chapter 5, MobileMe also keeps those in sync.

Apple did not stop with just e-mail, contacts, and calendars, however. The MobileMe synchronization service also synchronizes your Safari bookmarks, keychains, Dock items, dashboard widgets, and system preferences. If you

FIGURE 21–2

MobileMe's synchronization settings

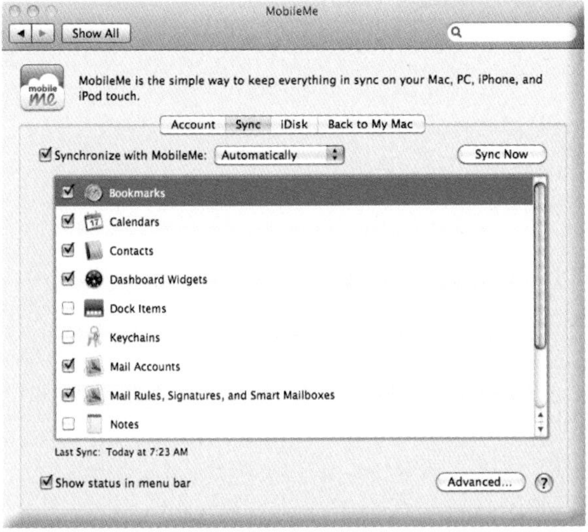

fully embrace the MobileMe synchronization settings, you can have identical preferences on all your Macs.

Apple also opened MobileMe synchronization to third-party application developers, so other applications can tap into MobileMe to sync data and settings. For example, TextExpander, covered in Chapter 3, allows you to synchronize your text snippets database through the MobileMe service. Once you add a snippet on any Mac, MobileMe synchronizes it to your other Macs.

In the MobileMe system preference, shown in Figure 21-2, you can set the frequency of your MobileMe synchronization to a specific interval (like once every hour), manually on your command, or automatically whenever there is a change. I find automatic syncing is best: It helps prevent the same record being independently modified on two Macs before syncing, which can cause syncing conflicts.

Sometimes files become corrupt and MobileMe gets confused. When this happens, the MobileMe service gives you a warning message explaining that two versions of some bit of data (an Address Book entry, for example) are inconsistent. You are then prompted to choose which version is correct, and the MobileMe service then does its best to sort things out.

Sometimes, these simple measures are not enough and you need to reset the MobileMe database. Do so in the MobileMe system preference as follows:

1. **Click the Advanced button, as shown in Figure 21-2.**
2. **Once in the Advanced settings sheet, click the Reset Sync Data button to reset your database.** The best strategy for resetting the database is to have one Mac with the correct version of the data. I'll

call that the Correct Mac. You can then instruct MobileMe to replace all the data in the MobileMe database with the data from the Correct Mac.

3. **Once the master reset is completed, use the replaced MobileMe data to reset your other Macs again using the Reset Sync Data button.** But this time, have the MobileMe database *replace* the data on your other Macs.

The MobileMe service also ties directly into the Apple iLife applications. If you have a MobileMe account, it is easy to share your photographs from iPhoto, your Web sites from iWeb, and your movies from iMovie directly to the Web. There are no settings to fiddle with or Internet protocols to master; you just click and share.

Apple also offers a Web interface for MobileMe, shown in Figure 21-3. You can log into your account from any computer (including Windows PCs) and have full access to your MobileMe calendar, contacts, and e-mail. You can also use the Web interface to send large files stored on your iDisk, as covered later in this chapter.

The MobileMe synchronization service ties all this data together with your Apple mobile devices such as iPhone, iPad, and iPod Touch. You can wirelessly share and synchronize your contacts, calendar, e-mail settings, and Safari bookmarks. Using the MobileMe service, you can remain connected no matter where you go. (Chapter 7 covers MobileMe's integration with Apple's mobile devices in greater detail.)

FIGURE 21-3

The MobileMe Web portal

With your MobileMe subscription, you also receive a 20GB allotment of space on the MobileMe servers, called iDisk, that can be split between file storage and mail storage. For the file storage, you can designate folders as public and make them available for friends, family, and co-workers to access; they can download files from your public folder and upload their files for you.

MobileMe also helps to tackle the problem of large e-mail attachments. Everyone has a war story about the time you sent a large proposal to a client or boss to find out the e-mail was not delivered because the attachment was too large, causing a missed deadline and leading to nothing but further misery and grief. Using MobileMe, you can store large files on your iDisk and then send them to clients and bosses with an e-mail that includes a download link to your iDisk file, as shown in Figure 21-4. You can even assign a password to keep the file secure. The recipient then clicks the link in his or her e-mail client to have the file downloaded. (This works for both PCs and Macs.) You can also place a time limit on the download link so it expires for time-sensitive files.

As with the rest of MobileMe, you can access your iDisk files from the Web interface. Before giving an important presentation, I often upload copies of the essential documents and Keynote files to my iDisk. If my computer does not work or the hard drive fails or there is some other last-minute problem, I can always get the files from another computer and keep marching forward. Apple has also released iPhone and iPad applications for iDisk that allow you to access the files from your mobile device and forward e-mail links to friends and colleagues.

The MobileMe settings allow you to keep a local copy of your MobileMe iDisk files on your Mac. This creates a second copy of your MobileMe data, one on your hard disk and the second on the MobileMe server. If you have your MobileMe account linked to an additional Mac and also have it set to keep local copies of your MobileMe data, you have a third copy. The MobileMe servers keep the computers synchronized. The next time you spend a few hours at the coffee shop working on your Pages sales proposal and then sync it to the MobileMe servers before closing the lid and heading to the office, your iMac at the office will download the most recent version while you drive back, and you will be able to continue where you left off.

MobileMe is a fantastic service for syncing Macs and does a great job with small data files, such as your address book, calendar, and individual documents. However, when synchronizing larger files, the MobileMe servers are simply too slow to keep up. If that sales proposal you worked on in the coffee shop includes video and music, you have to wait for it to finish syncing to the MobileMe server before closing your MacBook. Depending on the size of the file, that wait could be a long time. Although Apple does not control all the variables involved with

FIGURE 21-4

Sharing large files via iDisk

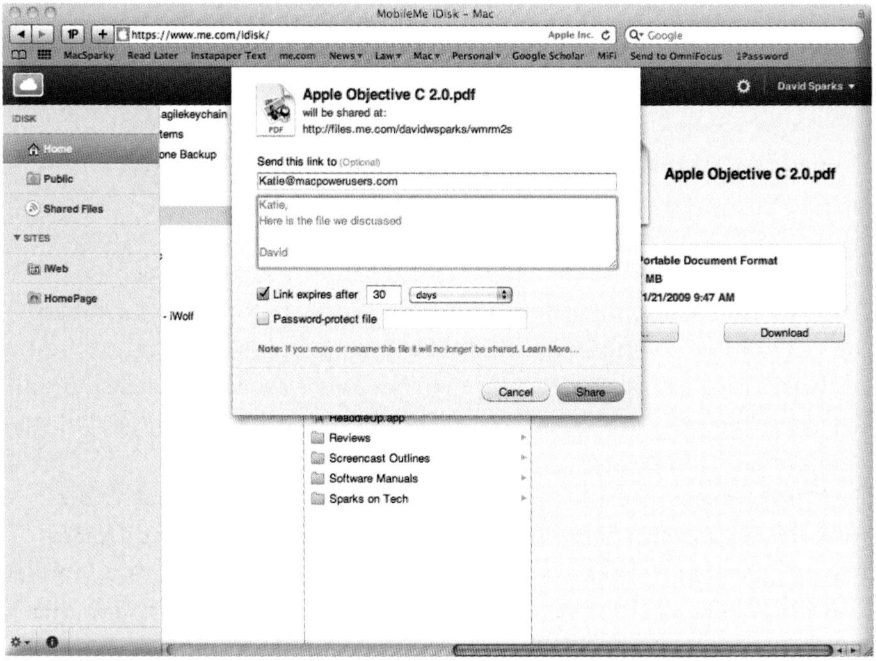

synchronizing data over the Internet (such as Internet speed, wireless network speed, and traffic), the bottleneck very often is the MobileMe service.

The Achilles heel of MobileMe is its lack of speed. As Apple releases even more mobile devices and becomes the hub of our digital lifestyle, I suspect it will address this problem in the future.

Despite my concerns with the MobileMe service's ability to quickly synchronize files, it is valuable to anyone who operates multiple Macs. The ability to sync so many elements of your computing experience among devices, plus the support for wireless synchronization of contact and calendar data with your iPhone, iPad, and iPod Touch, make the service worthwhile for many users in spite of its network speed issues.

Apple offers a 60-day free trial, so I recommend you give it a try and make your own decision. If you are looking for it only as a file-synchronization service, however, move on to a faster service such as Dropbox or Box.net.

Dropbox

Dropbox (`www.dropbox.com`) is the reigning champ of online file syncing services for the Mac. When you sign up for the service, it creates a local Dropbox folder on your Mac. On the free service, you can then load that folder with up to 2GB of data, which is copied to the Dropbox servers. (You can get more storage capacity if you pay for it: 50GB costs $10 per month and 100GB costs $20 per month.) When the upload completes, your files are in both your local Dropbox folder and the cloud-based Dropbox servers.

Working on the files is done from the local copies on your Mac. For example, if you are syncing a text file, you open the file from your local Dropbox folder. When you are finished working on the file and save it, the Dropbox application automatically syncs the updated version to the Dropbox cloud storage. In this sense, Dropbox gives you a backup in addition to syncing service. (For more about backup, see Chapter 2.)

If you have two computers, they can both synchronize to the Dropbox server. Dropbox creates a local Dropbox on your second computer just like on the first one. All the data is synced both locally and in the cloud, so you can share data and files between the computers. When you update a text file on one Mac, it gets synced to both the Dropbox server and to your other Mac (as soon as it connects to the Internet, of course).

The service also handles connectivity problems like a champ: If you lose your Internet connection in the middle of syncing, Dropbox resumes syncing the next time you connect in a way that protects the file integrity. In the years that I've been using Dropbox, I have never experienced data corruption despite lost Internet connections and my complete disregard for in-progress syncing operations when closing the lid of my laptop.

Although there are several competing services that do essentially the same thing as Dropbox, what makes Dropbox so popular among Mac users is its speed and reliability. Dropbox is incredibly fast. So fast that you can modify a file on your laptop and, in the time it takes for you to push your chair to your iMac, the

LIMITING THE DROPBOX SYNC

When using Dropbox, there is no way to limit the synchronization: It's everything or nothing. Although this normally is not a problem, it can be an issue if you have mixed personal and work data in your Dropbox files. By synchronizing with your office PC or Mac, you're making your personal data available to anyone who has access to that computer. Although Dropbox has promised it will add tools to limit the sync, it has not yet done so.

But there is a workaround: Run multiple Dropbox accounts. Keep your primary account on your Mac. Then add an additional free 2GB Dropbox account on the work computer under a different e-mail address and share a folder from the paid Dropbox account with the new account on the office PC. Just put files you want to share with the office computer in that shared folder. You can then control access of what gets synchronized and at the same time keep personal files off the work computer.

file is already synchronized. Dropbox accomplishes this speed by syncing only those parts of a file that have changed.

Your files stored on the Dropbox server are encrypted and inaccessible without your account password. All the data transmissions are done over an SSL-encrypted channel, which keeps your data safe from prying eyes.

The Dropbox service is not limited to Mac users. There are also clients for Windows and Linux, enabling you to easily share files between a work PC and your Mac laptop. Dropbox has also embraced the mobile operating systems with native applications for the iPhone, iPad, BlackBerry, and Android devices.

The iPad and iPhone applications are particularly good: They keep an index of all files in your Dropbox server and allow you to star any file as a favorite and keep it downloaded locally to your iPad or iPhone so you have access to it regardless of your Internet connection. Dropbox also allow you to easily e-mail and forward files from your Dropbox storage via an e-mail link; During lunch, I can send a contract to a colleague that is stored on my Dropbox by just pressing a few buttons on the Dropbox app on my iPhone.

If you are away from your computer, you can still access all your Dropbox files by logging into the Dropbox Web site, shown in Figure 21-5 with your user name and password. Once logged in, you can search your entire Dropbox for files, recover previous versions, undelete files, and create shared folders.

In addition to synchronizing, Dropbox is a great resource for sharing files. You can designate any folder in your Dropbox storage as a shared folder by creating a shared folder in the Dropbox Web interface. Dropbox then sends out invitations to the e-mail recipients you identify. Once they accept and install Dropbox on their computers, they will have the shared folder available on their computers.

A shared Dropbox folder allows you to get around the e-mail attachment size limitations that often plague telecommuters. Although you cannot place large attachments to your e-mail files, you can place large files in the Dropbox shared folder and send an e-mail to your colleagues informing them it has been loaded. But one note of caution when using a Dropbox shared file: Everyone in the shared group has administrative access to that folder and so can copy, modify, and delete the files.

Some businesses use a Dropbox account to replace their file server. They keep all their shared files on the Dropbox server where employees can access them from any location. A better tool for this, however, is Box.net, covered in the next section.

Another advantage of Dropbox is file versioning. The service keeps versions of your files for 30 days (or for an unlimited period with a paid account). This ability to fetch prior versions of files is similar to the Time Machine feature explained in Chapter 2. To obtain an earlier version of a document, log into the

FIGURE 21-5

Dropbox Web access

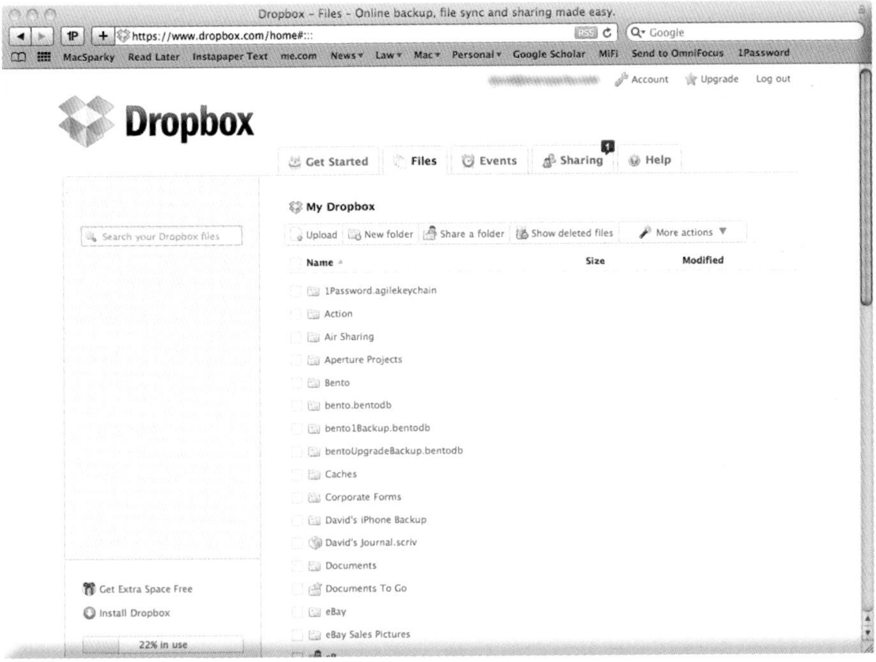

Dropbox Web interface and choose the desired version for download, as shown in Figure 21-6.

In addition to syncing your files, Dropbox is useful for syncing system and application files. For example, both 1Password (covered in Chapter 23) and TextExpander (covered in Chapter 3) allow you to sync your application database over Dropbox, which makes using these applications on multiple computers much easier. In the case of TextExpander, it is better to sync your data with Dropbox than with MobileMe because of Dropbox's speed advantages.

Box.net

Box.net (www.box.net) is another popular online collaboration tool similar to Dropbox. It allows you to securely upload and store your online files and folders using 256-bit encryption. Box.net, shown in Figure 21-7, is specifically aimed at businesses. Box.net offers a free 2GB account, as well as a 15GB account for $15 per month. For larger businesses, Box.net offers additional usage-based pricing tiers.

Box.net allows you to manage your files easily. You can create nested folders or even host your entire company file database on the Box.net server. You can then selectively set permissions for different users, such as edit, read only, or exclude

FIGURE 21-6

Restoring a previous version of a Dropbox file

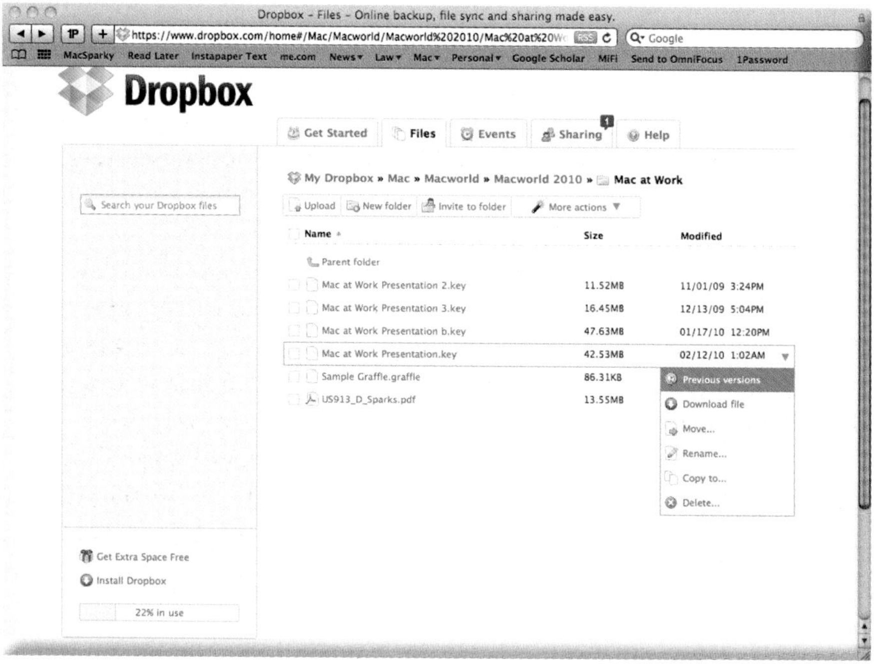

FIGURE 21-7

Box.net's Web interface

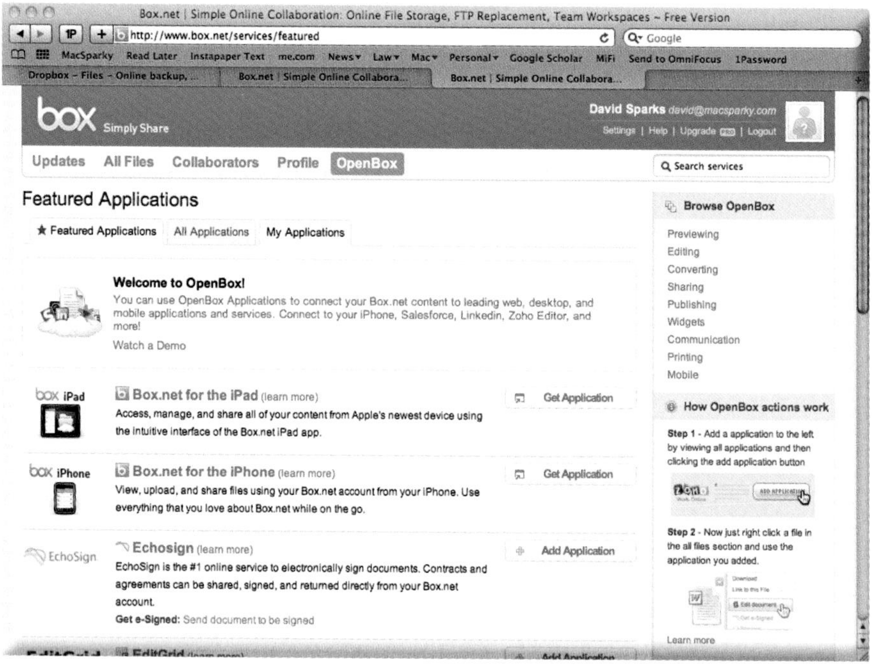

from certain files. Using a business account, you can search the text in your Box.net files and access them from mobile devices such as an iPhone or iPad.

Once your files are located on the Box.net server, you can take advantage of several collaboration tools useful for business. Box.net supports discussion and commenting threads on documents and keeps version histories. You can also set up tasks around specific files that all team members can review and update. Because Box.net tracks each team member who accesses its files, it can also send e-mail notifications when changes are made or there is other activity in the Box. net account.

Box.net is marketed as a Web-based server replacement, which is pretty remarkable. It includes server administrative tools so you can manage user settings and permissions, manage file security, and get reports including an audit trail of all activity on any file in your Box.net storage. You can also customize the Box.net interface for your company account to reflect your company brand.

We've come along way since synchronizing was accomplished with floppy disks and sneakers. Although Web-based syncing is an emerging technology, it holds much promise to make the seamless sharing of data among computers even easier.

Windows on Your Mac

I n 2006, Apple switched the Macintosh platform to Intel processors, which are the same processors used on most Windows PCs. Overnight, Macs and PCs got a lot more alike. Apple CEO Steve Jobs had not left the stage from making this announcement before people began speculating about how to run Windows on their new Intel Macs.

It didn't take long. Today there are several ways to run Windows on your Mac, including Apple's Boot Camp software, desktop virtualization software, and code interpretation. Now Macs can run Mac OS X, Windows, and Linux. Indeed, Apple computers are the only computers that easily run every major operating system on the same computer. You *can* have your cake and eat it too. In fact, the Mac is so good at running Windows that when Windows Vista was first released, some tests showed that the best hardware to run Vista was a Macintosh.

Why Windows?

So as we near the end of this book about working with your Mac in business, you may wonder why on earth you would want to run Windows on your Mac. After all, this book is full of Mac OS X applications that run circles around creaky old Windows applications. But sometimes there is that one application that you absolutely cannot live without that hasn't made the jump (yet) to Mac OS X. This may be true for an application you love or, more likely, your company loves and insists you use.

Another reason to load Windows is as a safety net. If you are a lifelong Windows user with a rebellious streak and you've decided to try a Mac, it is comforting to know that, in a jam, you can boot up Windows. I have set up new Macs for many switcher friends over the years and for all the times I've installed this Windows safety net, I have yet to hear from one switcher who still used Windows after three months on the Mac unless they were absolutely required to do so (kicking and screaming) for some specific Windows-only software.

MAC, WINDOWS, AND A FREE LUNCH

I once attended a seminar for a Windows-only application and during the first break the speaker practically sprinted toward me to argue how I couldn't possibly be running his application on a Mac. I bet him lunch that I could, and it was delicious. Once the other attendees saw how easily I was running Windows applications on my Mac, the seminar became more about Macs than the software we were there to learn. I think I sold about 10 Macs that day.

Boot Camp

Shortly after the Macs with the Intel chips started shipping, Apple released its own tool for running Windows on your Mac: Boot Camp. Boot Camp Assistant is a free utility (found in the Utilities folder) that ships on every new Mac that helps you install Windows on your Mac and then allows you to boot up directly into Microsoft Windows.

Installing Boot Camp

To run Boot Camp, you need an Intel-based Mac with the latest firmware running Mac OS X 10.5 Leopard or later. Your Mac's startup (internal) disk needs enough extra room for Windows, plus you'll need the installation discs for Microsoft Windows XP, Vista, or 7, along with the appropriate license.

One of the first steps in the Boot Camp installation is partitioning your startup disk for Windows; that is, reserving a chunk of space for holding the complete Windows environment, as shown in Figure 22-1. Under normal circumstances, partitioning your startup disk results in the destruction of all its data. Boot Camp, however, does a nondestructive partition, so your existing Mac

FIGURE 22-1

Partitioning a hard disk for Boot Camp installation

Boot Camp Assistant

Create a Partition for Windows

Each operating system requires its own partition on the disk. Drag the divider to set the size of the partitions, or click one of the buttons.

"Bird" will be partitioned as:

Mac OS X
440 GB
339 GB free

Windows
25 GB

(Divide Equally)   (Use 32 GB)

(Go Back)   (Partition)

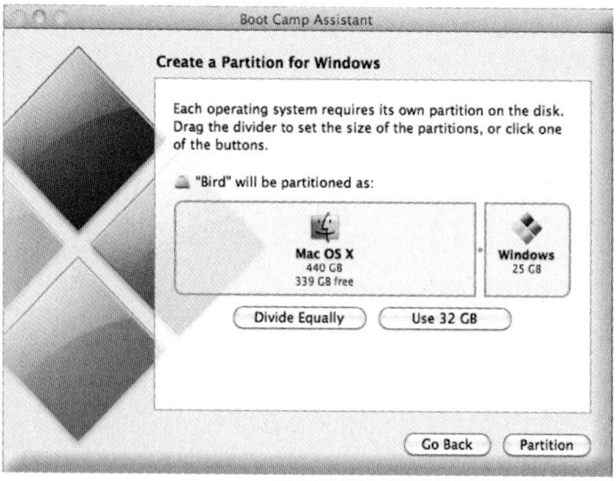

data is preserved. You need to have enough free space on your Mac's startup disk (Boot Camp can't create a Windows partition on other disks) for Windows.

So how big should this partition be? It depends. First, you'll need enough space to run Windows itself, which could require as much as 3GB. Then you must decide how much Windows software you intend to install and how many files you intend to hold on your Boot Camp partition. If you are planning on running Windows regularly and keep data files on the drive, the partition could be quite large. You can get a more precise estimate by looking at the specific applications you intend to install and their related data files to gauge the space required.

I know of one Mac worker who keeps a 200GB Boot Camp partition. In my case, I need Windows for only one application and very little data, so I made my Boot Camp partition just 10GB, and I have plenty of room left. The trick is to make the partition as big as it needs to be, but no larger. After all, you want to save space on your hard disk for all those great Mac OS X apps.

Make sure to leave at least 5GB of free space on the Mac OS X partition for memory swap files and other system requirements. (If you have less than 5GB of available space on the Mac OS X partition on your startup disk, it slows down your Mac.)

Once you choose your partition size, you can't change it. If you run out of space, you have to start over: wiping out your existing Windows partition, creating a new one, and reinstalling Windows and all its apps. So spend a few minutes deciding how big to make your partition.

After telling Boot Camp how much space to carve out for Windows, the rest of the installation is straightforward. You are asked to insert the Windows installation disc, as shown in Figure 22-2; clicking the Start Installation button reboots the Mac. It is important to remember that when prompted to install

FIGURE 22-2

Installing Windows with Boot Camp

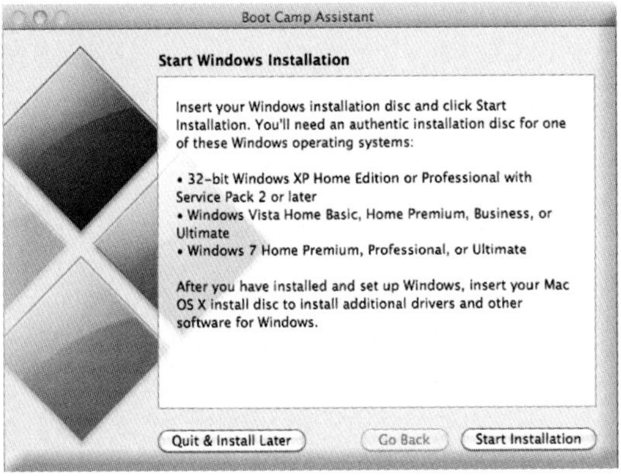

Windows, you do so on the BOOTCAMP partition. If you make a new partition or install Windows in your existing Mac OS X partition, you will wipe out all your Mac OS X data.

One of the unenviable challenges Microsoft faces with Windows is the driver problem. Unlike Apple, which controls the hardware platforms on which Mac OS X operates, Microsoft releases Windows to the world with a seemingly infinite number of different computers and hardware combinations. That means Microsoft's driver support burden is practically unimaginable.

For Mac users, that problem has a direct implication: Microsoft doesn't have drivers for the Mac's hardware or Mac peripherals. Fortunately, Apple has created the drivers for Windows to support Mac hardware, and Boot Camp installs them for you. Depending on the age of your Mac, the drivers on your Mac OS X installation disc may be out of date, so run the Apple Software Update application in Windows to update your drivers.

When you are done, your hard disk will have its own Windows partition with a full Windows installation ready for use. Having set up a lot of PC computers in my day, I can assure you that installing Windows with Boot Camp is one of the most painless Windows installations I have ever experienced.

Using Boot Camp

Holding down the Option key while booting a Boot Camp-enabled Mac brings up the Boot Manager. The Boot Manager allows you to choose which disk or partition to boot from; use the → and ← keys to move among the options and press Return to select the desired one, or just click the desired option with the mouse. If you select a Mac OS X disk or partition, your system boots as normal into familiar Mac OS X. If you select a Windows partition, your Mac will transform itself into a Windows PC before your eyes.

Running Windows under Boot Camp is no different from running Windows on any PC. You can download and install Windows software and data files. And with Boot Camp 3.0 (the version that comes with Mac OS X 10.6 Snow Leopard), you can open, read, and copy files from the Mac OS X partition when booted into Windows.

When running Windows, Boot Camp devotes the entire resources of your Mac to operating Windows. This is both good and bad. Any computer that runs just one operating system at a time has more available resources than one that is running multiple operating systems.

If you are running a resource-intensive graphics application or 3D modeling application under Windows, you will want all your system's processors, memory, and resources available to support it.

Most Mac workers, however, do not run Windows applications that are so resource-intensive. Instead, they run office suites and basic graphics applications that are not so taxing on their Mac. For them, the inconvenience of having to reboot the computer every time they want to switch between operating systems outweighs any benefit of having a single operating system running optimally. You can avoid having to reboot to switch between Mac OS X and Windows by using third-party desktop virtualization software.

Desktop Virtualization Software

Although Boot Camp is a great tool, rebooting the Mac to run a Windows application is a pain. Especially when the Windows application is something simple like Microsoft Access or Intuit QuickBooks. As soon as Apple made the Intel transition for the Mac, software developers began releasing products that allow you to run Windows as an application inside Mac OS X. This creates a virtual Windows computer inside your Mac OS X operating system (thus the name "desktop virtualization").

Once you have Windows running inside Mac OS X, you can run, for example, Microsoft Access for Windows at the same time as iWork Keynote for Mac OS X. You can access the same files and even copy and paste among them. The best desktop virtualization applications on the Mac are Parallels Desktop, VMware Fusion, and the open source VirtualBox. Table 22-1 summarizes the benefits of each application.

TABLE 22-1

Products for Running Windows on a Mac					
Product	Cost	Runs Windows and Mac OS X Simultaneously	Requires Windows License?	Runs Graphics-Intensive Applications	Runs Typical Windows Work Related Software
Apple Boot Camp	included with Mac OS X	—	✔	✔	✔
Parallels Desktop	$80	✔	✔	✔	✔
EMC VMware Fusion	$80	✔	✔	✔	✔
Virtual Box	free*	✔	✔	—	✔
CrossOver Mac Standard	$40	✔	—	✔**	✔
*personal use only; commercial cost varies			**only with $70 CrossOver Pro		

WINDOWS ANTIVIRUS SOFTWARE AND BACKUP

Although there is a legitimate debate about whether to run antivirus software on a Mac (see Chapter 23), there is no question of the need for antivirus software in Windows.

Whether you are running Windows through Boot Camp or through desktop virtualization, you really need to have an antivirus program installed in Windows if it is ever connected to the Internet, accesses e-mail, or accesses shared files. Windows, whether run on a PC or on a Mac, is susceptible to all the viruses, worms, Trojan horses, key loggers, and other malicious software every other Windows computer faces. One free option is Microsoft's Security Essentials, found at www.microsoft.com/security_essentials.

If your Windows Boot Camp partition or virtual machine becomes infected, it is generally not an issue for your Mac OS X partition. The malicious code is usually specifically written for Windows and thus cannot execute in Mac OS X.

Parallels Desktop

Parallels Desktop ($80; www.parallels.com), shown in Figure 22-3, was the first commercial desktop virtualization application for the Mac. It can install various editions of Linux and Windows 2000 through Windows 7.

Parallels Desktop walks you through the Windows installation, streamlining the process where possible. Parallels Desktop also installs Parallels Tools on the Windows virtual machine, which helps deal with the integration between Windows and Mac OS X.

The default setting when installing a Parallels virtual Windows machine is to fully integrate your data files between Windows and Mac OS X, as shown in Figure 22-4. This setting allows the PC virtual machine to access your Mac OS X files. Although sharing files can be convenient if you frequently work in both operating systems, it is not necessary if you are only running Windows for a few application. Moreover, there is at least a theoretical security risk if a shared data file was written to corrupt Mac OS X. Although I've never heard of such a virus, it is worth noting. Regardless, I recommend that you disable the file-integration option when setting up Parallels Desktop unless you have a good reason to keep it.

Another installation default behavior is to boot Windows in Parallels Desktop's Coherence mode, shown in Figure 22-5, which integrates your Windows applications into Mac OS X. This mode allows Windows applications to run in Mac OS X as if they were Mac applications, and it gets rid of a lot of the Windows trappings of a separate desktop. If you prefer to work in the traditional Windows desktop, turn off Coherence mode.

Parallels Desktop running Windows 7

The Parallels Desktop installer's file-sharing setting

FIGURE 22-5

Parallels Desktop running Windows in Coherence mode

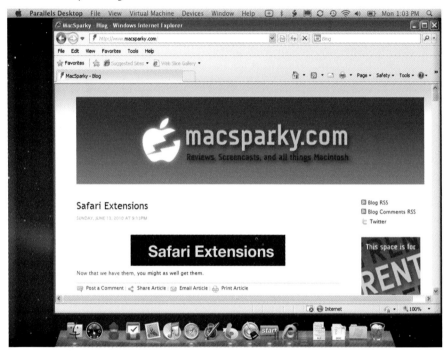

Parallels Desktop provides a great Windows experience. As of this writing, Parallels Desktop is generally considered to be the fastest Windows virtualization application. It wins most benchmark tests for graphics performance and for more nuts-and-bolts tasks like copying files and rebooting.

The newest version of Parallels includes the Crystal View mode, which integrates Windows even deeper into the Mac OS X Desktop. The Crystal View mode is similar to the Coherence mode but hides Windows even more. In Crystal View mode, all Parallels Desktop controls, icons, and menus are hidden, except for the Parallels icon in the Mac menu bar and Windows Applications folder in the Dock. Although Parallels can hide Windows, Crystal View mode does not magically turn your Windows applications into Mac OS X applications. For example, Windows applications still don't work with the Mac OS X Dock's Exposé feature. However, Crystal Mode view does remove nearly all traces of Windows from your desktop.

Parallels Desktop runs the common Windows productivity applications, such as Microsoft Office for Windows, Internet Explorer, and QuickBooks without breaking a sweat. The most recent version of Parallels Desktop is even more graphics-friendly. Parallels Desktop also supports using up to eight cores (on Macs whose processors have eight cores). The ability to run up to eight

WHAT ABOUT LINUX?

Windows isn't the only alternative operating system you may want to run on your Mac. Linux is an alternative, open source, free operating system that comes in many variations. A user-friendly version of Linux popular among desktop virtualization users is Ubuntu, although many IT staff prefer Novell's Suse because it works well with some Windows administration tools. There are open-source applications, such as IBM's Symphony, for Ubuntu, Suse, and some Linux variants that work well with Microsoft Office files. The Firefox browser is available for Linux, and the Evolution e-mail client holds its own against Microsoft Outlook and Entourage.

If you are running desktop virtualization software on your Mac, you can load Linux as a virtual machine and kick the tires for yourself.

cores substantially increases the computing power of Windows processor-heavy applications such as graphics and video applications.

There was a time when Windows video processing and graphics applications could only run on a Mac by rebooting into Windows on a Boot Camp partition, thus turning your entire Mac over to Windows. This is not true any more. Parallels Desktop now uses Mac OS X's OpenGL graphics protocols to deliver acceptable performance for high-end graphics applications.

A nice feature in Parallels Desktop (as well as in VMware Fusion, covered later), is multimonitor support. If you have two monitors hooked up to your Mac, you can use one for a Windows screen and the other as a Mac OS X screen. If you often work in both operating systems, it is nice having each platform on its own screen — plus it provides a constant source of amusement as you watch co-workers' reactions.

If you have a multitouch Apple Magic Trackpad or Magic Mouse, Parallels Desktop supports gestures. But I have to warn you: After using gestures in Windows on a Mac through Parallels Desktop, it feels strange to lose that ability when you sit at a traditional Windows PC.

Parallels Desktop was the first virtualization application on the Mac, and its maturity is repeatedly evident as recent versions continue to add useful tools and additional spit and polish to an already stable desktop virtualization environment.

Fusion

EMC VMware is an experienced virtualization software developer, with several virtualization products on other platforms. It's in the Mac desktop virtualization business with its Fusion ($80; www.vmware.com/fusion) product, shown in Figure 22-6.

Although Fusion was later to the Mac virtualization game than Parallels Desktop, the company's virtualization experience allowed Fusion to hit the

FIGURE 22-6

EMC VMware's Fusion running Windows 7

ground running. Fusion has many of the same features as Parallels, including multicore and 64-bit support to take advantage of the latest Macs' performance capabilities. Like Parallels Desktop, Fusion streamlines the Windows installation process by offering an easy-install option that automates several steps. Once Windows is installed, you can manage your virtual machines with the Fusion Virtual Machine Library panel, shown in Figure 22-7.

VMware also provides a free application, VMware Migration Assistant, that allows you to clone your existing PC onto your Fusion-equipped Mac. To make the transfer, both computers need to be attached to the same network. Although VMware states this can be done wirelessly, it is much faster (and likely to succeed) if both computers are wired to the network with Ethernet cables. This is ideal for Windows switchers who want to have the safety blanket of that old PC available on their Mac, even if they no longer have the actual PC around.

Fusion does not have the feature-creep that you find in Parallels Desktop: The interface is more streamlined and more comprehensible for new users, making it easier to use and configure.

Fusion's Unity view, shown in Figure 22-8, helps you run Windows applications while getting rid of much of the Windows interface. Using the Unity view, you can hide the Windows Start menu and the Windows taskbar.

FIGURE 22-7

Fusion's Machine Library panel

FIGURE 22-8

Microsoft Internet Explorer in Fusion's Unity view

Unity view can also run Windows applications directly from the Mac OS X Dock.

Fusion lets you drag and drop files between Windows and Mac OS X. For easier sharing, you can make files available to both operating systems via shared folders. I'm more in favor of copying files as needed. Move the file onto your Windows desktop and when you are finished working with the file in Windows, copy it back to Mac OS X. Chalk it up to superstition but I prefer to keep my data files exclusively in Mac OS X whenever possible.

One of Fusion's more interesting features is the ability to install preconfigured virtual machines. Fusion virtual machines are portable, so they can be installed on other VMware products. VMware has its own Virtual Appliance Marketplace, found at www.vmware.com/appliances, with more than 1,000 ready-made operating-system-and-application combinations. You just download the virtual machine of your choice and plug it into Fusion. This is great if you want to experiment with other operating systems, such as Linux.

Fusion's application upgrade process is more reliable than Parallels Desktop's. With Fusion, you are prompted when there is a software update, and the application does all the work. In my experience, Parallels Desktop's autoinstaller is not as reliable and often requires me to manually install updates.

An important feature recently added to Fusion, which Parallels Desktop also offers, is application sharing. You can set certain file types to launch with specific Mac or Windows applications. For example, you can open all PDF files — even those on your Windows virtual machine — with Mac OS X's Preview application. Likewise, it allows you to open all QuickBooks files — even those in Mac OS X folders — in QuickBooks under Windows. You can even drag a Windows file on to a Mac OS X application in the Mac OS X Dock and, assuming the file type is supported by the application, have it opened in that application.

The newest version of Fusion adds support for Mac OS X 10.6 Snow Leopard's OpenGL graphics acceleration. As in Parallels Desktop, this means you don't need to use a Boot Camp partition to run Windows by itself for many graphics-heavy applications. Fusion's graphics performance, however, generally trails slightly behind Parallels Desktop's on most benchmark tests.

Both Parallels Desktop and Fusion support installation of Mac OS X 10.6 Server clients. If you have a license to run Mac OS X Server, you can do it virtually on your "regular" Mac. The ability to run Mac OS X Server is useful for network administrators and software developers.

VirtualBox

Several years ago, the now-defunct Sun Microsystems created a Mac OS X virtualization product called VirtualBox, shown in Figure 22-9. Now managed as an open source project, VirtualBox (www.virtualbox.org) is available through a free license for personal and educational use and through a paid license for commercial use.

Although VirtualBox can adequately run Windows applications, it lacks many of the features as well as the speed found in Parallels Desktop and Fusion.

For example, VirtualBox does not assist you with the Windows installation. Both Parallels Desktop and Fusion allow you to run a Boot Camp Windows partition as if it were their own virtual machine, VirtualBox does not.

The most notable deficiency in VirtualBox is the inability to run graphics-intense applications. Although VirtualBox has some graphics support, the performance is noticeably slower than that of Parallels Desktop and Fusion. VirtualBox is also glitchy when you try to watch video in the Windows virtual machine.

Which virtual machine application?

Deciding which virtual machine application to use depends on your needs. If you only run QuickBooks for Windows or similar Windows-only application specific to your work that does not overly tax your Mac, any of the three desktop virtualization products will work. However, VirtualBox is a little more tricky to set

FIGURE 22-9

VirtualBox running Windows XP

up and a bit slower, so I believe it is worth paying for Parallels Desktop or Fusion. For the additional expense, Parallels Desktop and Fusion give you better ease of use, migration between operating systems, and better graphics performance.

But choosing between Parallels Desktop and Fusion is not so easy. Generally, Parallels Desktop wins on power and tools, whereas Fusion wins on usability. But neither victory is by a large margin; both applications are very good. VMware's Virtual Machine Marketplace is also extremely convenient if you plan on loading Linux operating systems. Fortunately, both Parallels Desktop and Fusion have free trial periods, so you can try them before making your decision.

I have been using Parallels Desktop since it was released on the Mac and thus am most comfortable with it. However, when working with Fusion for this book, I was able to duplicate all the functionality I use in Parallels Desktop with very little effort, and I haven't gone back to Parallels Desktop.

Whichever you choose, one thing is clear: Both applications have made so many advances with graphics performance that there is little need for Apple's Boot Camp except for the most performance-intensive applications.

CrossOver Mac

Whether you run Boot Camp or a virtualization application to put Windows on your Mac, you need to buy a full Microsoft Windows license and install Windows on your Mac. CrossOver Mac allows you to avoid that.

A long time ago, there was an open source project called Wine that sought to get Windows applications running in Linux without Windows. The idea was to duplicate the Windows commands in Linux. For example, when a Windows program loaded and told the computer to print, the software could translate that command into the Print command for Linux, effectively bypassing the need for Windows. The Wine project sought to do the same thing on a Mac. It worked, but only sort of.

Since then, CodeWeavers built on the Wine project to release CrossOver Mac (`www.codeweavers.com/products/cxmac`), which allows you to install and run Windows software without having Windows. CrossOver Mac Standard costs $40, and a professional version costs $70, offering better technical support and a copy of CrossOver Games so you can run Windows games on the Mac.

CrossOver acts as an intermediary between the Windows software and the Mac OS, translating Windows instructions into their counterparts on the Mac OS. The result is surreal, as Figure 22-10 shows as the Windows application appears on your Mac using the Mac OS X user interface.

The trouble is that not all Windows applications are programmed the same way, so — as a simple example — how Microsoft Word handles printing can differ

FIGURE 22-10

CrossOver running Microsoft Word for Windows in Mac OS X

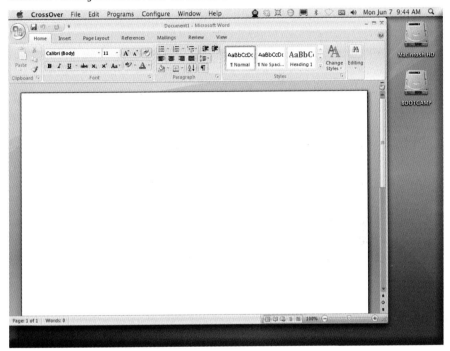

from how Intuit's Quicken does. As a result, CodeWeavers would have to do a lot of work to ensure the huge variety of Windows applications will run in CrossOver.

The result is that only a few actually do run in CrossOver, and even then not all their capabilities work. CodeWeavers has the most popular Windows applications — such as Microsoft Office, Microsoft Project, several Adobe applications, and Quicken — working in CrossOver. Sadly, QuickBooks — one of best reasons to install Windows on a Mac — works only in a limited fashion with CrossOver: QuickBooks 2005 and 2006 run, but no version since has been certified to run at all.

The CodeWeavers Web site has a complete list of tested and untested Windows applications at www.codeweavers.com/compatibility. If the Windows applications you need works in CrossOver, download the free trial and decide for yourself whether you can forego installing Windows.

Running Windows on your Mac gives you the best of both worlds: a stable secure operating system and the ability to run any software you may need. If you play your cards right, it may also one day get you a free lunch.

Security

Gone are the days when we can use our computers without concern for security. Your Mac is important to you; it is an expensive machine containing important data that allows you to get ahead at work. You need to take steps to protect both the Mac and the data on it. The Mac features some useful security tools, both built-in and from independent developers, to keep your computer and your data safe. This chapter explains the best practices for securing your Mac.

Physical Security

When addressing computer security, the importance of physical security is often overlooked. It is much easier to steal your data, ideas, and information if someone has physical possession of your Mac than through some indirect Internet-based attack. So how do you keep prying hands off your Mac?

The best tool to protect your computer's physical security is your own common sense. If you find yourself in a coffee shop and want a refill, do not walk across the room leaving your computer on the table. Shut the lid and carry it with you. Also, spend some time thinking about where you want to sit in a public place with your expensive computer. Right next to the door is a bad idea. In the corner, where a potential thief would have to navigate through a room full of patrons to escape with your machine, is a much better one.

Every Mac laptop has built-in support for a Kensington lock (www. kensington.com). This computer lock allows you to bolt your computer to a fixed device, such as a table leg. For example, you can lock your Mac to the desk in your hotel room while you are out. A Kensington lock may also be helpful at an unsecured workplace.

There are several software packages and services available that track the location of your Mac. One is Undercover ($49; www.orbicule.com/ undercover/mac). Undercover uses Wi-Fi positioning to locate your stolen or missing Mac. It also sends screenshots from your Mac and snaps pictures every eight minutes using the built-in iSight Web camera. Plus, Undercover simulates

THE COFFEE SHOP SNATCH AND GRAB

A law enforcement friend once told me about one of the most common criminal gambits for stealing laptops. The criminals work coffee shops as a team and look for someone near an exit. The first team member, usually an attractive woman, approaches and distracts the unwitting victim. The other team member then snatches the laptop and runs out the door. When done properly, the laptop is halfway down the street before the owner realizes it's gone. Be careful.

a hardware failure, which may prompt the thief to take it in for repair. Your Mac then posts a message on the screen explaining it is stolen.

The important thing is to remember that while you have good intentions, not everyone else does. There are crooks looking for low-hanging fruit, and Apples are particularly juicy. When you leave home with your Mac, you need to take steps to protect yourself and your Mac.

Insuring Your Mac

It is expensive to replace your computer, so insuring your investment may be a good idea. There are two types of insurance: the AppleCare Protection Plan and third-party insurance.

AppleCare

AppleCare (www.apple.com/applecare) is Apple's own insurance for your Apple hardware. Every new Mac includes a one-year warranty. Purchasing an AppleCare warranty (prices vary between $200 and $350) allows you to extend the insurance to three years. You can purchase an AppleCare warranty at any time within the first year of ownership. Quite often you can get a slight discount on AppleCare if you buy it with a new Mac or shop for it online from resellers such as Amazon.com.

An AppleCare warranty covers manufacturing problems and normal wear. If, after two and a half years, your hard drive fails, Apple will install a new one if you have the extended AppleCare warranty. However, AppleCare does not cover accidental damage. If you drop your Mac and crack the screen, the AppleCare warranty does not cover the repair. It also does not cover theft or loss.

Although opinions are mixed concerning the need for AppleCare with desktop Macs, it is a good idea with laptops. The electronics on laptops are crammed into a small package and take a lot of abuse as you carry them around and are more likely than the desktop Macs to have problems within the first three years of ownership. The cost of just about any service performed on a laptop will exceed the expense of AppleCare. Also, Apple is pretty fair about warranty service. I once had a laptop that had several problems. After three attempts to repair it, Apple simply gave me a new one.

Theft, loss, and damage policies

Because AppleCare does not cover accidental damage, theft, and loss, additional insurance coverage may be appropriate. If you have a homeowner's or renter's insurance policy, you can often purchase an insurance rider policy that covers accidental damage, theft, and loss of your Mac. If you can't get insurance through an existing policy, you can purchase a specific policy for your Mac. There are several reputable insurance brokers that specialize in portable electronics. I keep one on my MacBook that costs about $100 a year. If I lose my computer, or it gets run over by a truck, I get a replacement. If you take your Mac out often, the premium may be worth the peace of mind.

An important point is that AppleCare and a damage and loss policy cover two separate problems. Most accidental damage, theft, and loss policies do not cover warranty repairs. You need to check with your insurer but you may need both types of policies for full coverage.

Data Security

In addition to physical security, Mac workers need to protect the data on their machines. There are several tools built into Mac OS X and available from third-party vendors for just this purpose.

System password

The very first thing you should do with any Mac is install a system password. A system password, set up in the Accounts system preference shown in Figure 23-1, is the first level of defense on your Mac. Although well-motivated hackers can get past a system password, it will keep honest people honest. Moreover, when combined with PGP or FileVault encryption, explained later, your security becomes formidable. (You get to the system preferences by choosing ▸ System Preferences.)

After setting your system password, you can add security to it in the Security system preference, as shown in Figure 23-2.

You can set your Mac to require a password immediately or within a set time after your screen saver begins. You can also disable automatic login and set a timer to lock your Mac after a set period.

The secure virtual memory setting encrypts your data as the contents of your Mac's memory (including passwords and other sensitive data) are swapped out

Setting a new password in the Accounts system preference

Old password:	••••••
New password:	••••••••
Verify:	••••••••
Password hint: (Recommended)	

Cancel Change Password

The Security system preference's password settings

Security

Show All

General   FileVault   Firewall

☑ Require password [1 minute] after sleep or screen saver begins

For all accounts on this computer:
☑ Disable automatic login
☐ Require a password to unlock each System Preferences pane
☑ Log out after [30] minutes of inactivity
☑ Use secure virtual memory

☐ Disable Location Services   Reset Warnings
☑ Disable remote control infrared receiver
This computer will not work with any remote.   Pair...

Click the lock to prevent further changes.   ⑦

to your hard disk. This setting causes a slight performance hit to your Mac but is worth it for the security-conscious. While you are in this system preference, also disable your Mac's infrared receiver unless you plan on using an Apple remote with your Mac. Besides subjecting you to unplanned computer activity if there is surrounding infrared noise, this receiver also provides hackers one more vector into your Mac.

Data encryption

One of the best ways to protect your data is to encrypt it. Encryption scrambles your data, preventing others from reading it without the encryption key. There are two ways to accomplish this with Apple's built-in software, File Vault, and by using secured disk images.

File Vault

FileVault is Apple's disk encryption utility. It is built into Mac OS X and available on every Mac currently sold. It can be accessed through the Security system preference's FileVault tab, as shown in Figure 23-3. Once enabled, FileVault encrypts your Home folder. The data kept within the FileVault is not accessible without a password.

With FileVault enabled, it is difficult for someone to access files in your Home folder. But FileVault encryption has a cost: It increases the amount of space used on your hard disk by your home directory. FileVault also limits your ability to use a Time Machine backup. When using FileVault, you can't restore individual files; you can only restore the entire FileVault database. There are also claims by some researchers that the FileVault encryption algorithm can be hacked. I've never heard of anyone actually breaking through FileVault's encryption and suspect it would be quite difficult. Finally, make sure to keep track of your FileVault password. If you lose the password, you also lose all your data.

Perhaps the biggest shortcoming with FileVault is that you cannot select which data to encrypt. FileVault encrypts only the entire Home folder: your Documents, Downloads, Movies, Music, and Pictures folders, as well as any folders and files inside them. Any data outside your Home folder is not encrypted.

If FileVault is not enough for your privacy needs, there is a paid product, PGP (covered later in this chapter), that offers more complete data encryption.

FIGURE 23-3

The FileVault options for data encryption in the Security system preference

![Security system preference FileVault tab showing General, FileVault, and Firewall options. Text reads: "FileVault secures your home folder by encrypting its contents. It automatically encrypts and decrypts your files while you're using them. WARNING: Your files will be encrypted using your login password. If you forget your login password and you don't know the master password, your data will be lost. A master password is not set for this computer. This is a "safety net" password. It lets you unlock any account on this computer. FileVault protection is off for this account. Turning on FileVault may take a while." With buttons "Set Master Password..." and "Turn On FileVault..." and at bottom "Click the lock to make changes."]

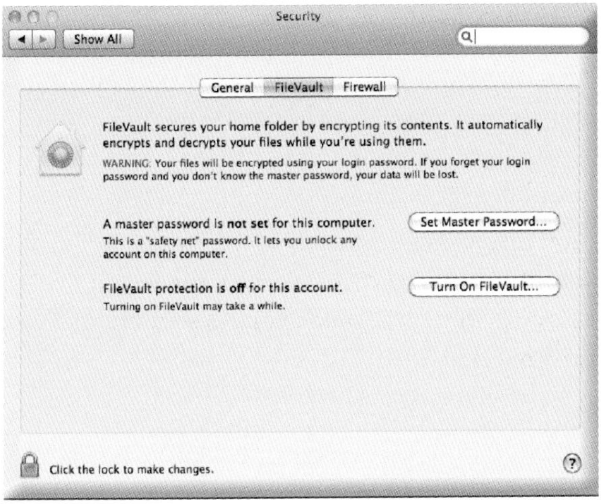

Mac OS X secured disk images

One little-known feature of Mac OS X is the ability to create secured disk images without any additional software. These are small (or large) virtual drives that you create and encrypt. It takes just minutes to create such a password-protected disk. Once created, you can fill the encrypted disk with confidential data and, once the secured disk image is closed, no prying eyes can return to the data without the password.

Many users keep several secured disk images with particular data such as client information, financial data, and personal information. Let's walk through the creation of an encrypted disk image:

1. **Open Disk Utility.** Go to your Utilities folder (found inside the Applications folder; you can press Shift+⌘+U to get there quickly) and double-click Disk Utility to open the application. Disk Utility comes free with Mac OS X to manage, modify, and monitor your hard disk. It also is the application from which you create a secured disk image.

2. **Create the disk image.** In the sidebar of Disk Utility is a list of all the disks on your computer. It is important to verify that none of the existing disks are selected when creating a new disk image; you can ensure nothing is selected by clicking in the white space below the list of disks. Once you are certain that no disks are selected, click the New Image icon at the top.

3. **Specify the disk image settings.** You are then presented with the Save As dialog box that has all the parameters for your secured disk image. They should be filled in as follows (see Figure 23-4):

    ▶ **Name:** Give your secure image a distinctive name so you will remember what it is in the future. Alternatively, you can give it a generic name to confuse prying eyes.

    ▶ **Size:** There are several built-in default sizes. You can choose any of these or create your own custom size. Once the encrypted disk image is formed, you cannot change the size, so make sure you make it large enough to hold any anticipated needs. If your sparse image begins to run out of room, make a new, larger one and copy the data into the new image before discarding the old one.

    ▶ **Format:** Leave this at the default setting: Mac OS Extended (Journaled).

    ▶ **Encryption:** Choose your encryption method, 128- or 256-bit encryption. I normally use 128-bit encryption, but for the strongest possible security, use the slower 256-bit method.

    ▶ **Partitions:** Leave this at the default: Single Partition – Apple Partition Map.

FIGURE 23-4

Secure sparse image settings

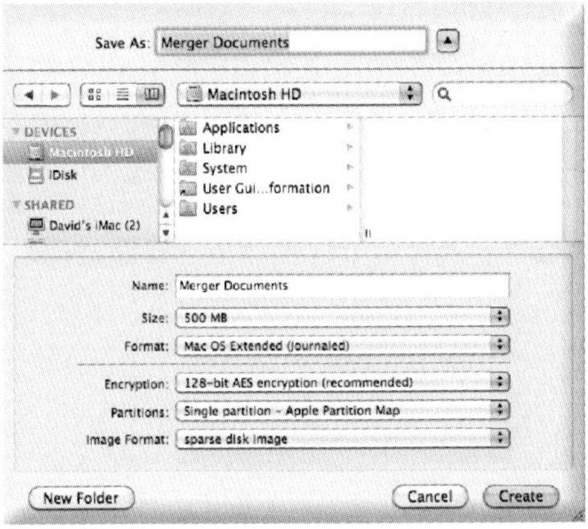

▶ **Image Format:** Select Sparse Disk Image, which allows you to keep the size of the drive to the actual data stored inside it. If you make a 5GB sparse image but only place 200MB of data in it, the disk image's file size is 200MB. The disk image's file can grow to 5GB as you add data, but you don't use the full 5GB until you need to. Note that sparse disk images don't get smaller as you delete files.

4. **Pick a location for your new image, and then click Create.**

5. **Enter a password.** Make it a good one. Do not check Remember Password in My Keychain; otherwise, someone with Keychain access to your Mac can open the secure image. Once you have entered your password and clicked OK, Mac OS X builds the secure sparse image.

If you open the Finder, you will see the image is already mounted and ready to be filled with your confidential data. Once you have loaded your confidential data into the sparse image, you can eject it to lock it. When you need to access the data, simply double-click the sparse image file to open a dialog box that asks for your password. When you are finished, eject the disk to lock it again.

The sparse image file can be copied, relocated, moved, and otherwise treated like any Mac OS X file. It is a good idea to make several copies of the sparse image and place them on backup disks, thumb drives, or other locations.

Secure sparse images are great for keeping data sets confidential. Because they are so portable, they are an excellent option for storing data on cloud-based servers, like MobileMe or Dropbox, with an extra layer of protection. If you have limited amounts of secure data, a secure sparse image might be all the protection you need.

PGP encryption

In addition to the Apple tools, several companies have released Mac-based encryption products. One of the best is PGP Whole Disk Encryption.

PGP (Pretty Good Privacy) encryption ($150; www.pgp.com) is an established encryption company in the PC world but a relative newcomer to the Mac. Unlike FileVault, which just encrypts the Home folder's contents, PGP Whole Disk Encryption encrypts the entire disk. Everything is secured.

Setting up PGP is simple: You install the software and allow it to encrypt the disk. Depending on the size of your disk, this can take several hours. Once the process is complete, the disk completely encrypts itself every time you shut it down. When you turn on your Mac, you are prompted for your PGP password. Without it, the disk is locked up tight. Unless the thief has your password, he can't get access to the disk's contents, even if he boots from a different disk. PGP also gives you the ability to securely encrypt e-mail and iChat communications.

PGP works at the root level of the disk, so it can limit some functionality. For example, when making a major operating system upgrade, such as from Mac OS X 10.5 Leopard to Mac OS X 10.6 Snow Leopard, PGP requires that you uninstall it first. I have used PGP on my MacBook since it was first released and I have never had any significant issue or degradation in performance. It is very comforting knowing that if my MacBook is stolen or lost, confidential data will remain confidential.

PGP is an enterprise-friendly company: If you are running a Mac network, you can buy site licenses to cover your entire office. Although there are no perfect tools and hackers are always probing for ways to access encrypted data, PGP is one of the most complete tools available on Mac OS X.

Viruses and Other Malware

Apple spends a lot of time bragging how the Mac platform is safer than Windows. That is true, to a certain point. Although Mac OS X has not experienced the types of security problems that plague Windows, there are still risks to Mac users.

Viruses and antivirus software

One of the most frequent questions asked by Windows switchers to the Mac OS X platform is "What antivirus program should I run?" The answer depends on several factors. Although Mac OS X certainly isn't impervious to viruses, the fact remains there have been very few documented cases of viruses in the wild on Mac OS X. There are several reasons for there have been few viruses in Mac OS X.

First, Mac OS X isn't as friendly to viruses as other operating systems. Because it is based on Unix, Mac OS X compartmentalizes a lot of the data it holds. Although a virus could get into certain parts of memory, that doesn't mean it will find its way into others. Mac OS X is very good at segregating its memory, also called *sandboxing*. Mac OS X also requires you to enter your name and system password for the installation of any new software. This act of requiring you to actively approve installation of new software is useful to prevent installation of viruses and malicious code.

Another reason Mac OS X doesn't have the virus problems Windows does is market share: Even with its recent success, the Mac is a very small portion of the overall computing market. When an operating system is only on one of every 20 computers, virus programmers are less likely to target it. But this could change given the Mac's recent popularity (it now accounts for about one in 10 new PCs sold). At some point, Mac market share is going to rise so high that viruses will be targeted at Mac OS X.

Several software vendors sell antivirus software for the Macintosh. Two of the more notable products are Norton AntiVirus for Macintosh ($50; www. norton.com/mac) and Kaspersky Anti-Virus for Mac ($40; www.kaspersky. com). These products not only detect known Macintosh viruses but also Windows viruses. Quite often, Windows viruses are spread using e-mail attachments, so Mac workers may unwittingly help distribute these viruses when forwarding e-mail with Windows virus attachments.

In addition to security tools on your Mac, your company may have its own IT-imposed security policies. These often require installation of software endpoint security tools for IT staff. The same companies that make desktop virus software usually design these tools, and most have Mac support. In that case, you need to check with your IT department to make certain it gets the right tools on your Mac.

The decision to install virus software requires a balancing of the necessity for the additional protection against the impact on system resources and is different for every person. If you do run antivirus software, you should not have a false sense of security. Even with antivirus software installed, you are still vulnerable to Trojan and phishing attacks explained later.

Trojan horse attacks

A Trojan horse, named after the mythological trickery in Homer's and Virgil's epic poems, is something attractive to the user that, once installed, creates all sorts of mischief. Trojan infection involves some action by the Mac user. The user unwittingly downloads and approves the malicious code. Trojans are useful to virus writers for data theft, keyboard logging (tracking your keystrokes to get passwords and other secrets), creating botnets (a network of computers used for spamming), or even the malicious destruction of your hard disk.

Trojans have been distributed on the Mac OS X platform. In 2009, following Apple's release of iWork, an illegal unlocked copy found its way onto the Bit Torrent file-sharing site. Many users downloaded copies and, when installing them, unwittingly installed a Trojan horse on their Macs. Both the Norton and Kapersky antivirus programs were quickly updated to catch the iWork Trojan.

The best practice for avoiding Trojan horses is to practice safe computing. The iWork incident is a good example. It infected only people downloading illegal software. Trojans are often distributed through illegal software downloads and pornography Web sites. Anyone who downloads software from the Internet is at risk of allowing a Trojan onto his or her Mac. Again, the best defense is common sense: Only download and install software from trusted sources. Like your mother always told you: If something seems too good to be true, it probably is.

Phishing

Phishing (pronounced "fishing") is the fraudulent acquisition of your sensitive data. Phishing is not a form of virus. Instead it is a subterfuge where the bad guys masquerade as a trustworthy Web site to get you to provide credit card, financial information, or other sensitive data. Phishing attacks often start with you receiving an e-mail that informs you of some important change to your bank account. When you click the link, you are presented a Web site that looks

USING THE FIREWALL

Mac OS X has a built-in firewall that, oddly, is turned off by default. The Mac OS X firewall, found in the Security system preference, exists to monitor the communications entering your Mac and block unauthorized access. The idea is to allow you to communicate with the outside world using tools like iChat and Safari while preventing malicious attacks from the outside.

Although some firewalls are extremely complex, the built-in Mac OS X firewall is not. In Mac OS X, the firewall is either on or off. You can make adjustments for specific applications under the Advanced tab but otherwise there is nothing to configure. If, while using your firewall, you find a certain application cannot send or receive data from the Internet, check your firewall's Advanced tab and add that application to the list.

Although Apple's firewall is not the strongest, it does afford some protection. Most office networks have their own hardware firewall built into their network. In those instances, the firewall may be unnecessary on your Mac. However, whenever accessing coffee shop, airport, or other public Wi-Fi hot spots, you should have your firewall turned on.

identical to your bank's Web site but in reality is an entirely different site hosted, quite frequently, on the other side of the world. You dutifully type in your account information and password — and you are compromised.

These attacks aren't just limited to banking. Phishing attacks are also engineered around any financial or other transaction such as PayPal and MobileMe account information. Mac users are just as vulnerable to phishing attacks as any other computer user on the Internet.

Phishing attacks are becoming more sophisticated and on the rise. You used to be able to determine a phishing attack by looking at your address bar in your browser. If, for example, you believed you were going to Bank of America but your address bar showed some Web site in Russia, you knew you had a problem. Unfortunately, phishers have now figured out how to spoof (fake) those addresses.

No legitimate financial institution is going to e-mail you and ask you to click a link to give sensitive data. When you get an e-mail from your bank or other financial institution, don't click any links. Instead open your browser and use your own bookmarks or type in the address yourself. Another clue is how the e-mail is addressed. When your bank writes an e-mail, it generally includes your account name in the e-mail. If the user name isn't present and the e-mail is simply addressed to "valued customer," your defense shields should immediately go up. Finally, if you are ever informed of any account problems, close the lid on your Mac and call the bank. Don't call the number in your e-mail. Open your address book or look at your last statement and call the number that you know is good.

Managing Passwords

When using your Mac, it is essential that you have a reliable password management system. Using modern computers, a hacker can easily throw the entire dictionary at a password field. Gone are the days when "pencil" was good enough. Many users don't give passwords enough thought and end up defaulting to the same two or three passwords over and over again. The trouble is that the hackers know this: Once they get your password anywhere, they have it nearly everywhere.

That's why you need a reliable password generation and management system. Some users keep a text file on their computer with a list of sites and passwords. Although this may be sufficient, it is insecure. Anyone with five minutes at your machine could access and copy your entire list.

Another solution is to have your browser keep your login passwords in the built-in Mac OS X Keychain utility. This is a better solution but also has its

FIGURE 23-5

1Password's Password Generator

![Strong Password Generator dialog]

security risks. Also, because Mac workers often find themselves using multiple Web browsers, the passwords and logins may not always be available.

One of the best password tools on the Mac is 1Password ($40; www.1password.com). This application, which also has Windows, iPhone, and iPad versions, installs as a standalone application in Mac OS X and creates shortcuts in your browsers. When you sign up for a new Web site, 1Password creates a password with a random string of characters extremely difficult to crack. You can even set parameters to the password such as length and avoidance of confusingly similar characters, as shown in Figure 23-5.

1Password then inserts your new super password and creates its own login in the 1Password database. Forever after, when you visit that site, you can click on the 1Password icon in your browser bar and automatically fill in your user name and the insanely complicated password. Because everything is automated, you can use a different password for every login.

An additional benefit of using 1Password is that it helps avoid phishing attacks. 1Password only offers to fill in passwords for sites you have already registered. So, if you are directed to your bank's alleged Web site but 1Password is not offering to log in, you may not be at your bank's Web site and red flags should go up.

1Password also stores your biographical and credit card information so you can fill in Web forms directly from your 1Password data store. Finally, 1Password also keeps other data such as e-mail and FTP logins and secure notes where you can keep any confidential data that is locked behind the 1Password wall, as shown in Figure 23-6.

FIGURE 23-6

1Password's application window

Security and Mac OS X Server

If you are running a Mac office, Mac OS X Server adds several network wide security tools. The server administration tools provide the IT staff remote administration and granular file management and communication privileges. Mac OS X Server also integrates a 128-bit encrypted channel between systems and file authentication services, limiting access to particular data. In addition to its own strong firewall, Mac OS X Server also incorporates the open standard Common Data Security Architecture (CDSA) that includes the ability to create security-enabled applications. As you can see, Mac OS X Server has many advanced security tools.

Although you are generally safer on a Mac than a Windows PC, Mac users still need to take security seriously. Using the tools in this chapter and a bit of common sense, you should be able to work with your Mac securely.

Mac Automation

When you need a new feature for your Mac, you usually go out and find the software that will do the job. Indeed, most of this book is about finding the right application. But what about making your own applications or enhancing the features of your existing applications?

Normally, creating an app or adding features to an application requires that you write your own software. Programming is not easy; it takes years of training and experience to do well. For those of us without the time and patience to learn how to program, Apple has created several tools to help us automate our Macs. These automation tools let you create a type of mini-program that performs specialized tasks and let you connect existing applications to make them work in new and better ways. This chapter covers the two primary automation tools on the Mac: Automator and AppleScript.

Automator

Automator is installed on all Macs for one purpose: to simplify repetitive tasks. Consider it your own personal robot. (Indeed, the Automator icon is a robot named Otto.) The idea behind Automator is to allow anyone, without a lick of programming experience, to create his or her Automator actions. Creating Automator workflows requires no computer programming whatsoever. With its drag-and-drop functionality, Automator lets you quickly create actions and start saving time. So let's create an Automator action.

Resizing images

Imagine you just returned from your company's latest retreat and your boss walks into your office and hands you a disc full of pictures that she wants posted on the company Web site before the day is over. You open the disk on your Mac to discover there are 638 pictures and they are all 3,888 by 2,592 pixels — much too large for the Web. So you have one hour to resize 638 images. No problem! Automator to the rescue.

The secret is to build a workflow in Automator to resize those photos. First open Automator (found in the Applications folder). Upon launch, Automator

FIGURE 24-1

Types of Automator workflows

gives you an option window to choose the type of workflow you are going to build (shown in Figure 24-1).

There are several types of Automator workflows:

▸ **Workflow:** A workflow is a set of Automator instructions that can be run from within Automator and is often the starting point for making new automation workflows. You can explore and experiment with available actions, as covered later in this chapter. A workflow is also the easiest place to build and run one time scripts, that you don't anticipate needing in the future. In order to run a workflow, Automator must be open.

▸ **Application:** Applications are workflows that do not need Automator running to work. When you perfect your workflow, save it as an application. (To do this, choose File ▸ Save As and select Application in the Automator Save As dialog box.) You can then keep the application in a folder (or on your Mac OS X Dock) and run it by dragging files onto the application icon. Using the resizing example, you could drag images onto the completed Automator resizing application.

▸ **Service:** Services are a new addition to Automator with Mac OS X 10.6 Snow Leopard. Services are handy: They install themselves in the contextual menu (accessed by Control+clicking or right-clicking a file).

They accept text, images, or other files and perform specific actions on them. (We are going to build a service later in this chapter.)

▶ **Folder action:** Folder actions are workflows installed in a folder. Whenever you drag a file into the folder, the Automator script runs on the file. If, for example, you often need to resize photos to a specified size, you could create a folder with an folder action that resizes images dropped in it.

▶ **Print Plug-in:** Print plug-ins are workflows in the Print dialog box. They install to the PDF output menu (covered in Chapter 12). The Print Plug-in workflow makes a PDF version of your document and lets you take further actions, such as filing and e-mailing.

▶ **iCal alarm:** These Automator workflows run when triggered by an event in iCal. For example, you could have Automator send a file to your staff every day at 7:00 a.m. To make this work, create an iCal appointment and, in iCal, select the Run Script option in the event's alarm menu. When the alarm triggers, iCal runs the selected workflow.

▶ **Image Capture plug-in:** Mac OS X includes Image Capture, an application to manage images from external devices like cameras and iOS devices. When you plug the devices into your Mac, you can use Image Capture to move, manage, and delete images on your Mac and the attached device. Using Automator you can automate this process by creating an Image Capture plug-in.

For the Web-resizing example, choose Workflow.

The left pane in the main Automator window, shown in Figure 24-2, holds a list of Automator actions. Apple has assembled an exhaustive set of actions for a variety of contexts, such as managing contacts, changing file names, and using iTunes. In addition to the Automator actions supplied by Apple, third-party developers have created actions you can install in Automator. Microsoft Office, for example, automatically installs several Automator actions that let you automate actions in the Microsoft Office applications.

The right side of the screen is where you build your Automator routines. Using Automator reminds me of playing with Lego blocks. The left side of the Automator screen is like the bucket of blocks and the right side is like your building mat. Creating an Automator workflow is no more difficult than finding the correct blocks on the left side and then stacking them in the correct order on the right side.

Creating an action

So let's get back to the images. Create a new Automator project by choosing File ▶ New or pressing ⌘+N. Then select Workflow from the settings sheet.

Before Automator can resize anything, it needs to first find the images. Automator actions that deal with files are found in the Files & Folders list in

FIGURE 24-2

Automator's main window

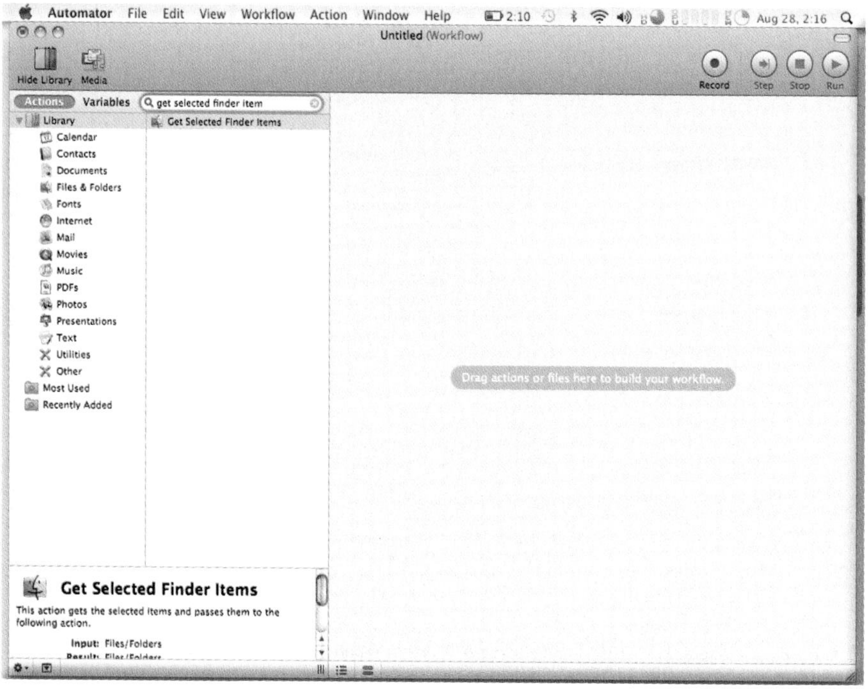

the left pane. Rather than digging through the lists of potential actions, you can search them out, if you know all or part of the action's name: Click on the search window, indicated in Figure 24-2, and type Get Selected Finder Items. Automator will display the Get Selected Finder Items action for you. Click and drag the action onto the right side of the screen. You've just laid your first block.

Once you have the Get Selected Finder Items Action in your workflow, click Description so Automator opens a description of what the action does. In this case, it simply takes the selected Finder items and passes them to the next action.

So now that you have selected the items, what next? It's time to resize. Type the word scale in the Automator search bar; the Scale Images action should appear in the left pane. Drag it onto your workflow. The screen should now look like that in Figure 24-3. The Scale Images action gives you the option to set the desired width of the images. Because these images will be published on the Web, set it to 400 pixels.

At this point, the Automator workflow has selected and resized the images. Just so there's no confusion as to the fact that the images have been resized for the Web and are not the original versions, you should rename the resized images; here, add the words for Web at the end. To do so, type rename in the Automator search bar and drag the Rename Finder Items action to the workflow. This action gives

FIGURE 24-3

Scaling images with Automator

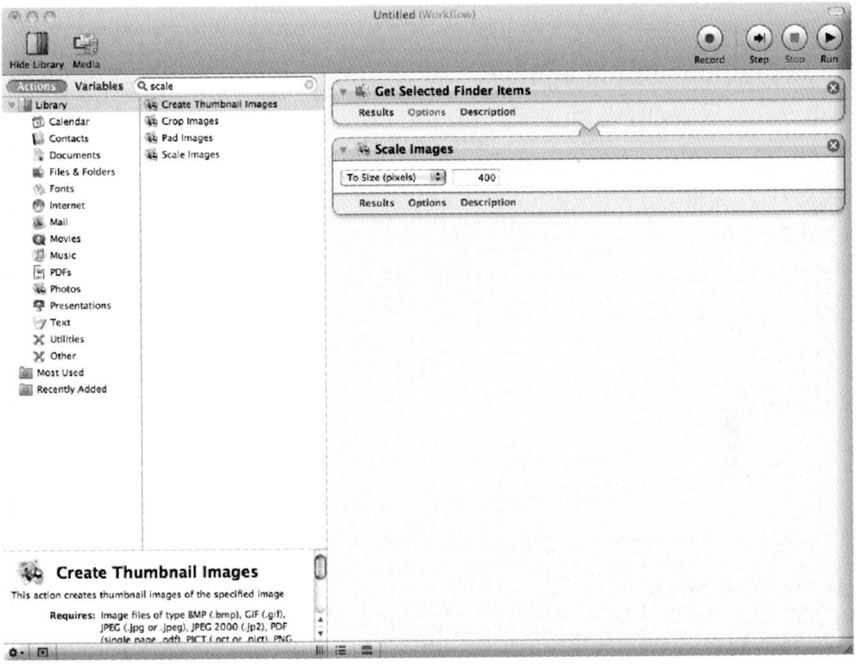

FIGURE 24-4

The completed image-resizing Automator workflow

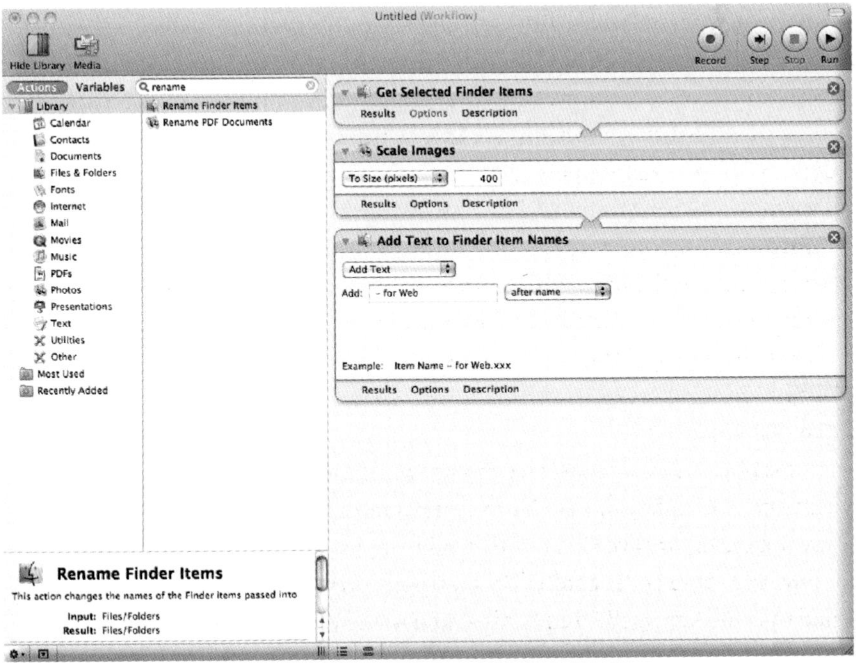

you several options: You can add a date or time, change the case, make file names sequentially numbered, replace text, name a single item, or add text. In this case, let's add text at the end of the resized image: Select Add Text and type the words for Web in the Add field. Finally, make certain the action knows to add the text after (as opposed to before) the file name by selecting After Name in the Automator action. The final Automator workflow should look like that in Figure 24-4.

Now you're finished. Open the folder containing all the image files. Select all the images with the mouse (or press ⌘+A) and then switch to Automator. Press the Run iconic button in the toolbar and Automator will resize your images, lickety-split. When you're done, you'll have a folder full of resized, 400-pixel-wide images ready for publication to the Web.

Now let's build an Automator service.

Creating a service

A lot of Mac workers have more reading materials than they have time: You are flooded with documents and extended e-mails that require reading. Let's use Automator to take written text and convert it into an audio file so you can listen to it on your iPod or iPhone during your commute.

This time, rather than make a workflow, you are going to create a service. Services let you to create a custom Automator script that resides in the contextual

FIGURE 24-5

Creating a text-based service in Automator

menu (activated when you Control+click or right-click an object). A service is always available, even when Automator is not running.

Create a new Automator project by choosing File ▶ New or pressing ⌘+N. This time, instead of selecting Workflow in the settings sheet, select Service. The Automator window opens and should look like that in Figure 24-5.

This service is going to work on blocks of selected text, so Automator should be instructed that the service receives selected text from any application, as shown in Figure 24-5.

The next step is to convert the selected text into an audio file. Automator has an action for this called, not surprisingly, Text to Audio File. You can find this action using the Automator search bar. Locate the action and drag it onto your Automator service. Your screen should now look like that in Figure 24-6.

You have several options when converting text to an audio file. First, you choose a voice. Mac OS X has several built-in computerized voices; the most natural-sounding voice is Alex. Several of the other voices, however, are entertaining; I particularly like Bruce and Zarvox. You can select various voices and press the Play button to get an example of each.

Once you've chosen a voice, create a name for the file. In this case, call it `text2speech -`. Include the hyphen at the end because the service will later add a time stamp (to avoid duplicate file names). You can save the file anywhere on your Mac. In the example, I'm putting it on the desktop. Your Automator window should now look like that in Figure 24-6.

At this stage, you have selected text, converted it to an audio file, and saved it to the desktop. Next you need to add a date and time stamp. To do this, use two instances of the Rename Finder Items action covered in the previous section's example of an image-resizing workflow. The first instance adds the date, and the second instance adds the time.

Next, use the Import Audio Files action to convert the audio file to the standard iTunes format, AAC. Search out the action and drag it onto your service. Finally, import the AAC audio file into iTunes, using the Import Files into iTunes action. You can import the audio file into an existing playlist or create a new one. (The example creates a new playlist called Text to Speech.) The completed service is shown in Figure 24-7.

The service is completed. Now you just need to save it. Choose File ▶ Save or press ⌘+S. Automator prompts you to provide a name for your new service; use `Text to Speech`.

Now, test it. Open your e-mail application or Web browser and find a large block of text. Select the text with your mouse, then Control+click or right-click the selected text to open the contextual menu. In that menu, mouse down to the Services directory and choose the Text to Speech suboption.

FIGURE 24-6

The Text to Audio action in Automator

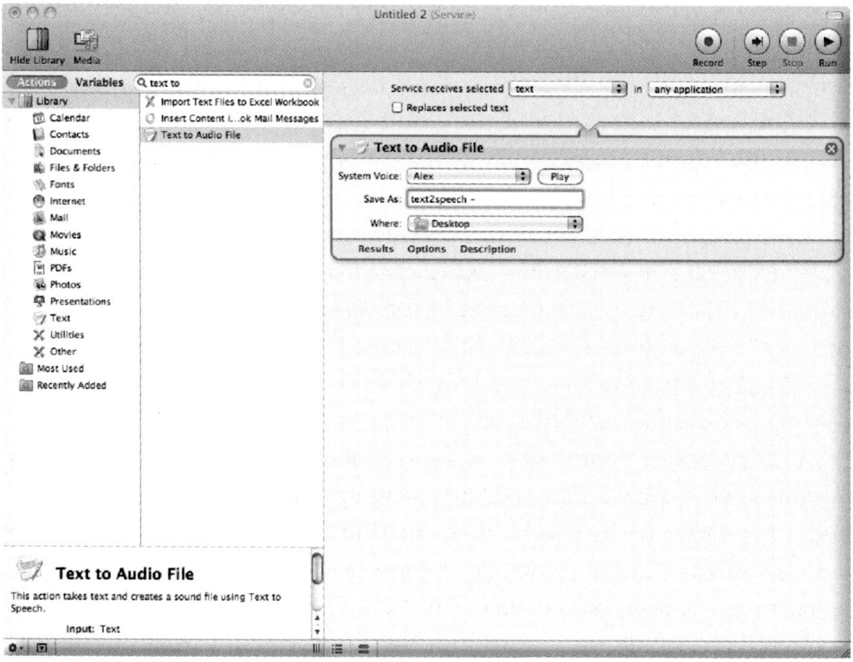

FIGURE 24-7

The completed Text to Speech Automator service

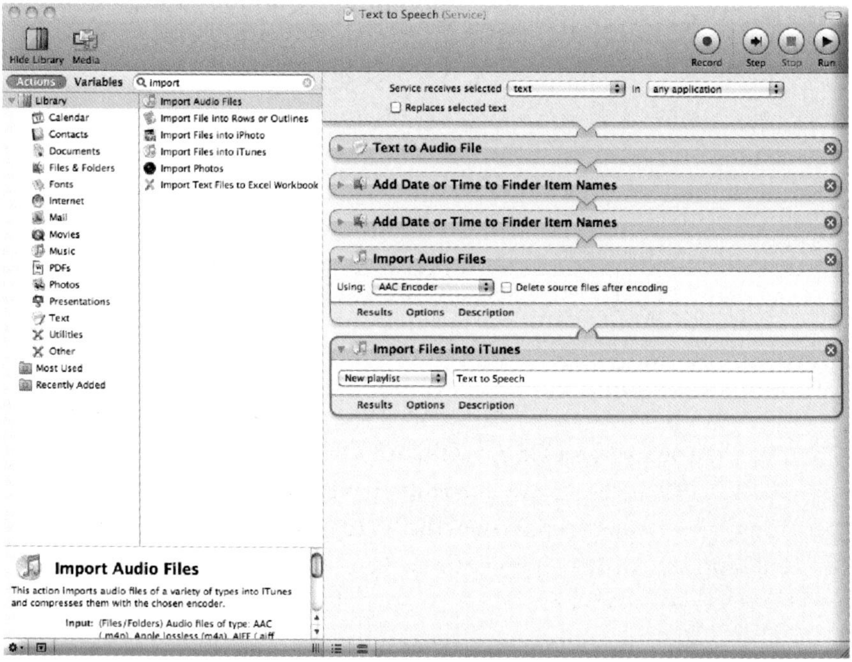

As soon as you activate the service, Automator goes to work: It takes the selected text, converts it to an audio file, renames it, converts it to AAC format, and brings it into iTunes in a matter of seconds. You can then synchronize that playlist to your iPod, iPhone, or iPad and listen to it on your ride home. I spend an hour a day commuting and get a lot of my "reading" done while behind the wheel.

If you don't want to fiddle with Automator but still want the benefit of using services, there are many services available for download and installation on your Mac. The best resource is `www.macosxautomation.com/services`.

Automator is amazing. You can, in essence, program your Mac without any programming knowledge. It does, however, have its limits: Automator is linear. When creating more sophisticated computer programs, you can instruct the program to jump around and make decisions for you. Automator doesn't work that way. It is more like an assembly line: You put a file in one end, and something else comes out the other.

Automator is also limited by its available actions. Although third-party software developers and Apple are always adding actions to Automator, if your workflow needs a step for which there is no action, you're probably out of luck. There is a way to create your own custom actions, but doing so requires programming knowledge of AppleScript (covered later) or one of the Unix shell scripting languages (such as Bash, Perl, Ruby, and Python), which goes beyond the scope of this book.

AppleScript

So what if you hit the wall of Automator's limitations? In that case, it is time to step up your game and learn AppleScript. AppleScript is a scripting language designed by Apple for Mac OS X. Unlike most programming languages, AppleScript tries to use a natural-language model so commands are easier to understand.

You won't learn AppleScript in an afternoon and a few pages of this book. Despite its simplicity, AppleScript is still a computer language, after all, and several lengthy books are published on mastering it. Nevertheless, let me give you a taste of AppleScript through a few AppleScript projects.

AppleScript Editor

AppleScript Editor, found in the Utilities folder of the Application folder on your Mac, is the built-in Mac OS X application for writing and executing scripts. Shown in Figure 24-8, the AppleScript editor has two panes. The top pane is where you type your AppleScript code. The bottom pane has two subpanes where you can display either a description of your AppleScript or an event log showing the results of your AppleScript.

Some simple scripts

The idea behind AppleScript is to make it as comprehensible to nonprogrammers as possible. As a result, the syntax works largely with natural (English) language. For example, programming your computer to talk is normally a pretty complicated task. Not so with AppleScript. Type the following in the script editor:

```
say "I can be used for work"
```

Click the Compile iconic button in the toolbar. Then make sure the volume is turned up on your Mac and click the Run iconic button in the toolbar.

Guess what? You just wrote your first AppleScript. Let's change the computer voice now. Type the following in the AppleScript Editor window, as shown in Figure 24-9.

```
say "shall we play a game?" using "Zarvox"
```

Now compile and run the script.

As you can see, AppleScript is more accessible to nonprogrammers than more traditional computing languages.

As another example, if you want AppleScript to open your startup disk, type the following script.

```
tell application "Finder" to open the startup disk
```

Here is a more complex example:

```
set text_entry to "I like to use my Mac at work!"
```

FIGURE 24-8

AppleScript Editor's main window

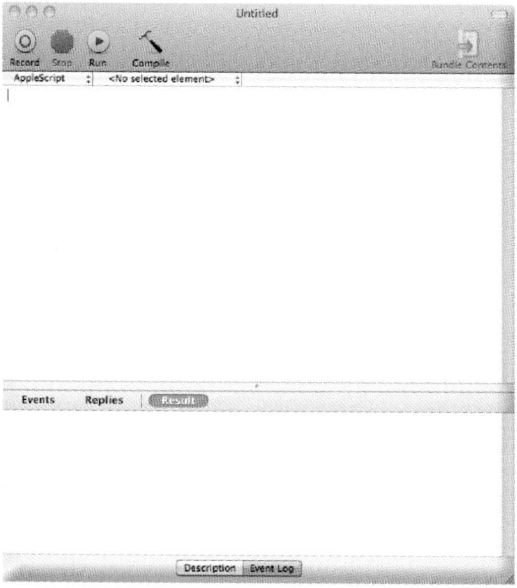

```
display dialog "Ready to Script?"
tell application "TextEdit"
    activate
    make new document with properties {text:text_entry}
end tell
```

Taking the above example, let's look at each line of AppleScript code to see what it does.

```
set text_entry to "I like to use my Mac at work!"
```

First, the script sets a variable called text_entry and fills it with the words "I like to use my Mac at Work!"

```
display dialog "Ready to Script?"
```

Next, the script creates a dialog box.

```
tell application "TextEdit"
```

The `tell` command is how AppleScript works with specific applications. In this instance, AppleScript is telling TextEdit, "I'm about to give you some work."

```
Activate
```

Activate is the AppleScript command to start the application. TextEdit will launch upon this command.

```
make new document with properties {text:text_entry}
```

This is an example of AppleScript's plain-language scripting. To make a new document, the command is `make new document`. The rest of this command adds the text from the `text_entry` variable to the new document.

FIGURE 24-9

The AppleScript Say command

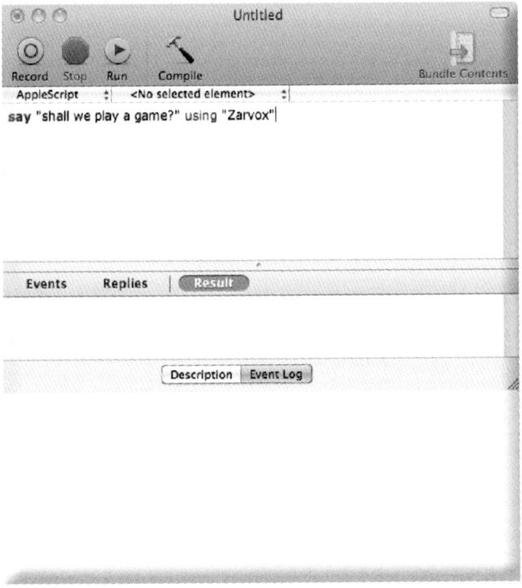

Finally, we tell TextEdit we are done working with it:

```
end tell
```

Although these examples are admittedly simple, they do show the utility of AppleScript. Many Mac OS X software developers include AppleScript support in their software code, meaning that they include AppleScript commands in their software that AppleScript can address and thus you can access from an AppleScript you write. Apple Mail, for example, has an AppleScript command to pull an e-mail address from a mail message. (The command is `Extract Address From`.) This command is useful if you have 700 e-mails and want to pull their e-mail addresses and add them to an Address Book contact group.

AppleScript includes a dictionary that lists all the available commands for your installed applications. You can access the dictionary in the AppleScript Editor by choosing File ▶ Open Dictionary. Figure 24-10, shows the Extract Address From entry in Mail's AppleScript dictionary.

Once you become proficient in AppleScript, you can use the dictionary terms to string together AppleScript commands on your Mac. Because many software developers implement AppleScript commands, you can have applications talk to one another. For example, you can have Preview modify a photograph and then drop that image into a Microsoft Word document. Experienced scripters can perform magic on their Macs with AppleScript.

You can even save bits of AppleScript code and install them as actions in Automator workflows. For example, to add voice prompts to your Automator workflows, use the Run AppleScript action in Automator, as shown in Figure 24-11. This is a useful script because there is no built-in Automator action to speak.

If you want the benefit of AppleScript but don't want to be bothered to learn how, there are several useful scripts available on the Web that you can download and run in AppleScript Editor. Two of my favorite AppleScript and Automator Web sites are `www.macosxautomation.com` and `www.macscripter.net`. Both sites have a rich assortment of downloadable AppleScripts and Automator Workflows. MacScripter also has an active user community, so you can get advice and help with your automation.

Script Debugger

AppleScript Editor is a great tool to learn AppleScript, and it comes free with every new Mac. But if you really enjoy working with AppleScript, upgrade to a more advanced AppleScript editing application. The best one is Script Debugger ($200; `www.latenightsw.com`). Script Debugger includes tools not available in AppleScript Editor. Script Debugger's dictionary support, for example, runs circles around the standard AppleScript Editor dictionary, providing more

FIGURE 24-10

The AppleScript dictionary

FIGURE 24-11

Running an AppleScript in Automator

detailed information about the available commands in each of your applications, such as usage examples and syntax.

Script Debugger also lets you run your AppleScript code one step at a time so you know exactly what is going right (and wrong) when debugging. Script Debugger is a necessary tool for any power scripter.

Using Automator and AppleScript, you'll be surprised how much more efficient you can be on your Mac. Good luck!

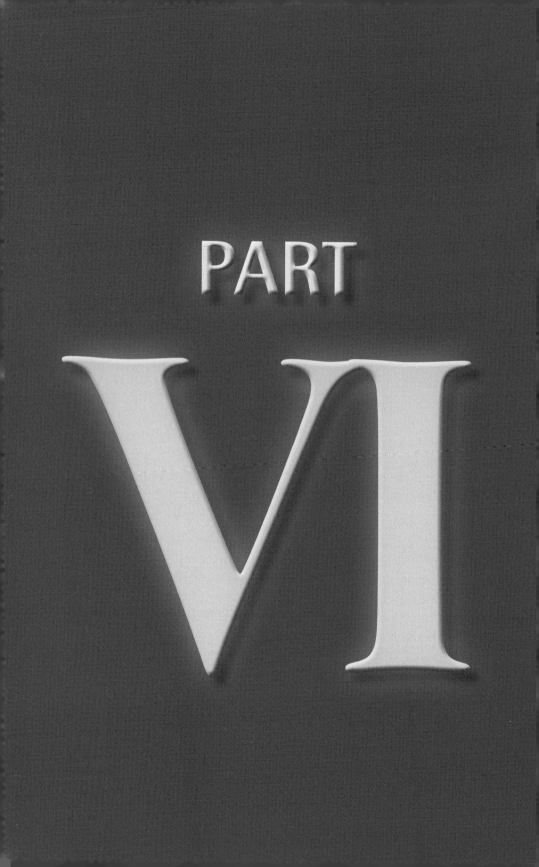

PART

VI

Appendixes

Debunking Myths about Macs

S adly, many information technology professionals get this special frown on their faces when you show up at work with your Mac. I have a theory about this. I once spoke with an IT manager for a big company that had an equal number of Macs and PCs. He explained that his IT staff spent four times as much time keeping the PCs running as they did the Macs. In other words, computers that don't break aren't necessarily a good thing if you earn your living fixing computers. This, of course, is not fair to IT professionals. Many are forward thinking and love Macs. Nevertheless, there are some common misconceptions you may hear from misguided IT professionals. Here are some of the most popular myths and how to debunk them.

Macs aren't secure

Macs are secure. Mac OS X will not let you install and run new software without first entering your system password. Furthermore, because there are so few Mac OS X computers (in comparison with Windows), the rotten scoundrels who create malicious software largely ignore the Mac. Finally, there are several enterprise-friendly antivirus tools for the Mac. Read Chapter 23. Quite often, the real source of this myth is that IT workers — who deal with PC issues every day — are unsure of the Mac security issues and how to address them. Their ignorance of Mac security issues makes them look worse than they actually are.

Macs can't be managed as easily as PCs

This is another myth born of unfamiliarity. Macs have built-in tools to pla nicely on a network. They ship with Exchange support (see Chapters 6, 7, and 20) and they use the same networking protocols as PCs. Macs can even run Windows software using virtualization (see Chapter 22). If your IT person s some time familiarizing herself with the tools available to manage a Mac c predominantly PC network, there should be no problems.

Macs will slow down the network

This rumor predates Mac OS X. Over the years, Apple has released networking protocols for its computers. Not all of them were efficien for example, was notoriously slow. These outdated network conventions are all irrelevant now. Apple uses the same networking protocols as Windows and there is no difference between the network speed of the two operating systems. See Chapter 20.

Macs aren't standards-compliant

"Standards" is such a nebulous term that this myth doesn't mean anything. What standards are they talking about? The Mac can network with the rest of them (Chapter 20). Web browsers on the Mac can open any standards-compliant Web site, which is just about everything on the Internet these days (Chapter 4). Running a virtual machine or Boot Camp, Macs can run Windows like a champ (Chapter 22). Macs support the standard PC interfaces such as USB, Ethernet, Wi-Fi, Bluetooth, and, via an adapter, VGA, as well as PC-formatted hard disks, CDs, flash drives, and DVDs. It's been more than 10 years since Macs came with proprietary interfaces.

Macs won't work with ActiveX

This myth is true. For a long time, Microsoft thought it could redefine the Web experience by including its own specific tools in Microsoft Explorer unavailable to other Web browsers, called ActiveX. This didn't work and Microsoft has returned to using Web standards with recent versions of Microsoft Internet Explorer. Nevertheless, some antiquated Web sites still depend on ActiveX controls. Even Microsoft now encourages people to abandon these old sites and recode them for the modern standards-compliant Web browsers. If you must run se older Web sites, you can always install an old version of Internet Explorer a virtual machine, assuming Microsoft will still support and release these rsions.

e not PCs

or "personal computer." Macs are PCs. It is just that they run system, Mac OS X. Macs don't run Windows, unless you want r 22.

nsive

ple tax." People often compare an Apple laptop with e same size and declare the Mac overpriced. When ut the components inside the computers. It is economy car. They both are about the same including price. You can buy a PC for $300, but done on it. When you compare a high-end Windows

PC with a Mac, the features, components, *and price* are competitive. The difference is, Apple doesn't make junk.

Smart businesses don't buy the cheapest PCs because, in the long run, maintenance costs and down-time far exceed any perceived up front savings. Quality PCs with similar components to Macs are largely priced the same. This, combined with the lower management costs of Macs (the annual cost of managing a Windows PC is estimated to be about $2,000 per year), make the Macs cheaper in the long run.

Finally, this argument ignores the Mac's lower cost of ownership. Macs usually last longer, have a higher resale value, and are less likely to break. Macs just work.

Macs don't run Windows

Macs are better Windows PCs' than most Windows PCs. See Chapter 22.

Macs don't work with Exchange Server

Mac OS X Snow Leopard ships with Microsoft Exchange support. Microsoft's Outlook, part of Microsoft Office for Mac, also includes Microsoft Exchange support. See Chapters 6 and 20.

There are no work applications for the Mac

Although Mac OS X does not have the quantity of applications available to the Windows platform, the quality of Mac applications is amazing. Instruct anyone who spouts this myth to buy two copies of this book.

Macs are a fad. It'll never last

The first Macintosh computer was sold on January 24, 1984. Apple reports selling more than 3 million Macs in the first quarter of 2010. Pretty good for fad!

The Mac is a toy, not a real computer

This rumor has a lot to do with the reason why I wrote this book. Somewhere along the line, the concept of the Mac as a toy entered the collective conscious. As you can see from this book, nothing could be farther from the truth. Your Mac can turn you into a productivity ninja if you give it a chance.

This is the one Mac myth I usually don't argue with. When an opposing lawyer sees my Mac and calls it a toy, I smile back serenely and then proceed to win my case with all the great tools covered in this book.

Index